BRITAIN AND SOUTH AFRICA

The Royal Institute of International Affairs is an unofficial body which promotes the scientific study of international questions and does not express opinions of its own. The opinions expressed in this publication are the responsibility of the author.

The Institute gratefully acknowledges the comments and suggestions of the following who read the manuscript on behalf of the Research Committee: Gordon Lawrie, Sir John Maud, Sir Arnold Plant.

Britain and South Africa

DENNIS AUSTIN

Institute of Commonwealth Studies,
London University

Issued under the auspices of the
Royal Institute of International Affairs

OXFORD UNIVERSITY PRESS

LONDON NEW YORK TORONTO

1966

Oxford University Press, Ely House, London W. 1

GLASGOW NEW YORK TORONTO MELBOURNE WELLINGTON
CAPE TOWN SALISBURY IBADAN NAIROBI LUSAKA ADDIS ABABA
BOMBAY CALCUTTA MADRAS KARACHI LAHORE DACCA
KUALA LUMPUR HONG KONG

Printed in Great Britain

Contents

Foreword

THIS short account of British interests in South Africa took shape during meetings of a study group at Chatham House. It has benefited enormously from discussions round the table, and from papers submitted for examination, but the conclusions set down in these chapters are not those of the group: indeed, I think it is very doubtful whether a consensus of opinion of the members who met at regular intervals during the greater part of 1964 and early 1965 would have been possible except in the most general terms of an agreement that the range of British interests in South Africa presents the United Kingdom government with a peculiarly difficult problem. I have tried, therefore, to express my own views, within the compass of my understanding of the interests involved, based on the arguments which took place among the members of the seminar. They included Philip Mason (chairman), Peter Calvocoressi, Noel Garson, William Gutteridge, Rosalyn Higgins, Catherine Hoskyns, Christopher Johnson, Roy Lewis, Sir John Maud, Hermia Oliver, Kenneth Robinson, Noel Salter, Tom Soper, J. E. Spence, and David Williams. In addition the group had the advantage of the presence of members from government departments and commercial firms who took part in the discussions on a personal basis. Two meetings between the Royal Institute of International Affairs and the Council on Foreign Relations (New York), for which funds were generously provided by the Carnegie Endowment for International Peace, were very helpful. I would also like to thank the Carnegie Endowment most warmly for their financial help in enabling me to visit the Republic of South Africa in September and October 1964.

The inclusion of a chapter on 'The Rhodesia Parallel' requires some explanation, since the primary aim of this study—as will be stated in the opening chapter—has been to try and 'measure the extent of British interests in South Africa, and the degree to which they are likely to influence United Kingdom policy towards the Republic'. In November 1965, however, Mr Ian Smith's unilateral declaration of independence offered the writer an opportunity, in the narrower setting of Rhodesia, of examining a number of the problems raised in relation to South Africa; the temptation to turn aside from the Republic proved too strong to resist. An additional chapter was included, therefore, in the hope that some of the lessons of the Rhodesian crisis might throw light on the wider problem of South Africa. It was written quickly during the latter part of November, and the writer offers his apologies to the reader if he has been unable, at proof stage, to remove every mark of haste.

I wish to express my thanks particularly to Philip Mason, an indefatigable chairman and wise counsellor. He too must be absolved of any individual responsibility for the expressions of opinions in these pages. I am also indebted to the three readers who commented on the draft as a whole: Mr Gordon Lawrie, Sir John Maud, and Sir Arnold Plant.

To Gordon Lawrie, his wife Audrey, and Deborah Lavin I owe a debt of gratitude greater than I can express: whatever merit this study has belongs in large part to them: only the faults are mine.

I should also like to say how indebted I am to Miss Hermia Oliver of the Royal Institute of International Affairs whose understanding of the South African scene enabled me to avoid many errors, and whose personal interest in the study enabled it to be prepared for the press far more quickly and efficiently than I could have done unaided. There are many others whose help I acknowledge gratefully: Michael Bell, Gwen Carter of North-western University, Sean Gervasi, Ernest Gross, Col. Donald Humphries, Vernon McKay of Johns Hopkins University, Joe Johnson of the Carnegie Endowment for International Peace, Waldemar Nielsen, William Diebold and Dave MacEachron of the Council on Foreign Relations, William Tordoff and Denis Osborne of the University College Dar es Salaam, Peter Canham and Selby Ncgobo of the University College Salisbury, Keith Hunt of Rhodes University, Professor N. Olivier of Stellenbosch, Professor Weiss of Pretoria, Helen Suzman M.P., and Edgar and Mary Mangion of Tx Biex, Gzira. Finally, I should like to record my debt to Miss Margaret Youdle of Chatham House whose patience matched her skill in typing the numerous papers and draft chapters which were presented to the study group as the basis for its discussions.

January 1966 D. A.

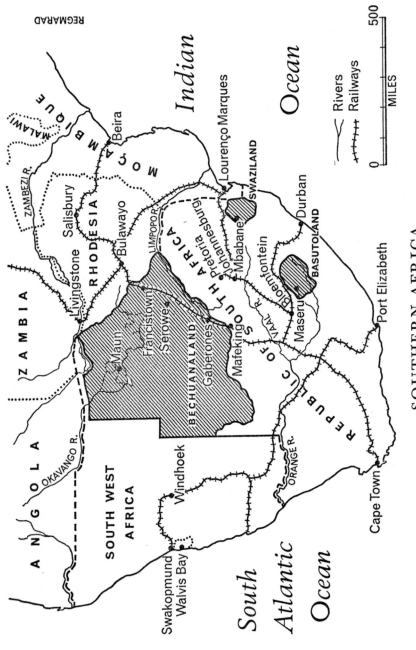

SOUTHERN AFRICA

I
British Interests

BRITISH interests in South Africa are of long standing, rooted in the history of the two countries and maintained by a close working relationship over many years. When the Act of Union united the four self-governing colonies in 1909 it continued the ties between the English-speaking and Afrikaner communities and the new Dominion and Britain; South Africa became a Commonwealth country under non-British leadership, preceding the achievement of responsible government by non-European peoples—India in 1947 and Ghana in 1957: an irony of history which must evoke wry comment in Pretoria. Under Smuts's leadership, South Africa was also a founding member first of the League and then of the United Nations, and in the early post-war years it was welcomed as a distant ally of the North Atlantic powers. It is true that the National Party, which has been in office since 1948, can hardly claim any special ties of friendship with Britain. A number of its leaders were interned during the second world war because of their sympathies with the Nazis. Yet the Commonwealth loyalties which linked the two countries for over half a century included far more than the English-speaking minority, as the names of those who fought on the allied side during both world wars would show.[1] And it was not until the second half of the 1950s that relations between Britain and South Africa began to show signs of strain. The change followed a more ruthless application by the Nationalist government of its racial policies and the assertion of nationalist demands by African leaders throughout the continent. Today the South African government is isolated in the international community, and both the English-speaking population and the Afrikaners are condemned for their support of a legalized racialism. It is this mounting condemnation of Dr Verwoerd's government which has raised the need to assess Britain's interests in the Republic in a new context. Hence the general theme of this study. The writer does not propose to pass detailed judgements on the South

[1] Including both Coloured and Africans.

African scene. There has been ample comment on apartheid, and there is little point in going over the same ground again. The aim is more modest: to measure the extent of British interests in South Africa, and the degree to which they are likely to influence United Kingdom policy towards the Republic.

These interests are discussed in subsequent chapters, but may be summarized briefly. They are surprisingly diverse. The United Kingdom continues to be involved with the Republic because of emigration to South Africa, adding to the numbers of the English-speaking community there who are still British subjects.[2] It has a substantial responsibility still for the three Southern African Territories—Basutoland, Swaziland, and Bechuanaland. There are joint defence arrangements between the two countries. There is the very large investment by British companies in the Republic, and a rich market for British goods at a time when United Kingdom exports are in great need of wider outlets. Britain is also involved internationally as a permanent member of the Security Council, where it is under attack precisely because of its long-established interests in South Africa. It may soon have to reach a decision on the case brought before the International Court by Liberia and Ethiopia over the mandated territory in South West Africa, should the judgement go substantially against the Republic and the matter be brought to the Security Council. Britain is further affected by its Commonwealth ties. This extraordinary association now includes among its twenty-two member countries five Asian, nine African, and two Caribbean states whose governments are incensed by the racial policies of the Nationalist regime and critical of Britain's continuing relations with the Republic.

[2]

Immigrants by Country of Previous Permanent Residence

Year	Total	Rhodesias	UK
1946	11,256	430	7,470
1950	12,803	546	5,097
1955	16,199	1,814	4,444
1960	9,789	2,166	2,292
1961	16,309	5,760	2,323
1962	20,916	7,180	4,970
1963	37,964	15,419	10,135
1964	40,865	8,453	12,807 (prov. fig.)

Sources: SA Statistical Year Book 1964 and *Monthly Bull. of Statistics,* July 1965.

It is easy to deprecate competition in international morality over South Africa among those whose own domestic policies are at best illiberal. Yet there are legitimate grounds for anxiety about the future of the Republic, so sharp are the racial antagonisms which confront it. South Africa stands as an extreme warning of the evil effects of man's lack of love for his neighbour. For there is a peculiar violence in racial conflict to which it is difficult to set limits in the modern world. Mankind has learnt to live with political oppression for many centuries—it has been the unhappy lot of ordinary people over the greater part of the world—but conflict between racial groups has deep roots; its poison spreads quickly beyond the control of governments to infect society in general, and there is a particular uncertainty about the South African scene because of the extraordinary plurality of its peoples—Afrikaner, English, African, Coloured, and Asian.[3] Racial discrimination is entrenched in law. Violence is held in check by a harsh system of controls whereby a narrow Afrikaner élite asserts its authority over the rest of the country by increasingly totalitarian methods. There is often a grotesque absurdity about the indignity which is inflicted on the non-white population of the Republic—many of whom would willingly enter white South African society on equal terms if it were open to them; but it is an absurdity which angers the leaders of the newly independent states and substantial coloured minorities in both America and Britain. The extreme insecurity among the

---

[3] On the other hand the very plurality of South African society may produce a balance of forces and, thereby, check the domination of one race over the others. It would certainly be wrong to assume that the Coloured and Indian populations will always be on the side of the African against the white.

Population 1963 estimate

	Total	Per cent		Total	Per cent
Afrikaner	2,037,000	12·0	Coloured	1,650,000	9·6
English	1,213,000	7·1	Asians	520,000	3·0
Total European	3,250,000	19·1	African	11,640,000	68·3

Source: SA Bureau of Statistics.

Note: It is virtually impossible to define what is meant by 'English South Africans' except in terms of language. By no means all are or were from Britain; on the other hand there are a number who still have dual (S. African and British) nationality.

majority of South Africans, in terms of housing, employment, family ties, and educational opportunities for their children, mocks the claim by the minority white population to be upholding European standards of civilization. The daily arrest of large numbers of Africans for infringements of the pass laws, and the compulsory removal of local communities from one part of the country to another, or from the townships to the reserves, are evils which must daily increase the hostility of the non-European population towards the Nationalist government. White South Africa rests on the enforced subjection of its non-white inhabitants. It rules by the sword, and refuses to accept the lesson of the parable on the plight of the militarist:

> When a strong man armed keepeth his palace, his goods are in peace; but when a stronger than he shall come upon him and overcome him, he taketh from him all his armour wherein he trusted, and divideth his spoils.

Because the likelihood of a violent insurrection seems remote, the white South African voter continues to trust in the strength of an an armed and oppressive regime. But the regime itself is more than a reflection of a privileged white minority. It rests on a stubborn Afrikaner nationalism, itself the product of a fierce anti-colonialism. It fought its own 'war of liberation',[4] to replace the Imperial power as a successor government, and it would be foolish to underestimate the determination of the Nationalist Afrikaner to beat down every challenge to his rule. Having at last won the Anglo-Boer War—and able to enlist growing support from his former English opponents—he is now confronted at the very moment of victory by demands that he should give up what he struggled for so long to achieve. One ought not to be surprised, therefore, at the intransigence of his leaders. 'Ons Voortrekkers het die land skoongemaak; ons is geregtig tot die vet van die land.'[5] The uncertainty, however, which clouds the South African scene is not whether the Afrikaner (and his recently acquired English allies) is determined to enjoy the fat of the land, but whether he will be able to defend what Professor

---

[4] The 'tweede Vryheidsoorlog' (the 'second Freedom War')=the 'Anglo-Boer War', the first being the Boer Republics' victory in 1880–1 at Majuba hill.

[5] 'Our Voortrekkers cleared the land; we are entitled to the fat of the land' (President Kruger, quoted in Vatcher, *White Laager* (1965), p. 20).

de Kiewiet has called his 'new laager of laws and restraints'.[6]

The immediate question, therefore, which faces any attempt to reassess Britain's relations with South Africa is how stable white rule is likely to prove. It is hard to answer because of the difficulty of judging between short and long-term possibilities. On the one hand there are few signs at present of any major shift in power between the whites and non-whites; on the other it is difficult not to believe that the weight of numbers will tell 'in the end'. The difficulty is how to define 'the end'. One can list the chances of revolution or reform as they now appear, and they are worth discussing briefly; but the catalogue is bound to be incomplete, while simply to note the possibilities is very different from being able to judge whether or not they will take place. What follows, therefore, is at best a very tentative assessment.

The most obvious source of revolution is among opponents of the Nationalist regime within South Africa itself. The government has not always seemed as impregnable as it does today. The range of political protests has included the United Party, the small Progressive and Liberal Parties, the African National Congress, the Indian and Coloured Congresses, the Pan-African Congress, the organized sabotage of *Umkonto We Sizwe*, and *Poqo* terrorism.[7] The main weight of opposition came in the 1950s, over a very broad front of dissent. There were legal challenges to the Senate Act, the successful defence of those accused during the 1956–61 Treason Trial, and popular protests among both English and Afrikaner, as in the Torch Commando and the Black Sash movement. Among the non-white communities (and a handful of Europeans) there was the Defiance Campaign

---

[6] 'In the old days of native wars, Voortrekkers drew their wagons into a circle or laager. Within its protection men defended themselves against the impis of the Zulus or the Matabele. Today their descendants seek to retreat within a new laager made up of laws and restraints, as if they could thereby be protected against the turmoil of a multi-racial society' (C. W. de Kiewiet, *The Anatomy of S. African Misery* (1956)).

[7] African political organizations in South Africa have a very long history: the SA Native National Congress was formed in 1912 and renamed the African National Congress in 1925; the Industrial and Commercial Workers' Union was inaugurated in 1919; the PAC was formed on a more overtly African basis by Robert Sobukwe and 'the Africanists' in March 1959 in rivalry to the ANC under Albert Luthuli. *Umkonto We Sizwe* (Spear of the Nation) came into being some time in December 1961, almost certainly linked with the banned ANC. *Poqo* is the name attached to apparently random, unrelated groups of Africans engaged in terrorist activity.

against the 'seven unjust acts' of apartheid legislation, the attempt at a bus boycott, and a number of abortive 'stay-at-homes'. By 1960, when the Sharpeville shootings took place, it was feared that they were the bloody dawn of a long day of African unrest. It seemed reasonable to argue that there would be 'more Sharpevilles', in an unending conflict between the government and its enemies. Both 1960 and 1961 were anxious years. They included not only Sharpeville but the declaration of a State of Emergency, the attempt on Verwoerd's life, a panic flight of capital from the country, pan-African meetings among the newly independent states, and South Africa's withdrawal from the Commonwealth after the referendum for a republic in which the Nationalists secured only a narrow majority of votes.[8]

None of these events seriously weakened the regime. Indeed, by 1965 the government appeared more strongly placed than at any time since it came to power. The United Party showed every sign of being in decline; the small multi-racial parties were harassed out of existence or crippled by government action; the two main African movements were banned and their leaders under restriction or in prison. In retrospect, Sharpeville appeared as the end of a long period of open opposition: but when the ANC and PAC were driven underground and new movements appeared—*Umkonto We Sizwe, Poqo*, the National Committee of Liberation (later the African Resistance Movement)—they were destroyed by a government which had learnt more effectively than its opponents how to deal with this new phase of the struggle. The Rivonia Trial in 1964, in which Nelson Mandela, Walter Sisulu, and their associates were sentenced to life imprisonment, was only the most dramatic episode in a number

---

[8] 5 Oct. 1960. For the Republic—850,458; against—775,878. It is only right, however, to add that many Nationalists were delighted to leave the Commonwealth and gratified at having won the referendum on the Republic. The following year a general election took place—the fourth time the electorate has gone to the polls in a little over three years. The results were:

	Seats	Votes
Nats.	105*	370,431
UP	49	302,875
Progressives	1	69,042
Nat. Union	1	35,903
Conservative Workers' Party	0	6,229
Liberals	0	2,461

* Incl. a number of unopposed seats.

of conflicts from which the Special Branch emerged clear victors. The struggle is not likely to end so long as white minority rule continues, since it is impossible to prevent every act of sabotage, or the sudden upheaval of local violence in the townships; mass arrests will probably continue and new movements will be formed. But one may doubt whether they will fundamentally alter the balance of power for many years to come. In short, revolution was not and has never been 'just round the corner'— as Julius Lewin noted as early as 1958:

> Visitors from abroad . . . often ask me 'how long can it go on?' By 'it' they mean the present state of the Union. They are always surprised at my answer, because I tell them that I see no reason why 'it' should not go on almost indefinitely, and certainly for a good many years. . . . It is my contention that the signs of discontent in South Africa, when added up, do not amount to a serious situation in the sense of a prelude to revolution.[9]

Professor Lewin was right in the 1950s; and the prospect today, in the 1960s, of any major internal convulsion still seems very distant.

If revolution from below is improbable—a proposition subject to the caveat that in so dramatic a situation as South Africa nothing can be taken for granted—what can be said of reform from above? If changes come, they will be generated among the European minority, more particularly among the ruling Afrikaner element, and it can be argued that since white society is by no means as united as it appears on the surface, there may be greater room for shifts in policy than is generally supposed.[10] There are minor centres of opposition to the extreme apartheid programme of the Nationalist government among both English and Afrikaners. There is a courageous, outspoken English-language press still, a tradition of protest in the Catholic and Protestant Churches, and a strong liberal element in the English-speaking universities, including the National Union of South African Students (NUSAS). Within Afrikanerdom itself, there

[9] 'No Revolution Round the Corner', *Africa South*, Oct.–Dec. 1958.
[10] Hence the need to examine the nature of Afrikanerdom and the stresses to which it is subject by its own dilemmas. See, for example, the interesting article by Miss Deborah Lavin, 'The Dilemma of Christian-National Education in S. Africa', *World Today*, Oct. 1965, and the plea by Mr Joe Rogaly for a close study of 'the internal movements inside the Afrikaners' National Party', *The Economist*, Southern Africa Survey, 7–15 Aug. 1965.

are stirrings of an uneasy conscience among the Dutch Reformed Churches, including scattered protests against too harsh an application of apartheid laws, and an anxious desire to find a Christian answer to racial issues.[11] There are a number of Cape Afrikaners who are prepared to see the integration into white society of the Coloured community. There is a general uneasiness over the present isolation of South Africa, whether in matters of sport or at international gatherings, over a broad range of activities. Of more practical consequence, there is the effect of the long-term growth of the economy. Three and a half million whites may possibly be able to exercise political control over the rest of the population, but they are hardly likely to be able to supply all the skills needed to maintain the present rate of de-

[11] There are many examples of the struggle which continues between the provinces, as in the resignation of Professor Olivier of Stellenbosch from the chairmanship of SABRA (the South African Bureau of Racial Affairs) and its removal to Pretoria under Professor Weiss. It was also the Cape Synod of the Afrikaner Churches which was most troubled in its conscience when the four synods decided to end their membership of the World Council of Churches. Two quotations must suffice to illustrate the argument over inter-racial membership:

'To my mind separate churches for the different racial groups in a country like our own can have very positive results: it can help the African Christian to develop initiative and relate his Christian faith to his own thought forms and cultural heritage; it can help him to make Christianity his own in a more real and vital way; for reasons of language, etc., much can be said for separate churches.

'Such churches need not ruin or destroy real Christian unity and brotherhood—as long as they do not become segregated or apartheid churches.

'What is the difference between a separate and a segregated or apartheid church? The difference is very meaningful. A segregated church is an exclusive church. It is for Whites only. Non-Whites are not welcome and excluded. This practical exclusion is unchristian' (Dr Ben Marais, *Cape Argus*, 14 June 1960).

'We must obey God rather than man. . . Now I realise that there are many today who say: This is not the time to speak—even if many things are not right or not morally defensible: this is the time to keep silent and to stand by your people. Brethren, no matter how well-intentioned such a view may be, do we not as Christians understand that such an attitude is born of fear, and that fear is a sign of unbelief?. . . Whose kingdom comes first: The Kingdom of God, or that of our people? If the Dutch Reformed Church will not take heed and carry out this obedience which God demands, then we shall suffer endless damage and sorrow' (Rev. Beyers Naude, Sermon (22 Sept. 1963) when appointed Director of the Christian Institute and after he had had to give up office in the Nederduitse Gereformeerde Kerk. By 1965 Dr Naude was calling on South Africa's Churches to form an inter-denominational movement as in Germany in the 1930's because of the 'parallels (which) exist between the situation in Nazi Germany and in South Africa' (*Pro Veritate*, July 1965)).

velopment for the whole of South Africa's 17 million inhabitants. The former president of the Trades Union Council has been reported as saying that in the past two or three years some 12,000 non-whites have taken over skilled or semi-skilled jobs that were formerly closed to them. The economic development plan published by the South African government in December 1964 envisages an annual growth of 5½ per cent in the gross national product down to 1969; the effect will be to create nearly 50,000 vacancies in jobs at present reserved for whites, with only the unemployed non-whites on which to draw.[12] Politicians legislate to keep the races apart, but (it may be said) the economy is forcing them to live together in greater mutual dependence on prosperity.

One may note these stresses within the structure of white rule, but the political effect is hard to calculate. The small number of *predikants* who have spoken out against the government have been moved quickly from positions of influence: the centre of Nationalist rule continues to remain in the Transvaal. The effect of the current rate of economic growth is also hard to interpret in political terms. It opposes economic good sense to deep political convictions but ideologies are not easily abandoned (though they may grow and take different forms) particularly when they draw strength from fear—the fear of white society in South Africa for its survival. Inroads into the practice of job reservation have been grudgingly conceded or ignored by the government, which is pulled in opposite directions by the more militant of its own followers and the demands of a modern economy. It is true that a failure to meet the need for skilled (and, therefore, educated) non-white labour may destroy the prosperity which has helped both to persuade the white electorate to support the Nationalists and to ease the plight of the disfranchised majority. But too many concessions may upset the *platteland* Afrikaner whose influence is felt strongly at local and provincial levels, and the white trade unions in the towns. Part of the answer to the problem may depend on whether the government feels confident that political control can be kept in white hands distinct from and unaffected by economic concessions. If it does, and if it is justified in its belief, the economy may then work to the consolidation of white rule rather than its destruction. It is at least as plausible a view

[12] *Economist* Survey, Aug. 1965.

as the argument more commonly expressed that industrial forces will 'make nonsense of apartheid'.[13] For economic answers to political questions are rare, and the rate of growth of the economy is unlikely by itself to convert Europeans and non-Europeans to a policy of mutual tolerance, however much it may oblige them to live in greater mutual dependence.

The extreme difficulty of prediction in these circumstances is shown most clearly in relation to the present scheme of Bantustans. One may note the shifts in policy, but it is not easy to say what political conclusions should be drawn from them. There has been an important verbal change from the early insistence by Afrikaner leaders on 'baasskap' to the more subtle advocacy of 'separate development', and although one can argue that the Transkei and other Bantustans are no more than an experiment in control at local government level, at least the experiment is there. And it may possibly lead the government along paths it once refused even to contemplate. It is worth quoting Dr Verwoerd's own words to show the extent of the change:

> Now a Senator wants to know whether the series of self-governing areas would be sovereign. The answer is obvious. It stands to reason that White South Africa must remain their guardian. We are spending all the money on those developments. How could small scattered States arise? The areas will be economically dependent on the Union. It stands to reason that when we talk about the Natives' rights of self-government in those areas, we cannot mean that we intend by that to cut large slices out of South Africa and turn them into independent States. (Statement in the Senate, 1 May 1951, when Minister of Native Affairs.)

> ... In the first place we must appreciate that in adopting the standpoint that we are prepared to give the Bantu areas their independence and to help them develop gradually to full independence, we have undertaken to assist their economic development, even at our own expense. However, we have emphasized that we are only doing so to achieve certainty that we still have a White South Africa by virtue of the fact that all the Bantu will be given their political rights in these homelands. Consequently this settlement must include the provision that the urban Bantu in our midst will also exercise their rights

[13] A belief expressed, for example, by the London Press Exchange early in 1964: 'external political and economic pressures will only harden the republic's racial policies. On the other hand, trade and continued prosperity can lead in the long run towards relaxation and tolerance' (*The Times*, 6 Jan. 1964).

and will be accommodated to an ever-increasing extent in those areas. (Speech in the House of Assembly, 11 Apr. 1961.)

. . . The moral problem, just like the political problem, is to find a way out of the extremely difficult and complicated situation, caused by the fact that no longer is the black man incapable or undesirous of participation in the control of his destiny. Nor is there any longer anyone prepared to refuse the fulfilment of such ambitions in a form that is fair to all. . . . I envisage development along the lines similar to that of the Commonwealth. In other words, I perceive the development of a Commonwealth of South Africa, in which the White State and the Black States can co-operate together, without being joined in a federation, and therefore without being under a central government, but co-operating as separate and independent States. In such an association no State will lord it over any other. They will live rather as good neighbours. (UN Doc. 5/5723, 28 May 1964.)

Again, one may say that the change is merely one of vocabulary. Local homelands and a white South Africa are unlikely to meet the demand for political rights among the Indian population in Natal, or the millions of Africans in the towns and white farming areas. However rigorously control regulations under the Bantu Laws Amendment Act are applied, the number of Africans in the white areas will continue to grow, and they are unlikely to be content with absentee voting rights.[14] Yet the difference in terminology may one day help to promote more fundamental changes—stemming not from the desire for reform, but a determination on the part of the present leaders to stay in office. Here too there is room for speculation. For the present strength of the Nationalist government lies in its growing support among both English and Afrikaners. Yet much of the support is conditional—law and order have to be imposed without too overt a show of force, and the present level of prosperity must be maintained.

The measure of Nationalist power lies in the extent of its success, and as long as sabotage is held in check there is no compelling reason—from the point of view of the white electorate—

---

[14] In 1950 about 28 per cent of the African population lived in the towns; by 1960 the figure was 37 per cent; by 1970 it is likely to be 45 per cent of a growing African population. In 1963 the proportions were: total African population $11\frac{1}{2}$ m.; no. in white farming areas $3\frac{1}{2}$ m.; no. in urban areas 4 m.; no. in Bantu homelands 4 m.

why changes should be introduced. If, however, these pre-
conditions of Nationalist support began to disappear, one might
see major changes of policy governing the relations between
white and non-white, in which still harsher measures of control
alternated with substantial measures of responsibility being extended to the non-European communities. There are two major
uncertainties, therefore, about the long-term future, each to
some extent contradicting the other. The first is that one does
not know whether there is any limit in time, even in conditions as
difficult as South Africa, to the ability of a regime to maintain
itself in power when it has all the resources of a modern industrial
state at its disposal. The second is that it is impossible to foretell
how white society may react if the present policy of race con-
tainment fails to hold back violence, or to preserve the existing
level of the economy.

In the *short* run, the position is plain. Neither revolution nor
reform is likely. And it is anger with the present situation in
South Africa, coupled with prophecies of a racial civil war,
which has brought the demand for 'external pressure'—to
achieve what cannot be done by South Africans themselves. The
demand is justified partly in moral terms, partly on grounds of
expediency. It is stated, on the one hand, that apartheid is an
evil which the rest of the world community has a moral duty to
eradicate. But it is also argued that a fundamental conflict exists
in South Africa which is absolutely beyond the ability of either
side to resolve and the outside world will one day be forced to
intervene. The question, therefore, is not whether the United
Nations or the west should act against South Africa, but whether
they should intervene on their own terms now, or wait until they
are forced to do so later. If now, there may be a chance of the
peaceful dismantling of apartheid. But if Britain and the United
States remain inactive, the time will come when open bloody conflict will have destroyed not only the basis of white rule but the
possibility of a multiracial alternative. Nor will the passions and
hatred aroused be confined to the Republic: they will infect the
rest of the world, most virulently where there is already a danger
of racial conflict. Lastly, it is argued that Britain and the west
must face the probability that if they do not act today it will be
their enemies in Peking or Moscow who will act tomorrow. In
sum, it is a plea for preventive action by the west not only to end

a particularly cruel form of government—although that would be a justifiable end in itself—but to avert the danger of a 'race war', or a communist victory among the Afro-Asian states, or both.[15] These are the primary arguments behind the advocacy of economic sanctions, by which the Nationalist government is to be forced either to abandon its racialist policies, and to accept the demand for a 'multiracial Convention', or be replaced by leaders who are prepared to move in that direction.

The effect of the campaign has been to bring the United Kingdom under direct pressure at the United Nations and Commonwealth meetings, since it is the Republic's main export market and chief source of supply. The different stages in the attack will be examined later. But one may note here that, to date, both Britain and the United States have opposed the Afro-Asian states (except on the sale of arms) primarily on the grounds that the evils which are likely to follow the application of full economic sanctions—at least in the present situation in South Africa—would exceed the dangers of inaction. It is an unheroic stand, and subjected to a great deal of criticism by the more militant opponents of apartheid: but it is not without strength, as the following argument shows.

Firstly, there is the fact that the world is already sufficiently troubled along the broad front of international relations without adding intervention in South Africa to its list. Not only must it live close to the terror of nuclear war; it is also divided by local conflicts, between and within states, and time will not have a stop to allow the world to 'deal with South Africa', even if one knew what was meant by such a phrase. Indeed, if the United States or Britain were engaged with South Africa others might be tempted to push their own interests against local rivals. Nor is the United Kingdom or the United States likely to be free to turn aside from Malaysia or Vietnam, Cyprus or the Dominican Republic, Aden or Cuba, Kashmir, Israel, or the many potential areas of local war, to take 'preventive action' in South Africa, where the full weight of crisis has yet to be felt. Even the United States, despite its immense resources, must be reluctant to create by its own actions a whole new area of responsibility where today a relatively prosperous society exists, however harsh the laws and however anxiously one may ponder its future.

[15] On the idea of 'race war' see below, pp. 54 ff.

One may also argue that neither the Soviet Union nor China is likely to intervene to any effect in the present situation.[16] China is absorbed in South East Asia, on the borders of its own immense territory; the USSR is feeling its way as hopefully as it can towards a *détente* with the west. Neither power can be said to have had much success as yet in attempts to convert or supplant the leaders of the independent African states. This is not to say that Africa, including southern Africa, will escape the competing pressures of east and west, since the departure of the colonial governments has naturally opened the way to the entry of outside powers, and both China and the Soviet Union will look for an easy dividend for a small outlay of capital. Both have little to lose materially and everything to gain morally by their support for sanctions, particularly since they are in competition for the role of champion of the anti-colonialists. But both have also been rebuffed on occasions by nationalist governments suspicions of all outside influence. Nor is it clear what the East Germans or the Chinese have been able to achieve in Zanzibar other than to alarm the mainland African governments.[17] The prospect of an African communist revolution, for all Chou En-lai's brave words, still seems remote, and both Moscow and Peking are likely to be chary of any major commitment in South Africa. To attempt to sponsor a revolution several thousand miles away, in a hardly known situation, is a very different undertaking from extending Soviet or Chinese influence across the borders of a communist homeland in territories where revolutionary movements are already in being. It may be said in reply that the most likely threat over the next few years is of a 'flank attack' on South Africa, opening the way for direct subversion under Soviet or Chinese influence from a liberated Angola, Moçambique, or Rhodesia; but even if Portugal (whether under Salazar or his successor) were expelled from Africa, or majority rule were introduced in Rhodesia, the successor governments in these territories are unlikely to be in a position to act any more strongly against

[16] The position of the Organization of African Unity is examined in the following chapter.

[17] The extent of communist influence in a number of African countries has to be seen in proportion: it is often exaggerated simply because it exists, but 'there are, for example, more American Peace Corps teachers in Tanganyika secondary schools than there are Chinese technicians in the whole country' (W. Tordoff, 'Politics in Tanzania', *World Today*, Aug. 1965).

South Africa than Tanzania has been able to do against Moçambique.

There is a second major difficulty facing any attempt at collective action against South Africa—the absence of any agreement on the ends to be gained. Criticism of the Nationalist government often implies that there is a just solution to the country's racial problems lying close at hand if only the government would move towards it. But what is a 'just solution' in terms of the plurality of South African society? What measures need to be introduced in South Africa in order to produce a free and prosperous community in which racial attitudes are subordinated to national needs? Where is the model in other parts of the world from which South Africa could take its copy? The United States? But the nature of the problem there, in terms of the proportion of white to non-white, is vastly different from South Africa's, and the time available for change has been very much greater. The United Kingdom—where the addition of a tiny percentage of coloured immigrants to the population has brought protests, shifts in government policy, and great heart-searchings? The communist countries—where demonstrations have been staged by the small number of African students against racial discrimination? Cyprus? British Guiana? Ceylon? Malaysia? The hopeful cases, perhaps, have been in the Caribbean—but, again, the time for change has been greater than is allowed South Africa and, in respect of the British West Indies, there was a strong Imperial factor which bridged the slow transition from white to black rule. Where would the equivalent to the Imperial power be in South Africa, even supposing that there was a surrender of control on the part of its present rulers? The answer is clear. There is none, and it is difficult to see any agreement between the USSR and the west, or between South African leaders and the powers imposing sanctions, on the nature of the regime which should hold power in the new Republic. The Great Powers were divided over the Congo by their support of rival factions among the African leaders: how much more are they likely to be divided over South Africa? There would be the danger, therefore, of a conflict of policies,[18] damaging not only to any agreement to act

---

[18] As, for example, over the report of the UN Committee of Experts (S/6120, 2 Mar. 1965), appointed in 1964 to examine 'the feasibility, effectiveness and implications' of sanctions against South Africa. Members were Bolivia, Brazil,

against South Africa but to the present delicate area of tacit
agreement between the Soviet Union and the west.

Thirdly, both Britain and the United States have every right—
since they would be the principal agents in any action against
South Africa—to ask those who call for coercive measures, first,
how they would be applied and, secondly, what the result is
likely to be. Suppose, for example, it were possible to reach agreement among members of the United Nations on the denial of
goods to South Africa, or on a refusal to buy its exports. The embargo might be evaded by unscrupulous states, of which there
are many in the world: oil might be sold since there is a glut on
the world's markets, or gold might be bought since it has its
own intrinsic value.[19] Suitable United Nations machinery would
have to be devised, therefore, to try and stop this illicit traffic and
to prevent if possible the transhipment of goods through third
countries, including Angola and Moçambique. It would not be
easy to create the machinery, and it would take time. Nevertheless, if the United Kingdom and the United States agreed to impose a boycott, many would follow suit, and South Africa would
undoubtedly suffer. It might not, however, suffer immediately.
A boycott could not be imposed all at once, and the South
African government would have ample time—if it were determined to resist—to stock essential goods and withstand a siege.
The majority report of the Committee of Experts on Sanctions
noted 'that some means of alleviation, such as substitution,
rationing and redeployment of resources could have significant
results' in respect of South Africa's capacity to withstand an
embargo, and that 'it was not possible to draw precise conclusions
as to the degree to which [sanctions] might affect South Africa's
economic activity, or as to the length of time it would take for

China, Czechoslovakia, Ivory Coast, Morocco, Norway, USSR, UK, and
USA. The western countries, and China, submitted a majority report in which
they expressed cautious agreement that sanctions 'could prove feasible' under
certain conditions but that 'evaluation of their applicability and effectiveness
in the political and psychological context lies within the province of the
Security Council'. The Czech and Soviet members dissented and declared
that sanctions 'will have the necessary effect' on South Africa. They were
supported by the Moroccan and Ivory Coast delegations, whose own draft
conclusions were also published as part of the report.

[19] The recent sterling crisis led to substantial buying of gold shares and gold with
few questions asked about their origin—e.g. the Chinese sold sterling and
bought gold bars instead, in 1965.

their effects to be felt'.[20] In the meantime, certain conditions would presumably have been put before the South African government and white society: 'Release your political prisoners and bring them and yourselves to the conference table'; or perhaps 'Introduce reforms of a kind which will satisfy the minimum demands [which would have to be listed] of the boycott powers'. At this point, no one knows what might happen. The South African government might 'give in', although this is unlikely, at least at first. It might, on the other hand, rally the white elector-ate behind it, put the country on a war footing, and impose severe restrictions on the whole population particularly (one would suppose) on the non-white communities, including those of the three Southern African Territories. Under such conditions, and with the help of clandestine sales of gold and diamonds, it might succeed in defying even a total embargo for a long period of time running into years. It might also attempt to break the boycott with its own ships. The boycott powers would then have to impose a blockade, a formidable undertaking and an act of war. If the South African government continued to resist, it might be necessary to use force directly by landing troops; there would be fighting and people killed on both sides, until an army of occupation was in uneasy control—as in 1900.[21] By this time, it is probable that the internal economy of the country would be in ruins. There might be starvation in the large cities, bread riots, and fierce repression. One may wonder whether the boycotting powers would be able to stand aloof from direct action even for

[20] UN Doc. S/6210, p. 7. The Ivory Coast and Morocco would have preferred a different wording, namely that any counter-measures taken by South Africa 'might temporarily lessen the impact of the measures envisaged' (p. 12).

[21] Most competent observers see a blockade and an occupying force as necessary concomitants of sanctions. Cf. Philip Mason: 'once sanctions were imposed there would be little likelihood of surrender until in fact military occupation became necessary' ('South Africa and the World—Some Maxims and Axioms', *Foreign Affairs*, Oct. 1964). The findings of the Committee of Experts on the practicability of sanctions noted the need for a blockade or 'partial blockade'. The South African forces are well equipped, and though their present fighting qualities are unknown there is no reason to suppose their per-formance would be inferior to their excellent war record. The army is about 21,500 strong of which 5,500 are regulars. There is also a Citizen Force of some 50,000 and the South African government claims to be able to mobilize 250,000 men at reasonably short notice. The defence budget has been in-creased from £60 m. in 1960–1 to over £100 m. in 1964–5. The police force consists of about 30,000 (including 15,000 non-whites) and half as many again as reservists.

an initial period. Once established, however, an occupying force would have to face the task of ruling a vast country in which the administration, in so far as it was effective, was still in Afrikaner hands. The period of fighting might be short (although one could not be sure of this); the length of time before a United Nations administration and supervisory force could be withdrawn might stretch out indefinitely.

Admittedly, events may not reach this point. The fearful spectacle of local revolution may force the Nationalist government, or its temporary successor, to surrender. It may 'come to the conference table'; it may even agree to the conditions imposed by the boycotting powers. If so, other difficulties would arise. Would the boycott be lifted—and then reimposed if further negotiations broke down, or if the white minority reneged on the agreements? It took several years to produce a compromise between the Nigerian regions before British rule could be withdrawn. How long would it take to reach agreement between racial groups in South Africa? And how long would it be possible to retain both the machinery of the boycott and the collective agreement on terms among the United Nations negotiating team which would be required to umpire the proceedings? It is difficult to believe that the Afro-Asian states, or the communist powers, would be content with limited concessions by the whites, and equally difficult to be confident that a white South African government would be able to carry through peacefully a brief transition to majority rule. If during the period of transfer the South African government, of whatever complexion, lost administrative control of the country, the United Nations would have to intervene—provided it could agree on the terms of intervention—whereupon many of the problems already indicated would be encountered.

Fourthly, there would be the immediate loss to the United Kingdom of an overseas market now worth over £200 million a year to British industry, at a time when the economy is in great need of increasing its exports. The overall loss is likely to be nearly 5 per cent of total British exports which for a country with a long record of favourable balance of payments might be of little account. Unhappily, Britain is in no such position.[22] Every

---

[22] It would not be 5 per cent for particular companies—e.g. the British Commonwealth and Shipping Company (the Union Castle Line); or of the dock labour force in Southampton.

market is valuable, each percentage growth in exports is anxiously recorded, and even the temporary(?) loss of the South African market must weigh heavily with those whose primary concern is to strengthen the British economy. There would be other consequences hardly less painful—for example, to the large British investment in the Republic, on which the income is now running at about £60 million a year. The Committee of Experts which tried to examine the implications of sanctions noted that there could be 'serious dislocations in the United Kingdom in the event of a general embargo on trade'; it concluded that it would be essential to establish a committee 'to mitigate proportionately the major hardships eventually caused on the economies of Member States', but one may be sceptical of the ability of such a committee to act.[23] The conclusion will be drawn in a later chapter that economic considerations alone are unlikely to be decisive in determining British policy towards the Republic, but they are also not likely to be dismissed as irrelevant by any government in Britain at the present time. Moreover to the loss on trade and investment would have to be added the cost of any United Nations or western-mounted action. If sanctions required a blockade, and a blockade led to the need for an occupying force, the cost would be high. If—and one must at least face the possibility—there was fighting, the cost might be very high in both money and men. The detailed assessments by the authors of the Carnegie study on *Apartheid and United Nations Collective Measures* put the figure at £60 million for a six months' naval and air blockade of South Africa's 1,800 miles of coastline; casualties might be between 19,000 and 38,000 for a 3–4-month period.[24] These figures involve a great deal of guesswork and interpolation from situations—Cuba and Korea—which may not be easily comparable.[25] Nor do they include the cost of a United Nations peace-keeping force in South Africa after the fighting had stopped. Who would pay? And which governments would face the casualty figures if military action became necessary? On the one hand, therefore, Britain would forfeit a valuable export market; on the other, it would have to help pay in money or men, or both, for the loss.

[23] UN Doc. S/6210, 2 Mar. 1965, pp. 8–9.
[24] Ed. by Amelia C. Leiss (1965, mimeo.), pp. 150 and 165–70.
[25] The limited 'quarantine' of Cuba cost approximately $44½ m. for the 28 days' operation.

Lastly, any United Kingdom government which agreed to sanctions would have to face its own electorate, many of whom have close ties with South Africa.[26] Families have relatives living there; there are widespread business connexions; there is the simple fact that many thousands of those resident in the Republic are still British subjects. If the Nationalist government in Pretoria were forced on the defensive under the threat (or reality) of sanctions, it might widen its ranks and form a coalition with the United Party, including many of its English-speaking members; if there were serious rioting, there might be considerable numbers of people killed, including British subjects. In these circumstances emotion would run high in Britain, and it is unlikely to be in support of a government, whether Labour or Conservative, which had actively helped to bring about such a situation.[27]

In sum, the case against coercion rests on the enormous difficulties involved in any attempt to change the South African situation from outside, and the heavy consequences that would follow intervention. And because of the difficulty in trying to predict what will happen, it is easy to conclude that there is little point in devising remedial policies for the Republic, and none at all in yielding to the demand for sanctions. These are practical observations. They are also in tune with the traditional British view that foreign policy should be determined by immediate interests rather than long-term predictions, and one can add to it the unpalatable fact that in 1966 Britain no longer has the power it had a hundred years ago to shape the world to its liking.

Yet when all the reservations are made, and the difficulties of trying to impose changes on the Republic are listed, one remains profoundly uneasy, moved by a deep sense of disquiet when confronted by the racial policies of the present government in South Africa. The argument set out in the previous paragraphs describes the obstacles to action in the present context of the Republic. It leaves out the unexpected and unpredictable, and argues the need to balance the dangers of intervention against the anger and moral indignation aroused by apartheid. It may be wise to be cautious, however, on both counts. For there have

---

[26] The USA, on the other hand, may have to face the anger of its 20 m. Negro Americans if it does *not* act.

[27] The difficulties which the Labour government faced in this respect over Rhodesia in November 1965 are discussed in Ch. VII.

been occasions in British history when large issues of morality clashed with economic and political interests, and the former prevailed. It was broadly true in the nineteenth century when the British government, and a large section of public opinion, turned in revulsion from the slave trade. There were sensible reasons then, too, in terms of the cost and effort involved in abolition, on the side of doing nothing; yet action was taken. And those who refuse to consider the possibility of intervention in South Africa, for all time, and in all circumstances, may find themselves as mistaken (in respect of the strength of public opinion) as the former opponents of abolition. If, for example, there were to be large-scale disorders in South Africa and harsh repression, a similar revulsion might compel the United Kingdom not merely to accept, but to give active support to, collective action. Nor can one be sure that the United Nations, including Britain and the United States, would be able to hold aloof if the South African government ceased to be able, amidst scenes of terror and violence, to control events in the Republic. The legal grounds for intervention might still be difficult to obtain unless it was at the invitation of a frightened government in Pretoria: but necessity may bend the law to what has to be done.[28]

The ugly possibility exists, therefore, that Britain and the United States may have to intervene. Should this point be reached, if events were to take this course, there would indeed be a case for intervention by the United Nations not simply in terms of an economic boycott but in the fullest sense of the word—not to 'exert pressure' but to impose a settlement. It would have to be both massive and long term, including the use of overwhelming military power, an occupying force, an indefinite period of administration, very large allocations of funds to cover the cost of the operation, and the resolute enforcement of whatever solution could be reached by international agreement. One has only to list these requirements to see the immense difficulties involved. For the almost universal condemnation today of apartheid would not prevent disputes between the great powers (or among United Nations' members in general) over the use of force, the provision of funds, the legal grounds for intervention, and the terms to be imposed on the Republic. Thus those who now support a policy of total sanctions draw back from advocating inter-

[28] The legal obstacles to UN intervention are described below, Ch. VI.

vention on this scale. But to assume that fundamental changes of
policy (and of heart?) can be achieved by external pressure alone
in the present circumstances of the Republic is simply to deceive
either oneself or those to whom the argument is addressed.[29] If,
therefore, it ever became possible to reach agreement in the
Security Council to intervene, in order (for example), to put a
stop to savage fighting between white and non-white, there
would be a strong case for arguing the need to use the full range
of coercive measures within the terms of the Charter. Then, and
only then perhaps, there might be the power available to work
towards those shadowy ends of federation, or partition, or the
evacuation of substantial sections of the population, which are
bound to draw near once white supremacy is lost.

If such a dramatic course were adopted, the United Kingdom
would clearly have to surrender its immediate interests in the
Republic—trade, investment, defence, and the three Southern
African Territories; they would be swept aside by the urgency of
the need to intervene, and many of the arguments used later in
this study would no longer be relevant. Yet it would also be mischievous to pretend that measures of this kind are capable of being taken at the present time. There is little in the existing situation in the Republic, or at the United Nations, or in the current
state of international relations, to warrant such a belief. All the
evidence points in the opposite direction, to an unstable international situation and the maintenance of white rule by the
Nationalist government in South Africa. While these circumstances last, therefore, Britain must learn to live with the pressure
from the African states for intervention. It must point out the
probable events that would follow in the wake of sanctions, and
argue the need—at least for the immediate future—for a continuing watching brief on developments in the Republic. There
is also little point in trying to isolate white South Africa by way of
a withdrawal of social contacts or diplomatic representation. The
United Kingdom government can do very little at present to
persuade National Party leaders of the dangers of sharpening the
knife that may one day be held against their own throats; but it
is equally unlikely to achieve very much by severing the ties
which now link South Africa with Britain. To try and turn aside
would be morally wrong and—in respect of the large number of

[29] Again, for the very different circumstances of Rhodesia, see below, Ch. VII.

voluntary links—virtually impossible to carry through in practice. Apartheid is an evil, but neither Britain nor the United
States—nor western Europe—has the right to wash its hands of
the responsibility for what may happen: indeed, the extremes of
racial prejudice there are a frightening example of what may be
found in weak or strong measure throughout western society—
and the world. There may also be long-term advantages in
resisting the temptation to turn away from the Republic. By refusing to isolate South Africa both Britain and the west may be
able to sustain hope among those who not only refuse to accept
apartheid but who keep alive the possibility of peaceful change.
For once hope is gone the worst may seem the best, and there will
be no alternative to violence. That may happen. Disaster may
sweep through the Republic: but in the end—however long it
may be in coming—there would have to be a slow and painful
period of reconstruction. It is then that the small number of
South Africans who now try to preserve a belief in the values of
a free society may be of inestimable value. They are there in
South Africa today, and the west ought not to abandon them.

II
Britain, South Africa, and the OAU

ALTHOUGH isolated in the south of Africa, the Republic is part of a continent to which both geography and politics ascribe a formal unity. A historian may wonder whether African countries have much in common with each other apart from their colonial origin, but pan-African sentiment insists on seeing the continent as one and indivisible, and there is a simple cartographical unity about the huge land mass that lends itself to a synoptic view. Moreover, it is generally agreed that the African states are united—if on no other issue—in their attack on apartheid. It is proposed in this chapter, therefore, to examine a wider theme: to inquire into the relative success and failure of the pan-African attack, and its bearing on British interests in Africa as a whole. Within this general frame of reference it will be useful to raise a number of related questions. Hitherto it has been possible for Britain to divorce its economic interests in southern Africa from those in the rest of the continent. The greater part of its trade is carried by sea without intermediate calls at other ports, and the threat by African governments of restrictions on the east coast route (and air travel) has been more verbal than real. But pressure may be exerted by other means, and it is no more than prudent to reckon with the possibility that the African attack on South Africa may be extended to affect British interests throughout the continent. One must ask, therefore, whether Britain will be obliged to choose between one side and the other; and, if it is forced to take such a decision, what the balance of British interests is between southern Africa and the independent African states.

The decade 1955–65 saw a remarkable change in the distribution of power in the continent, in which the African states have so far made the running. Within this short span of years, three empires in 'black Africa' have come to an end. British power has been transferred to successor governments in all its former colonies north of the Zambesi. France retains control only of the small enclave of French Somaliland. Belgium has surrendered its rule over the immense area of the Congo and the trust territories of Ruanda-Urundi. The force of African nationalism has reached and—one can argue—must surely soon overrun, the final frontiers of white settlement. The rate of African advance may be seen, too, in the extraordinary reversal of South African fortunes. It is difficult now to recall that in 1945 South Africa was the only country of international significance in Africa, a major part of which—between the Cape and the Kenya Highlands—was still under colonial/settler rule. Nor had earlier claims to a 'pan-African' interest by the South African government yet lost their force, i.e. that the areas of European civilization north of the Limpopo were in a sphere for which it had a special concern. The position today is very different. An 'Organization of African Unity' is in being, whose headquarters are at Addis Ababa; its Charter has been ratified by thirty-six independent African states, each pledged to 'eradicate all forms of colonialism from Africa'.[1] And it is the OAU leaders—unfolding the banner of popular sovereignty—who are now insisting that South Africa is an integral part of Africa. Behind the demand lie the assumptions of a successful anti-colonialism and (in sub-Saharan Africa) the emotion of *négritude*—including the belief that the independent African states have a special concern for what happens in the Republic because it is 'black man's country'; other communities may have their place there, but a subordinate place. This is the attack from which the South African government has been forced to retreat. Pushed back within its frontiers, challenged over its possession of the mandated territory of South West Africa, white South Africa now looks to its defences, raises the image of the laager, and has to assert its right to survive as 'a unique African nation that in outlook and descent is of Europe'.[2] One may easily understand the African leaders in recent years for believing that history is on their side, and that it needs very little in the way of help to complete the 'emancipation of Africa'. Rhodesia will fall; Angola and Moçambique will follow; then

---

[1] Charter of the OAU, Art. II (1) (d). The member states also 'solemnly affirm [their] absolute dedication to the total emancipation of the African territories which are still dependent' (Art. III (6)).

[2] *S. African Realities*. Booklet prepared by the Dept of Information, SA Embassy, n.d.

South West Africa: until South Africa itself is liberated. The exact timing and order may be difficult to foresee, but during the past decade it seemed logical to conclude that the end of white supremacy was in view.

Confident assertions of this kind still run through many of the declarations of the meetings of African heads of states and governments. None the less, pessimism keeps breaking in. For although the African states have numbers on their side, they lack power. They lack military power; they lack economic strength. The political will to concert measures against South Africa or Portuguese rule is also vitiated by quarrels among themselves. Many of the states are frail structures, whose regimes are easily challenged by local opponents—as in Senegal where Mamadou Dia and his associates are in prison for conspiracy, in Togo where Olympio was murdered, in Ghana where Nkrumah walks in fear of subversion, the Ivory Coast where plots against Hou-phoüet Boigny have been suppressed, the Congo (Brazzaville) where the Abbé Youlou was overthrown, Dahomey where Maga was replaced by the army, the Sudan where conflict between the north and the south forced Abboud out of office, Zanzibar where the Sultan was overthrown, Tanganyika, Uganda, and Kenya where army mutinies defied the newly established party regimes, and—above all—the Congo (Léopoldville) where the government seems always to stand near to the brink of collapse. The list is already long, and it is difficult to see many years of stability ahead. There are also disputes between the newly independent states which sap the governments' will to act together—Algeria–Morocco, Kenya–Somalia, Morocco–Mauritania, Ruanda–Burundi, Ghana–Togo; quarrels also over support for rival factions in the Congo, Angola, and Moçambique. These differences may not lead to sustained conflict, but they breed suspicion of neighbours' intentions and inhibit joint action. In sum, it is no longer so easy to be sure that time is on the side of the African states. The remarkable feature of the African scene was that all but Ethiopia, Liberia, Libya, and Egypt became independent within the same decade, 1956–66; twenty-four became independent within five years (1957–62) of each other. There has been a nominal unity of colonial origin, and a mutual awareness on the part of African leaders that they share the fact of a newly attained freedom; but this sentiment of belonging to a particular period of history is very likely to fade as they move farther away from the coincidence of their origins.

The African states lack military power. There are about 400,000 men in their armed forces, of whom some 250,000 are in the north African states, 34,000 in Ethiopia, and 30,000 at one time in the Congo. By contrast, the Republic of South Africa has a cadre-type defence force which is the nucleus of a citizen army of fairly well trained white men, backed by the most modern as well as the most experienced air force on the continent.[3] Mr Gutteridge adds: 'Not only is the military strength of the new African states minimal; they have not the ability to deploy it far from home. Transport aircraft and ships are not part of their equipment.'[4] There is an additional weakness on the African side. The armed forces of the leading military powers among the African states are not only situated at the other end of the continent but are actively engaged in local conflicts. The United Arab Republic is more conscious of Israel than of South Africa, and has large numbers of troops deployed in the Yemen. Ethiopia has a constant preoccupation with Somalia and the Somali nomads of the Ogaden. If there were to be a land frontier between South Africa and the independent African states the position might perhaps be different. But here, too, one must note the paradox: the more militant states are those at the greatest distance from South Africa; the weaker states are on its borders. Proximity has bred caution and has forced recognition of the need to reach at least a temporary *modus vivendi*—by Malawi with Moçambique, by the former High Commission Territories with South Africa, and—to date—by Zambia, even with Rhodesia. If the Portuguese were to withdraw from Moçambique, it is by no means certain that their successors would be either willing or able to become the advance base for military intervention in South Africa. Nor is it clear, even if an African government in Lourenço Marques were to be firmly in control throughout the country and was determined to forego the economic advantages of collaboration with Pretoria, whether the military strength would be there to undertake the overthrow of its powerful neighbour.

[3] & [4] Neville Brown and W. F. Gutteridge, *The African Military Balance* (Aug. 1964) and M. J. V. Bell, *Army and the Nation in Sub-Saharan Africa* (Aug. 1965), Adelphi Papers nos 12 and 21, published by the Inst. for Strategic Studies.

Direct intervention by military force in South Africa has there-fore to be ruled out by the independent African states. They would be thrown back if they tried, and it is difficult to see them being prepared to try. What can they do? Although divided among themselves, and absorbed in domestic disputes, their hos-tility to white supremacy rule has provided some common ground for action which is worth examining. They have attempt-ed a triple attack: by sponsoring resolutions at the United Nations designed to entangle Britain and the west with their own campaign against South Africa, by imposing an African boycott against South Africa, and by assisting clandestine groups in Angola, Moçambique, and South Africa.

The first prong of this attack was greatly helped by the forma-tion of an African Group of eight states at the United Nations in 1958. Powerfully reinforced as independence spread throughout tropical Africa, it enabled the growing number of Afro-Asian members to press for international action, whether on apartheid and colonialism in general, or the particular issue of South West Africa. The actual procedure will be looked at later; but one may note here a number of the steps taken. On 4 November 1960, for example, Ethiopia and Liberia entered their case over South West Africa against the South African government before the International Court. Two years later (21 December 1962) the Court decided by the slender majority of eight votes to seven that it had jurisdiction in the issue and proceeded to consider the merits of the dispute.[5] Within the General Assembly, the African delegations secured a resolution (for which Britain voted) in April 1961, by 96 votes to 1, which requested member states 'to consider taking such separate and collective action as was open to them to bring about the abandonment of these [apartheid] policies'. It was the first tentative approval by the Assembly of collective sanctions, and the appetite grew with feeding. At the inaugural meeting of the Organization of African Unity in Addis Ababa in May 1963 the thirty-two heads of states and govern-ments resolved to press home their attack in the Security Council on which the Ivory Coast and Morocco were represented,[6] and

[5] See below, Ch. IV.
[6] It was recognized that voting in the General Assembly could only produce recommendations: what was wanted was a mandatory resolution in the Security Council.

to campaign for the expulsion of South Africa from the Specialized Agencies of the United Nations. By 1964 they could register a number of successes in this strange world of resolutions, vetoes, abstentions, verbal manœuvres and—sometimes—action. They had secured general approval in the Assembly for the application of sanctions against South Africa where governments were willing to operate them. They had pushed Britain and the United States in the Security Council to the point where they agreed that the situation in South Africa was 'disturbing international peace and security'.[7] They had obtained a resolution in the Security Council against the sale of arms to South Africa.[8] There was also a decision by the Security Council on 4 December 1963 to establish 'a group of experts' to consider the situation in South Africa and what part the United Nations might play in resolving it; and, step by step, South Africa was excluded or forced to withdraw from a number of international bodies—the FAO, the ILO, the WHO, the International Olympics Committee, the Economic Commission for Africa. On the international front, therefore, the African states have gone some way towards isolating South Africa. Yet, despite these gains, the fact remains that the Afro-Asian states have so far failed in their principal object. They have not been able to edge the western powers—the United States and Britain in particular—beyond a general condemnation of apartheid, a readiness to support United Nations efforts to concern itself with the issue, and a qualified arms embargo. Both Britain and America have stopped short of critical phrases declaring the situation in South Africa 'a threat' to international peace. Both made it clear in the July meeting of the Security Council in 1963 that they would regard as illegal a resolution calling for mandatory sanctions.

In their second line of attack, the African states have tried to impose their own boycotts. Resolutions were passed both at the Addis Ababa and Cairo conferences declaring an embargo on trade with South Africa. They have closed their harbours and airports to South Africa, denying it (for example) landing facilities in Kenya and Libya, and forcing South African Airways to fly the longer, west coast route to London via Luanda and Las Palmas. At Lagos, in April 1964, the African foreign ministers agreed to examine the possibilities of a boycott of all ships and

[7] & [8] See below, Chs. IV and V.

aircraft going to and from South Africa, a decision endorsed by the second plenary meeting of the OAU at Cairo but not (at present) implemented; and at both meetings consideration was given to a postal and telecommunications ban on South Africa.[9] But on this front, too, the African states find themselves hampered. They have been able to vex the South African government; they can often isolate its representatives in international gatherings. They can restrict South Africa's trade with the rest of Africa, and stir the conscience of Scandinavian dockers and Scottish labour councillors over the handling of South African goods and contracts. But these are pinpricks rather than wounds. Moreover the Afro-Asian states were for long irresolute. If the official boycotts on South African exports were completely effective (it has been estimated)

the loss of trade to South Africa would be approximately R35,000,000 per annum or 4·5% the value of our merchandise exports. In actual fact the loss of trade between 1959 and 1962 was only about R12,500,000 per annum or 1·7% of South Africa's merchandise exports excluding gold (1% if gold is included). This is partly because some of the boycotts are of recent origin (e.g. Kenya and the Philippines) but also because not all the boycotts have been very effective so far. Malaya, for example, which officially began to boycott South Africa in mid-1960, still bought R3,900,000 worth of goods from us in 1962.[10]

Other evidence of a weakening of faith would not be difficult to find. Senegal continued to send its phosphates to South Africa at least until 1964.[11] Ghanaian hardwoods have been shipped to

---

[9] The Cairo heads of states and governments agreed 'to take the necessary steps to refuse any aeroplane or ship or any other means of communication going to or coming from South Africa the right to fly over the territories of member states or utilize their ports or any other facilities'. In 1963 Portugal had been included in similar resolutions by the Addis Ababa conference and the meeting of ministers at Dakar in August; it was omitted from the decisions reached at Lagos in February 1964 and at Cairo in July.

[10] 'Implications of Economic and other Boycotts for S. Africa', paper submitted by Mr Leo Katzen to the SA Inst. of Race Relations, Jan. 1964. (R1 = 10 shillings.) It is also clear, however, that if it were not for the African boycotts, South African trade with the rest of the continent would be much larger than it is. Trade with the African continent reached its highest level in 1957—and then declined. See D. Hobart Houghton, *The S. African Economy* (1964), pp. 170–1.

[11] Report in *Le Monde*, 15 May 1964: 'Répondant, à l'occasion de sa conférence de presse hebdomadaire, à la question d'un journaliste relative à la persis-

Lourenço Marques where they are reassigned to Durban. The Congo (Léopoldville) bought more from and exported more to South Africa in 1962 than it had done before independence in 1960.[12] The countries bordering on the 'strongholds of white colonialism' are obliged to recognize their interdependence with Moçambique or Rhodesia or South Africa. Dr Banda had to tell the second meeting of the OAU in Cairo in 1964 that, while fervently believing in the independence of Africa, he could not 'commit economic suicide to be a loyal OAU member'; compliance with a resolution demanding severance of ties with Portugal 'would mean economic strangulation'.[13] During Zambia's first years of independence President Kaunda was similarly cautious. A number of post-federal arrangements continued to link the Zambian and Rhodesian governments together, through a joint Railway Board of Management, common air services, and the supply of power from the Kariba dam; Zambian copper continued to find its main outlet through Rhodesia. The country's two principal suppliers of imports in 1964–5 were Rhodesia (£30 million—40 per cent) and South Africa (£16 million—21 per cent).[14] Whether these links can now be maintained after the

---

tance de courants commerciaux entre le Sénégal et la République Sud-Africaine, M. Lamine Diakhate, ministre sénégalais de l'information, a déclaré que le gouvernement sénégalais croyait devoir honorer ses contrats antérieurs aux décisions de boycottage économique. Il a fait valoir d'autre part que certains pays progressistes, qui font pression sur le Sénégal pour qu'il abandonne un client intéressant pour ses phosphates, feraient mieux de commencer par donner eux-mêmes l'exemple. Le ministre n'a nommé aucun État particulier, mais il faisait allusion, selon certains fonctionnaires de son ministère, à la Tchécoslovaquie et à Cuba. Le ministre a ajouté qu'au sein même de l'Organisation de l'unité africaine (OUA) de nombreux États non seulement continuaient comme par le passé à entretenir des relations commerciales avec l'Afrique du Sud, mais n'avaient même pris aucune décision officielle de boycottage.'

[12]

	Exports	Imports
1956	£9·43 m.	£3·3 m.
1962	£11·3 m.	£3·7 m.

(UN, Yearbook of International Trade, 1962)

[13] *Guardian*, 22 July 1964.

[14] In 1964 Zambia's external trade included (£ million):

	From Rhodesia	From S. Africa	Total
Imports	30	16	77
	To Rhodesia	To S. Africa	
Exports	7	13	168

unilateral declaration of independence by the Rhodesia Front may be questioned; but (at the time of writing) the economic unity of the region has continued to assert itself over political differences north and south of the Zambesi. Farther south still, Bechuanaland, Swaziland, and Basutoland are part of the customs union of South Africa, and could hardly stand alone without the wider market and employment opportunities available in the Republic.[15] There is thus a major difficulty for the African states in this context, namely the inequality of sacrifice that action against South Africa imposes on the other members. All can agree that measures must be taken, but not all are willing—or able—to meet the bill that may be submitted in respect of their own local economy.

The third line of attack by the OAU has been to assist opposition groups in Angola, Moçambique, Rhodesia, and South Africa with money, propaganda material, arms, the training of 'freedom fighters', and refuge for those seeking asylum: a 'sapping and mining operation' ranging from help given to those engaged in the revolt in northern Angola in 1962 to the encouragement of sabotage in South Africa. Promises of assistance to exiled leaders of African nationalist parties have included money and the offer of 'volunteers'. According to the evidence produced at the Rivonia Trial (which opened in Pretoria on 9 October 1963), Nelson Mandela was given or promised: '£10,000 from Nigeria, £5,000 from Tunisia, £3,000 in Morocco, £2,000 in Liberia would be yearly amount; £5,000 in Ethiopia and definite promises from Senegal and the Sudan'.[16] A Liberation Committee of the OAU was established at Dar es Salaam by nine member states—Algeria, Ethiopia, Guinea, Congo (Léopoldville), Nigeria, Senegal, Tanzania, UAR, and Uganda—to co-ordinate the help given to the various 'liberation movements'. It maintains contact with nationalist groups in exile and (one may assume) gives such help as it can to insurgent leaders in Moçambique and Angola.

Here too the African states cannot claim much success. The Liberation Committee was criticized by Nkrumah at the 1964 Cairo meeting of the OAU in terms which it was difficult to re-

---

[15] See below, Ch. III.
[16] Entry in Mandela's diary, quoted in H. H. W. de Villiers, *Rivonia* (1964), p. 86. See also N. Mandela, *No Easy Walk to Freedom* (1965).

fute except on the grounds that it was prompted more by resentment at Ghana's exclusion from the committee than by a concern for 'failures (which were) inexcusable because they were so unnecessary'. According to Nkrumah, there was

general dissatisfaction . . . regarding the functioning of this Committee. . . .

The choice of the Congo (Leopoldville) as a training base for freedom fighters was a logical one, and there was every reason to accept the offer of the Congolese Government to provide offices and accommodation for the representatives of the Liberation Committee. . . .

What could be the result of entrusting the training of freedom fighters against imperialism into the hands of an imperialist agent? Under the Liberation Committee set up at Addis Ababa, the freedom fighters had no real security, and were not provided with instruments for their struggle, nor were food, clothing and medicine given for the men in training. Thus, their training scheme collapsed within two months under the eyes of the Liberation Committee, and the freedom fighters became disappointed, disgruntled and frustrated.[17]

The charges were brushed aside. The OAU decided that the Liberation Committee should remain at Dar es Salaam, and that payment to the Committee of a minimum sum (based on members' contributions to the United Nations) should be made obligatory. There was point, however, in Nkrumah's general comment on the failure of the pan-African movement to alter the balance of power in southern Africa:

By raising a threat at Addis Ababa and not being able to take effective action against apartheid and colonialism, we have worsened

---

[17] 'Africa's Finest Hour', speech delivered by President Nkrumah at the Conference of African Heads of State and Government in Cairo on 19 July 1964, Supplement to *Ghana Today*, 29 July 1964. President Nyerere was equally blunt:

'The real reason [for the criticism] was extremely petty. The decision not to contribute funds was made at Addis Ababa as soon as the conference committed the unforgivable crime of not including Ghana on the committee and of choosing Dar es Salaam as its headquarters. . . . The great Osagyefo then asks the question: "What could be the result of entrusting the training of freedom fighters against Imperialism into the hands of an imperialist agent?" Firstly, Mr Chairman, if . . . the President of Ghana believes the liberation committee should have been housed in Leopoldville, then all I can do is ask you to imagine what the consequences would have been. Secondly, if the reference to an imperialist agent refers to my country or to any of its leaders, those who know my country, its leaders and its people, and all those who have any respect for the truth, know that it is a lie' (*The Times*, 21 July 1964).

the plight of our kinsmen in Angola, Mozambique, Southern Rhodesia and South Africa. We have frightened the imperialists sufficiently to strengthen their defences and repression in southern Africa, but we have not frightened them enough to abandon apartheid supremacy to its ill-fated doom.[18]

The primary reason for failure was clear, namely the inability of the African states—financially and militarily—to help anyone but themselves, and very often not being able to do that. After 1960 the outstanding illustration of the frustration of the OAU was the Congo—where the withdrawal of United Nations forces in 1963 left the OAU states powerless either to help the Léopold-ville government or to replace it with one more to their taste. It was perhaps an extreme example, baffling to the African governments and the great powers alike. None the less, it was also only the most dramatic demonstration of the fact that the OAU was unlikely to be any more effective as a regional organization in achieving its ends, or settling its troubles, than its counterparts in Latin America and the Arab world.

On each of these three fronts, therefore, the African states have been able to do no more than score minor successes without substantially advancing the anti-colonial, anti-apartheid aims set out in the OAU Charter. It is possible to argue that, in this respect at least, the Charter will remain a dead letter, that the effort required of the newly independent governments to defend their 'sovereignty and territorial integrity [against] political assassination, as well as . . . subversive activities on the part of neighbouring states or any other state'[19] will allow southern Africa to go to its own 'ill-fated doom' without pressure from outside. To each country its locally determined destiny? Perhaps. Yet the very weakness of the newly independent states may have the opposite effect. It may lead them—and the evidence is there already in the efforts made over the Rhodesian crisis and at the United Nations—to seek outside help for what they cannot do unaided. Pan-African sentiment is most easily generated in its anti-colonial setting, and finds strongest expression in the common ground of the leaders' hostility to white supremacy. It is unlikely, therefore, that the African states will be prepared to abandon the tie that helps to keep them together. Moreover, events in central and southern Africa itself may stiffen their determina-

[18] 'Africa's Finest Hour'.   [19] Charter of the OAU, Art. III, 3 (5).

tion. A renewal of the Angolan revolt, strikes and riots against Mr Smith's government in Rhodesia, and acts of sabotage in South Africa—countered by an increased severity of repression—may force the hands even of the most conservative of the African leaders. It is precisely in these circumstances, out of a frustration born of the desire to act and the failure to act effectively, that the African states are likely to try and exert pressure on those powers which have substantial interests throughout the continent.

Where does Britain stand in this situation? No longer a major colonial power, it might be thought to have escaped, by its own efforts and in good time, the obloquy which clings to Portugal and South Africa. 'Colonies', as Duncan Sandys once remarked, '. . . involve us in much unwelcome controversy with the outside world.'[20] If the illegal Rhodesia Front government can be forced out of power in Salisbury, and the three Southern African Territories be brought safely to independence, the future of British-African relations might be thought to augur well. There has been a long history between Britain and a large part of the continent. There are mutual interests in trade and investment; there are those special links of 'affection and affinity'[21] between Britain and the nine Commonwealth African members—Gambia, Ghana, Kenya, Malawi, Nigeria, Sierre Leone, Tanzania, Uganda, and Zambia. There are all the advantages on both sides—notwithstanding current charges of neo-colonialism—of a continuing relationship between an ex-Imperial country and its ex-colonies. In this possible Eden, however, white supremacy in South Africa and Rhodesia is very much the evil serpent. At the time of writing, it is impossible to say how Mr Smith's declaration of independence will affect relations between Britain and the African states. It could draw them closer together if Mr Wilson can convince the Commonwealth African leaders that he is determined to end the rebellion; it will strain them to breaking point if there is lasting suspicion of British intentions. South Africa is a different case since Britain has no formal responsibility there. Yet it is the Republic's biggest customer and by far its largest investor, and maintains with the Republic many of its former Commonwealth bonds. Hence the argument, heard more

[20] Duncan Sandys, *The Modern Commonwealth* (London, 1962), pp. 2–3.
[21] Ibid. p. 5.

and more in recent years, that Britain should push the process of disengagement, begun in 1961 when South Africa left the Commonwealth, still farther. A far worse storm than the rebellion in Rhodesia (it is said) is gathering over South Africa and Britain would be exceedingly foolish to draw the lightning down on itself, since it may destroy British interests not only in South Africa but in Africa as a whole. Thus we reach the questions raised at the beginning of this chapter, namely what is the balance of British interests between South Africa and Africa north of the Limpopo? What kind of pressures might the African states exert to force the United Kingdom to choose between them?

There are three overlapping groups of interests. There are those which are primarily economic. There are Commonwealth interests. And (it can be argued) there is the particular concern of Britain to retain the goodwill of African leaders and countries —born of the era of European colonialism—whose principal ties are still with the west.

Trade and Investment

We turn first to trade, and an immediate difficulty must be confessed. It is by no means easy to draw a satisfactory balance sheet between trading interests spread over a whole continent, and those concentrated in the single market of South Africa. Such conclusions, therefore, as may be reached must be tentative. Yet one can dispose of the simple argument from scale. It is tempting to rely on the assertion that South Africa is merely the tip of a vast continent of over 200 million people. The larger interest, therefore, must surely lie with the greater number of the African states than with the fortunes of a regime about whose future there is almost universal misgiving. The contrast is indeed vivid. But poverty is no respecter of size; nor is wealth always on the side of the large battalions. In the round, the United Kingdom's trade with the independent African countries is greater than it is with South Africa. Nevertheless, the Republic is comparatively rich and its economy is expanding; the African countries are relatively poor, and in many of them the economy is sluggish. Thus, by comparison, the advantages of the South African market stand out plainly, whereas its long-term uncertainty can only be conjectured.

The trade figures are reasonably clear. Exports from the

United Kingdom to the independent African states exceed those to southern Africa, though to a lesser extent than one might suppose, considering the disparity of population between them. Imports into Britain are much higher from the African states than from South Africa: indeed, there is an unfavourable balance of trade with most of the new countries. Investment is considerably greater in South Africa than in any other single African country but less impressive when placed against British investment in the continent as a whole.

The figures of British exports to Africa are:

UK Exports f.o.b. (£ million)

To	*1959*	*1960*	*1961*	*1962*	*1963*	*1964*
Commonwealth Africa	187·5	201·3	203·2	172·6	189·0	191·0
Other independent African states	66·9	80·5	87·1	95·5	97·3	98·7
TOTAL	254·4	281·8	290·3	268·1	286·3	289·7
South Africa	150·8	155·9	148·7	148·4	198·0	225·0
South West Africa	1·3	1·5	2·1	1·8	1·7	2·6
Bechuanaland, Basutoland, Swaziland	0·5	0·5	0·4	0·3	0·5	0·4
TOTAL	152·6	157·8	151·2	150·5	200·2	228·0

Source: Board of Trade, *Report on Overseas Trade 1964.*

These figures include rough estimates of exports to Zambia and Malawi, based on the proportion of British exports to Southern Rhodesia, Northern Rhodesia, and Nyasaland during the period 1946–53.[22] Even if one adds to the South African customs union total the value of British exports to Angola, Moçambique, Rhodesia, and the remaining colonial territories in Africa— Spanish Sahara, French Somaliland, Portuguese Guinea—the difference (though narrower) is still in favour of the African states:

[22] *Proportion of total Central African Imports from Britain.*

	per cent
S. Rhodesia	70
Zambia	23
Malawi	7

UK Exports f.o.b. (£ million)

To	1959	1960	1961	1962	1963	1964
South African customs union	152·6	157·8	151·2	150·5	200·2	228·0
Moçambique	5·2	6·5	5·3	4·8	6·3	6·7
Angola	3·6	4·3	4·6	5·0	5·7	5·9
Rhodesia	34·7	33·1	33·2	29·1	31·5	33·0
Other colonies	1·5	1·7	2·0	1·8	2·0	2·2
TOTAL	197·7	203·4	196·3	191·2	245·7	275·8
Independent African states	254·4	281·8	290·3	268·1	286·3	289·7

Source: Ibid.

UK Exports as Percentage of Total African Purchases (£ m.)*

To	1959			1960			1961			1962			1963			1964		
	Total	UK	%	Total	UK	%	Total	UK	%	Total	UK	%	Total	UK	%	Total	UK	%
Nigeria	178	81	46	215	91	42	221	85	38	203	74	36	207	71	36	253	79	31
Ghana	113	45	40	130	48	37	141	52	37	117	40	34	130	43	33	121	33	27
Sierra Leone	24	10	42	26	11	42	33	15	46	30	12	40	30	13	43	36	14	39
Tanganyika	36	11	31	39	10	26	42	12	29	42	10	24	43	11	26}	64	15	23
Zanzibar	6	1	20	53	1	19	6	1	23	52	1	21	5	1	17}			
Uganda†	21	5	24	21	5	24	22	6	27	22	5	23	28	6	21	46	11	24
Kenya	84	30	36	97	31	32	95	31	33	98	30	31	106	30	28	88	23	26
Rhod. Fed.‡	150	55	37	156	51	33	154	51	33	142	46	33	135	43	32	201	49	24
S. Africa	499	152	31	563	157	30	510	149	29	523	148	28	648	198	31	763	225	30

* Figures rounded. † Direct imports 1959–63; net imports 1964.

‡		Total	UK	%
1964	Zambia	77	13	17
	Rhodesia	110	33	30
	Malawi	14	3	21

Sources: Commonwealth Economic Committee, *Commonwealth Trade 1964* (1965); Board of Trade; Houghton, p. 242; Union Acceptances Ltd, *The Scope for Investment in S. Africa* (1964), pp. 5–6.

On closer inspection the picture is less favourable to the OAU countries. British exports to many of the larger African markets have remained stagnant or have declined. For although imports into the African states may have increased, the British share of the market has declined by up to 10 per cent of total imports between 1959 and 1964. Exports to South Africa, on the other hand, have maintained a reasonably steady proportion of the total market, and in the past two years sales have risen (and risen fast), the result not only of an increased purchasing power among all sections of the population but of the hold that United Kingdom exporters still have on this traditional market. The effect of independence in the African states has had the opposite result. It has led to a turning away from the traditional Imperial connexion to new sources of supply. If the figures are taken of imports from Britain into a number of Commonwealth African markets, the contrast with South Africa is plain (see second table on p. 38).

By 1963–4 South Africa was a larger market for British exports than the combined Commonwealth markets of Nigeria, Ghana, Sierra Leone, Tanzania, Uganda, and Kenya:

Imports from Britain (£ m.) into:	*1959*	*1963*	*1964*
Nigeria, Ghana, Sierra Leone, Tanzania, Uganda, Kenya	182	174	175
Republic of South Africa	152	198	225

Sources: Ibid.

The Commonwealth African pattern reproduced the global picture of the long downward trend (in the percentage of world trade) of British exports to the Commonwealth markets. The goods bought by South Africa, on the other hand, reflected the general increase in British overseas trade during 1963. The Republic is still dependent on the import of a large range of manufactures since its principal exports (like those of the independent African states) are of agricultural produce and industrial raw or semi-processed materials: in addition, its own rapid programme of industrialization has increased the demand for imports. Thus it helped in the general expansion of British sales of engineering products, transport equipment (including motor vehicles), and electrical machinery. One must add, too, that the Commonwealth African countries are in receipt of United Kingdom development aid; in addition, both Kenya and Malawi receive direct British subsidies of several million pounds.[23] South Africa benefits only from private investment from which there is a fair return on capital. Nor can one be optimistic that the next decade will see a substantial growth in demand in African markets despite the efforts made to assist the underdeveloped world. In

---

[23] In 1965 Britain provided £9¼ m. in aid to Malawi, of which £6¼ m. was needed to cover the deficit in the budget of £15¼ m. The balance of £3 m. was for development.

D

short, the argument from scale—'the handful of Europeans in South Africa compared with the many millions of Africa-north-of-the-Limpopo'—is less impressive in terms of markets for British exports than one might deduce from the plain fact of the numbers involved. A fairer conclusion would be that both groups of markets—'independent Africa' and southern Africa—are important. Together, they accounted for over 10 per cent of the total value of British exports between 1959 and 1963. But neither is so clearly superior to the other—even supposing a choice had to be made—that the loss on one side would far outweigh the loss on the other.

In terms of imports into Britain the picture is different:

UK Imports c.i.f. (£000)

From:	1959	1960	1961	1962	1963	1964
Commonwealth Africa	147,539	142,253	140,846	135,615	163,800	171,100
Other ind. African states	64,171	72,727	63,463	90,423	98,534	110,203
TOTAL	211,710	214,980	204,309	226,038	262,334	281,303
South Africa	89,264	96,410	103,302	103,144	115,080	126,000
South West Africa	8,037	9,611	7,485	11,656	12,031	13,042
Bech., Bas., Swaz.	1,446	3,656	3,799	3,642	3,721	3,694
Colonial territories	3,609	3,750	4,756	4,014	4,503	4,783
TOTAL	102,356	113,427	119,342	122,456	135,335	147,519

Source: Board of Trade, *Report on Overseas Trade 1964.*

Note: The table excludes the Federation of Rhodesia and Nyasaland from which imports into the UK were: 1959—£90,301,000; 1960—£103,047,000; 1961—£101,794,000; 1962—£95,511,000. Approximate proportion of imports from the three territories: Southern Rhodesia—25 per cent; Northern Rhodesia—68·5 per cent; Nyasaland—6·5 per cent.

Which is the more valuable source of supply? Wines and fruit from the Cape, or coffee and cocoa from Kenya and Ghana? Palm oil and cotton from Nigeria and Egypt, or sugar and wool from South Africa? It would be hard to say. Over the full range of British imports, the African states are important suppliers of tropical products, and many United Kingdom importers would clearly find it difficult—certainly in the short run—to turn to alternative sources to meet the full demand of the home market.

On the other hand, many of the principal commodities on which the economy of the African countries depend absolutely—cocoa, coffee, ground nuts, oil seeds—have outrun world demand in recent years. In 1964, for example, the Ghanaian government authorized a number of bonfires each of some 500 tons of cocoa in Accra in an attempt 'to increase the bargaining powers of producers'.[24] The moral is clear. Although the United Kingdom might find it difficult to procure alternative sources of supply, it would be impossible for the African countries to find alternative markets for their sales to the United Kingdom. One might note here too—the point is made more fully below—that whereas African imports into Britain are only about $4\frac{1}{2}$ per cent of total imports, all the Commonwealth African countries send a substantial proportion of their total exports to the United Kingdom.[25]

A number of the independent African states are valuable sources of minerals, including some of strategic value to Britain (and the west): but so is South Africa, and it is an impossible task to try and choose between them. The balance of importance tilts first to one side, then to the other, according to which particular mineral or precious metal is selected: no simple verdict can be reached in respect of South Africa on the one hand and the independent African countries on the other.[26]

A similar account emerges from a survey of investment. The figures of British private capital investment overseas are extraordinarily difficult to assess. But, taking those given by the Board of Trade—where the returns of investment in South Africa and selected Commonwealth African countries (though below the amount usually given for South Africa from local sources) have the merit of being calculated on a common base—the picture that emerges is of a near balance between Commonwealth Africa and South Africa (see table on p. 42 showing figures of direct investment abroad). Admittedly the figures are imprecise: they include an unscrambled figure for the now dismantled Central African Federation; and, since they exclude oil companies' activities, they omit the heavy capital investment in Nigeria by Shell International. As a proportion of the total direct

[24] Statement by Nana Sir Tsibu Darku, Chairman of the Cocoa Marketing Board, *The Times*, 12 Dec. 1964. The effect was nil.
[25] See table p. 46.   [26] See App. 4.

(*Book*) *Values of UK Companies' Direct Investment Abroad, 1962**
(£ m.)

South Africa		269
Fed. Rhodesia & Nyasaland	108	
Nigeria	79	
Sierra Leone	20	277
Ghana	50·5	
Kenya	30	
Canada		672
Australia		522
United States		341
India		256
Western Europe (of which EEC—69%; EFTA—23%)		356

* Excluding oil, insurance or banking.

Source: Board of Trade Journal, Aug. 1964, p. 293.

Note: the SA Reserve Bank, *Bull. of Statistics* (Dec. 1964) (Table 3, p. liii) gives the amount of British capital invested as: 1962—£912½ m. 1963—£927½ m. The Board of Trade omits non-direct UK investment (*c.* £250 m.), current liabilities (*c.* £240 m.), and UK companies registered in South Africa (*c.* £80 m.). Deducting these amounts from £900 m. leaves £330 m.—the balance between this amount and the £269 m. given in the table presumably being accounted for by investments of banking, oil, and insurance companies.

investment overseas by British companies, however, the amount of capital invested in South Africa (on the Board of Trade figures) is probably about 7·7 per cent.[27] The returns are high[28] but, like most of the independent African states, South Africa has imposed strict controls on the outward flow of capital, resulting in a high degree of reinvestment.

There is a further argument to be considered briefly. The African governments may be insecurely based but (it may be said) they are not faced with the possibility of total upheaval arising from a racial explosion. The events of 1960–1 in South Africa, on the other hand (when the economy was suddenly put under great restraint), might well be thought to be an ugly warning of far worse to come. There was rioting in Cato Manor, the shanty town on the outskirts of Durban; the PAC began its

[27] Total direct British investment overseas: £3,500 m.
[28] 17·1 per cent on direct investment in manufacturing, according to the US Dept of Commerce (*Scope for Investment in South Africa*, p. 39).

campaign against the pass laws, and the police opened fire on African demonstrators in the Sharpeville township near Vereeniging; further outbreaks of violence followed in Johannesburg and the Langa location outside Capetown. There was the imposition of a State of Emergency between March and August 1960, the attempt on Verwoerd's life on 9 April, unrest in Pondoland, the banning of the ANC and PAC, and the emergence in 1961 of new movements openly committed to sabotage. These sombre events appeared to many as the forerunners of a dreadful collapse of public order and, during the disturbances, capital fled the country. There was 'a huge outflow of capital of over R12 million per month during 1960 and the early part of 1961. Reserves of gold and foreign exchange were reduced to half; . . . there was the danger that fears of devaluation might accelerate the capital outflow'. It was the worst financial crisis since 1932, and 'during May 1961 the bank rate was raised, import controls were intensified, restrictions were imposed on commercial bank loans... and foreign exchange facilities were reduced.'[29] Future prosperity was seen to depend on political peace—the one commodity that seemed in short supply—and on the political expression of a racial ideology—job reservation, pass laws, Bantustans, border industries—which might combine to cripple the economy. On the other hand it had to be acknowledged that from 1962 onwards recovery was swift. The economic measures taken were paralleled by a tightening of repressive laws. There were no more than minor outbreaks of violence, if only because the ANC, PAC, and other leaders were under restriction, in prison or exile. Meanwhile capital, prevented from leaving the country, began to generate new growth; helped by an increased output from the new gold mines of the Far West Rand, Klerksdorp, the Evander district, and the Orange Free State, the effect was to lift the economy to a new level of expansion.[30]

Which of these two series of events was the more significant—

[29] Houghton, p. 179.
[30] 'These restrictive measures led to a spectacular improvement in the foreign-exchange position, a favourable balance on current account for the year 1961 of R190 million; and, despite a capital outflow of R72 million during the year, a recovery in the foreign-exchange reserves from R153 million in May 1961 to over R316 million in February 1962 . . . thus exceeding the figure at which they had stood in January 1960' (ibid. p. 179). By 1965 the reserves had dropped again because of the high level of imports.

the riots and financial panic of 1960–1, or the repressive peace and boom of 1962–4—it is impossible to say. The formula by which the outbreak of revolution may be predicted has yet to be discovered, and in relation to the particular problem of trade and investment there is a great deal to be said, in so unpredictable a field, for leaving decisions to the individual companies concerned. This is not to ignore the question, what attitude should the United Kingdom adopt in respect of collective measures against South Africa if the United Nations were to move in that direction? The writer is concerned here only with the problem of estimating the hazards involved in trading with and investing in South Africa; and whether they are different in kind (or so much greater in degree) than trade and investment in other troubled areas of the world—including the independent African states. To put money into South Africa may (perhaps) be to 'invest in a volcano' which is about to erupt;[31] but to invest in a number of newly independent states is to run the risk of expropriation and a legal battle for compensation. And on this narrow issue there can only be conflicting judgements. Certainly no two companies are likely to reach the same conclusions on the risks involved. Nor can one expect a clear statement of policy by the United Kingdom government other than the reiteration of the traditional argument of all trading nations; namely, that one must trade in the world as it is since it is unlikely ever to be as one would like to see it. For its own economic well-being, the United Kingdom has to insist that, except in times of emergency, markets are neutral; that goods for the most part (armaments excepted) are neutral; and that one trades not with 'friends' or 'enemies' but customers.

Are the independent African states likely to be able to by-pass these arguments, and to force the issue by exerting *economic* pressure on the United Kingdom? It is doubtful. The African leaders are committed to policies of economic development which are a matter of urgent concern to them, not only in respect of their own survival as governments but in terms of national needs. Faced with problems of unemployment,[32] falling prices for primary products, and the difficulties of attracting investment, they are un-

[31] *Investors' Chronicle*, 19 July 1963.
[32] The level of employment in Kenya, for example, fell by 13 per cent between December 1960 and December 1963.

likely to be eager to engage in economic conflict with their main trading partners. True, states do not act consistently with their economic self-interest: the world might be a great deal better off if they did. One should perhaps expect that some of the African governments will borrow from the Arab League the notion of selected boycotts of companies in Britain (and elsewhere) despite the injuries they may also inflict on themselves. The effect of such boycotts, however, is very difficult to calculate. There are, for example, firms whose main interests lie in South Africa and whose secondary interests in other parts of the continent are thus open to attack. In this category, the effect of a boycott would be to hurt not South Africa but the particular company and, possibly, the boycotting state.[33] There are other firms whose growing interests in Africa at large may possibly force them, under threats of a boycott, to forego their trade with South Africa.[34] Here again the effect on South Africa may not be very large since other firms—in Britain, EEC, Japan, the United States—are likely to fill the gap. The example of the Arab-Israeli boycott is not a particularly encouraging one for the African governments, although it can be argued that action of this nature helps to keep the conflict alive and does something to assuage radical opinion in the states which impose the restrictions. The scale of the problem in Africa is also very different from that elsewhere. *Collective* boycotts of individual companies by all the African states are difficult to imagine in the present state of African disunity. Boycotts of particular *countries*—notably the United Kingdom—which trade with South Africa would prove very difficult indeed, since they are also those—notably the United Kingdom—whose domestic markets are vital for African exports.[35] In general

---

[33] e.g. firms like Glaxo whose 'companies in South Africa . . . are on a larger scale than those in equatorial Africa' but which continue 'to invest modest sums in developing our business in the newly independent equatorial states [including] not only the incorporation of Glaxo-Allenburys (East Africa) Ltd but also the completion for the new company of a factory in Nairobi for the local manufacture of selected food and pharmaceutical products' (statement by the Chairman to the 30th Annual General Meeting, 7 Dec. 1964, *The Times*, 8 Dec. 1964).

[34] e.g. a number of the oil companies which compete for the right to build and manage oil refineries throughout the continent.

[35] The country most vulnerable in this respect is probably Japan, whose export trade both with the independent African states and South Africa is increasing fast, but which lacks the entrenched position occupied by Britain, Western Europe, and America as principal importers of African products.

terms the African states are in a poor bargaining position economically because of their great dependence on external trade and particular export markets. Which African government could deny its export to, or risk refusing to import from, Britain in an attempt to bring pressure to bear on British policy towards South Africa? Which African country could offer additional outlets for British goods in order to persuade the United Kingdom to act against South Africa? In respect of exports from Commonwealth Africa, the pattern is clear. Except for Uganda and (in 1964) Ghana, Britain is the largest single export market for the other member countries:[36]

Exports, 1964 (£ m.)

	UK	USA	West Germany	Nether-lands	(EEC)	Total exports	UK as per cent of total
Ghana	16	24	13	12	34	104	15
Nigeria	77	17	33	27	87	211	36
Sierra Leone	24	—	2	3	6	31	77
Kenya	11	5	7	2	12	77	14
Uganda	8	18	4	—	11	76	11
Tanganyika	21	6	6	4	16	80	24

Source: Commonwealth Economic Committee, *Commonwealth Trade 1964* (1965).

Commonwealth Ties

Opposition to British policy (or lack of policy) in southern Africa may take other forms. There are Commonwealth links between Britain and, at present, nine African states. Within the next decade the number may rise to twelve or thirteen, when the African states will comprise half, or more than half, the total membership.[37] By far the greater number of Commonwealth governments are fiercely hostile to the racial policies of South Africa, and one must reckon with the possibility that this hostility —powerless to bring about changes in Southern Africa—may be turned against the ties that link them with a Commonwealth in which Britain is thought by many to be the chief beneficiary. In 1961, discussion of South Africa's racial policies led a number of prime ministers to declare that they would have to consider

[36] If the EEC countries are taken together—all of whom trade with South Africa—the UK drops to second or third place.

[37] Assuming that by 1970, Basutoland, Bechuanaland, Swaziland (and Rhodesia?) are members of a Commonwealth of 25 states.

whether they could continue to belong to an association which included South Africa. To Nehru, 'it seemed quite improper for us to be a member of an organization which itself tolerated this kind of racial policies which are pursued by the South African Union Government'. Addressing the Lok Sabha, he went on to recognize that 'by South Africa going outside the Commonwealth, the South African policy of *apartheid* or segregation or racial discrimination does not diminish at all; . . . the evil continues and will continue in an aggravated form'. Nevertheless, he thought that South Africa's withdrawal had strengthened the Commonwealth and certainly not weakened it.[38]

In the short run, that was undoubtedly so. But in the long run? The 'evil continues', and other avenues of attack are being explored. In July 1964 the Commonwealth presidents and prime ministers agreed to differ over South Africa while jointly condemning 'the policy of apartheid practised by the Government of the Republic of South Africa'.

Some Commonwealth Prime Ministers felt very strongly that the only effective means of dealing with the problem of apartheid was the application of economic sanctions and an arms embargo. It was recognized however that there was a difference of opinion among Commonwealth countries as to the effectiveness of economic sanctions and as to the extent to which they regarded it as right or practicable to seek to secure the abandonment of apartheid by coercive action, of whatever kind.[39]

But may the day not come when some of the Commonwealth African members feel that they can no longer be associated with a (British) government which, either because it trades with, or opposes sanctions against, South Africa is condemned for 'condoning apartheid'? There is the very real danger that this may happen over Rhodesia: how much more is it likely over the wider problem of South Africa? The triumph of a left-wing government obliged to prove its radicalism, or of a right-wing government concerned to deny its conservatism, may, therefore, bring Commonwealth ties under attack. It is true that Britain is only

[38] N. Mansergh, *Documents and Speeches on Commonwealth Affairs, 1952–62* (1963), p. 390. See too the article in the *Observer* 21 Mar. 1961 by Julius Nyerere, in which he declared that Tanganyika could not 'join any' association of friends 'which includes a State deliberately and ruthlessly pursuing a racialist policy. . .'.

[39] Commonwealth premiers' communiqué, 15 July 1964, Cmnd 2441.

one of more than twenty member countries, of whom the great majority are non-European, and that there are practical advantages still, particularly to many of the newly independent states, in remaining within the association. Moreover by depriving themselves of membership, the African states would also forfeit the means whereby they could bring their influence to bear on British policy. But a movement that begins by trying to exert pressure in Commonwealth terms may none the less end in a formal fracture of the relationship. In short, reason may point to the advantages of Commonwealth membership; but emotion may still cause the break.

What importance should the United Kingdom give to such an attack? The Commonwealth might, as a result, be shaken by the withdrawal of one or more of its African members; at worst, it would lose its universal, multi-racial character and, thereby, much of its value as 'a unique experiment in international co-operation among peoples of several races and continents'.[40] True, the Commonwealth has been shown to have unexpected powers of survival. It learnt to live with Ireland and South Africa until 1949 and 1961; it also learnt to live without them. It could no doubt adjust itself to the departure of many of the African members. Yet much of value *would* be lost. For every break is a loss, it being 'always easier to break than to construct'—as was true of the withdrawal of South Africa itself.[41] Nor would it be easy, for Britain in particular, to contemplate the dissolution of Commonwealth ties which continue to bear witness to a remarkable decade which saw power transferred, amidst cordial ceremonies of farewell, to local rulers of a once immense empire.

Yet one must also note the changes that have taken place. The greater spread of membership has diluted even the appeal of the

---

[40] Ibid.

[41] 'Now, no one likes—at least most people do not like—breaking something. It is always easier to break than to construct' (Jawaharlal Nehru, 24 Mar. 1961 (Mansergh, p. 390)). And, as Mr Menzies observed: 'Under inexorable pressure, South Africa is out of the Commonwealth. It is not the Verwoerd Government that is out. It is the Union of South Africa' (ibid. p. 397, 11 Apr. 1961). The writer has no doubt that South Africa's withdrawal was necessary if the Commonwealth was to continue on its present path. Nor can the present rulers of South Africa lay claim to the comradeship of past Commonwealth ties between Britain and South Africa. Yet, although the Commonwealth may have been preserved by Verwoerd's withdrawal of South Africa's membership, the decision can hardly be said to have contributed to any improvement in the racial situation in South Africa.

old Dominions as a group of like-minded nations linked by a common allegiance to the Crown. And although the sentiment that informed these links may still be there between Britain, Australia, New Zealand, and Canada, the Commonwealth as a whole is not like that any more. 'There are some who view with apprehension the shifting composition of the association. It is a strange thing, but out goes Verwoerd and in comes Achbishop Makarios. . . The close intimacy of the days when the present Leader of the Opposition was secretary of state for external affairs . . . is ended'.[42] One may doubt, too, whether a 'common allegiance' will be replaced by 'a common idealism' since it is impossible to see what could form its base.[43] The Commonwealth is now an association in which a past Imperial relationship—however disguised—struggles against new interests which crowd in upon its individual members. Sometimes it is the language which is more expressive than the reality of these interests—as in the protestations by African leaders of prior loyalties to regional movements.[44] Sometimes, and more menacingly, deeds speak louder than words—as in the United Kingdom's application in 1962 to join the European Economic Community. And if one singles out the failure of the United Kingdom 'to join the Six' it is not because of the failure but because the application showed how far the founder member of the Commonwealth had travelled in its painful task of adjusting national interests to unfamiliar ends. The effect on Commonwealth ties of Britain's application is difficult to measure; but the comment of an early 'Commonwealth loyalist' is worth reproducing here to show how greatly attitudes have changed:

I think that twenty years ago I might have become more impas-

---

[42] Diefenbaker, 17 Mar. 1961 (ibid. p. 369).

[43] Macmillan's phrase: '. . . the whole concept of the Commonwealth has radically changed. In the past it was four or five countries populated by people of, broadly, British descent linked together by their common allegiance as subjects of the Crown. From 1949 onwards it has become more and more a group of countries associated historically with this island. . . This association must depend not on the old concept of a common allegiance but upon the new principle of a common idealism' (22 Mar. 1961, ibid. p. 374).

[44] e.g. Nkrumah: 'Even at this time, there may be certain advantages in maintaining a link which history has forged. . . Nonetheless, however loose such a relationship may be, if it should tend in the slightest degree to impinge upon the African state's relations with other African states its retention becomes indefensible' (*Africa Must Unite*, p. 187).

sioned about this matter, but the Commonwealth has changed a lot
since then. Its association has become looser. For most of its members,
the association is, in a sense, functional and occasional. The old hopes
of concerting policies have gone.[45]

On the other hand, merely to write the Commonwealth's
epitaph, on the assumption that the past decade of decolonization is as much as may be hoped for from a moribund association,
may also be over-pessimistic. History is always a long time dying.
There is point, too, in being aware (in R. G. Collingwood's
phrase) of the 'illusion of finality', of passing judgement too
quickly in contemporary terms on what may yet be a lasting
phenomenon. A 'functional and occasional' association is likely
to last as long as the self-interests of its members (in terms of education, aid, investment, trade, and collaboration in numerous
fields of voluntary action) give it life. On this basis, and at a
modest level of expectation, it may still be thought that there are
advantages to Britain in keeping Commonwealth links active,
and to the African countries in preserving working arrangements over a wide field of activity with each other and non-
African members. Under the special Commonwealth African
Assistance Plan, for example, £79 million was made available in
1961–2 to the African member countries.[46] There were over
16,000 students from Commonwealth Africa studying in Britain;
there are joint Commonwealth training schemes for army officers,
civil servants, members of the diplomatic corps, and a host of
other professional occupations.[47] There is the right of free entry
into the United Kingdom market for many Commonwealth
African products. There may be great potential yet in an
association which tries to preserve these special links between so
many diverse nations.

---

[45] Menzies, *Canberra Notes*, Sept.–Oct. 1962.

[46] *Capital Aid and Technical Assistance*	1960–1 (£ m.)	1961–2 (£ m.)
Grants	19·83	37·88
Loans, investments, &c.	31·72	41·04
	51·55	78·92

Source: SCAAP, *Report for the Year ending 31 March 1962* (1963).

[47] See *Overseas Students in Britain 1962*. Under the 'Special Commonwealth
African Assistance Plan' (devised in 1960) there were some 13,000 officers
retained (or recruited) for Commonwealth African countries in 1962.

Provided, therefore, that national interests are not held to be affected, and that emotion does not sweep away argument, both the United Kingdom and the African member governments may continue at least to suspend judgement, and at best to place a positive if modest value on the association. Yet the main point under discussion emerges clearly: that whatever estimate is put on Commonwealth ties in 1965–6 it is unlikely in relation to South Africa to give the African states any substantial lever against the United Kingdom.[48] Threats of withdrawal may be met with expressions of deep regret, but hardly with major concessions injurious to what are seen as the United Kingdom's own national interests.

African Stability

The third line of argument against United Kingdom policy as it stands at present is as follows. The practice of apartheid in South Africa is not only an affront to coloured peoples throughout the world but (it is argued) a dangerous irritant in the national life of the independent African states. The leaders are under pressure from radical opinion among their supporters to take measures against South Africa. They lack the power to do

---

[48] A good example of the extent to which Commonwealth ties are being critically examined today may be seen in Mr Kenneth Younger's Chatham House Essay, *Changing Perspectives in British Foreign Policy* (1964), in which the Commonwealth is described as at best irrelevant, at worst an obstacle, to its members. 'It is clear that, while good relations and expanding trade among member countries are as important as ever, the concept of the Commonwealth as a separate group possessing some distinctive common interest is outdated. . . . For what is now happening throughout the whole group is that each country is searching for a new identity and is inevitably finding it increasingly in relationships to which the Commonwealth as a group is, at best, irrelevant. At worst it may even be an obstacle, if any attempt is made to base defence or economic policies upon it' (p. 118). In 1956 the same author had spoken in different terms. 'With, I think, the single exception of the South African racial policy . . . there has always been, despite our differences, an underlying understanding between all of us in the Commonwealth about the common aims which we are seeking to pursue in our differing circumstances. . . . In a period when relations between Asia, Africa, Europe and America are all in the melting pot and changing at a tremendous speed, it is the intercontinental nature of our Commonwealth which makes it so great and useful a conception' (8 Nov. 1956, HC Deb. vol. 560, cols 266–8, when proposing an amendment to the Queen's Speech and calling for a Commonwealth Prime Ministers' conference in the wake of the Suez disaster). To current doubts in Britain about the Commonwealth may be added recent questioning of the advantages and disadvantages in Britain's maintenance of sterling as a reserve currency.

so. Yet they are continually urged on by threats that if *they* prove inadequate others will take their place. One must envisage a situation in which violence erupts in South Africa and is beaten down with fierce repression. The African governments will then face demands for action if not against South Africa at least against those powers, primarily in the west, which hold back from positive measures against the Verwoerd government. Indifference or caution will exact their price. The USSR and/or China will seize their opportunity, each spurring on the other. Communist influence will spread among the waiting, watchful critics of the post-independence regimes whose leaders will be unable to preserve the precarious balance of non-alignment that once seemed so daring a posture. Existing governments will then be seen—in retrospect—as moderates alongside their successors. For they will either be compelled to 'move to the left' or be swept from office and replaced by leaders hostile to our interests. Large areas of Africa may thus be 'lost' to the west. And 'the problem of the colour line', which Du Bois foretold some sixty years ago would become 'the problem of the twentieth century', will grow to terrifying proportions, the contagion of racialism spreading from continent to continent until it ends in a 'race war' engulfing the world. The west—that is Britain and the United States—must, therefore, act directly (and boldly) against South Africa to exorcise this fearful spectre.

It is an argument to make the flesh of western man creep. Is it valid? One can only repeat here what was said in the Introduction, that much of the strength of its case rests on the assumption that sooner or later 'race war' is inevitable in South Africa itself. But one can only argue to any point from what the position is now or has been in the past, and violence between racial groups in South Africa has so far been sporadic—on a minimum scale[49] —alongside upheavals in the Congo, Rwanda, the Sudan, or Zanzibar. In recent years it has been held in check by a tight web of repressive laws. The police are vigilant, the government determined, the white electorate unwilling at present to accept any alternative to Nationalist policy. Given these conditions, it is impossible to predict how long the present position will last, or from what direction change may come. Should violence break

[49] The cruellest event was Sharpeville where 67 Africans were killed and about 100 wounded.

out on a large scale, reaching the point of communal civil war, the situation would indeed be changed. But one must then suppose that opinion both in South Africa and abroad would also change—including opinion in the United Kingdom and America which, the crisis upon them, are likely to be far more open to the plea that they should intervene—and intervene in full force to stop the killing. At present, pressure from the OAU states is directed against Britain and America not to urge them to rescue a situation in which violence has outrun public control, but to impose sanctions in the hope of forcing change from outside. In African eyes, sanctions are called for in order to prevent a 'race war'. Less hopeful observers of the South African scene would argue that their most probable effect would be to provoke fierce conflict, and as long as the present situation in South Africa continues there are genuine grounds for disagreement between the African states and the west on the issue.[50]

What can be said of the dangers that may arise from this disagreement? There would be general endorsement of the argument that the African states are weak constructions whose stability rests on a number of imponderables—whether the resources of state power are sufficient to meet political requirements, whether the rate of economic growth will meet demands for employment and higher living standards, whether the newly independent governments can acquire a legitimate authority when the credit of having achieved self-government is exhausted, or whether a particular leader can hold the balance of power between competing groups which struggle to use his authority for their own ends. It is much less certain, however, whether problems of *external* policy are anything like as important in this respect as internal weaknesses. Although exasperation over the west's refusal to act against South Africa may injure relations between Africa and the west, it is likely to weigh much less heavily in the balance of national interests than the domestic struggle for power between individuals, party groups, racial communities, regions, districts, and tribes. Does this underestimate the

[50] Rhodesia is in a somewhat different category in this respect since it is clearly— and repeatedly stated by the Labour government to be—a United Kingdom responsibility. Nevertheless, if Mr Wilson is able to persuade the Commonwealth African governments that he really means to get rid of Mr Smith *in the long run,* and without damaging Zambia, he may be able to reach an accommodation with them (see below, Ch. VII).

strength of popular feeling against South Africa, of a kind that in the Arab world may oust a government from office or a regime from power? Is there a comparable hostility to apartheid—comparable, that is, to the hostility among Arab peoples towards Israel? Certainly, for many African leaders hatred of South African policy is 'felt in the heart and felt along the blood'; too open an accommodation to Portuguese, Rhodesian, or South African rule is always likely to be included in domestic criticism of a particular leader (as of Banda in Malawi). But local interests still dominate the African scene—understandably so at a time when national independence is newly acquired—and the main ground of criticism of a particular government is almost certainly to lie at home. It is also unlikely, to say the least, that any African leader will become communist, whether in Russian or Chinese guise, because of a particular quarrel with Britain and the west over their refusal to intervene in South Africa. Some may move closer towards communist positions on aspects of domestic policy or international affairs. Some may be able to combine their appeal to an 'African Personality' with ideological declarations in favour of Marxist–Leninism. Yet the primary concern—the point cannot be over-emphasized—of each African government is with the retention of power within its own borders and the manipulation of local interests to that end. The writer would conclude, therefore, that current forebodings that independent Africa will be swept by revolutions provoked by apartheid in South Africa are greatly exaggerated. Revolutions may occur: but their origins are much more likely to lie in the constantly shifting balance of domestic politics.

The further assumption, that the clash of policy over South Africa between the African states and the west will poison a broad field of international relations to the point of engendering a 'race war', may also be questioned. The dangers, to be sure, are clear. There is a nucleus of anti-western feeling in many African countries because it is still overwhelmingly a British, French, or American presence that is encountered throughout the continent. (The corollary is also true, that there is a large reservoir of goodwill, at individual and official level, for co-operative enterprises between many African states and the west.) Suspicion of western policy is fed by events in the Congo and southern Africa. And precisely because—on these issues in particular—the

African states are powerless, resentment may grow over the extent of power in European hands and the reluctance of western governments to use it for ends urged on them by (some) African leaders. Moreover, the charge that a large part of western society is racist minded may also be pressed more and more, and cannot easily be countered if only because the charge is one to which western man finds it hard to plead not guilty.[51] Yet it is necessary still to question what is meant by a 'race war', and similar emotional phrases to which it is difficult to give definition. Does it mean that the Asian and African states will refuse to employ 'white' technicians or advisers? Surely not. Does it imply that relations between Sinhalese and Tamils, Malays and Chinese, Ibo, Yoruba, and northerners in Nigeria, Indians and Negroes in British Guiana, Hindus and Muslims in India, Greek and Turkish Cypriots, will grow worse or better because of the repression by South Africa of non-whites? It is hardly likely. Is it conceivable that the Afro-Asian states will combine, in political and economic terms, against 'white countries' (including Russia or Latin America)? Again, surely not. National interests are very strong, and must be reckoned to override international concern for the maltreatment of non-Europeans in South Africa. And national interests, over a large part of Africa and Asia, not only reinforce trade ties with the west; they are also a source of fierce conflicts between states regardless of their racial composition— as today in Asia between China and India,[52] Indonesia and Malaysia, India and Pakistan. In general, international relations depend on a multiplicity of issues, and it would be naïve to suppose that the African states will deny themselves normal relations with western Europe or America over an immense range of interests because of a clash of policy—however sharp—over

---

[51] In the writer's view, racial discrimination in Britain, whether explicit in local politics or implicit in the parties' immigration policies, is more likely to injure our relations with Afro-Asian countries than differences over South Africa.

[52] Note the revealing comment by an Indian member of parliament on the Sino-Indian dispute. 'The recent London Conference of Commonwealth prime ministers could not be persuaded to say a word in sympathy or support of India in our China predicament because of the opposition of the African prime ministers; the colour of our skin did not help us there' (*The Statesman*, 13 Jan. 1965). When in India recently, the writer noticed that the Madras branch of the Indian Council on World Affairs heard a lecture on 24 March by Capt. Rajagopal on: 'The Yellow Peril and how to annihilate it'. On which side of a 'race war' would the Indians and Chinese be?

E

South Africa. Evidence for this view may be found in many of the
African states themselves. Between the Commonwealth African
countries and Britain there are innumerable ties of association
which, though they may be affected from time to time by quarrels at government level, are able to weather the storms that rage
above their heads because of the advantages to be gained from
maintaining them. It would also be very difficult to find any
substantial evidence even of strain, still less of rupture or 'war',
in African-French relations arising from the sale of French arms
to, or trade with, South Africa. That is not to say the French-
speaking states endorse apartheid. On the contrary, many of
their leaders may be among the first at the United Nations or in
the OAU to condemn 'racism'. But their opposition to racial
oppression in South Africa is not allowed to interfere with what
they believe to be their national interests, namely, close relations
with France and the European Economic Community.

In general, one may very well conclude that Britain would find
the world an easier place to live in, if South Africa did not exist,
or if the European minority there were to cease to practice
apartheid. The latter is hardly likely in the immediate future:
indeed, precisely because the economy is growing, support for
Dr Verwoerd's government has increased among the white
electorate. But if hopes are dupes, fears may yet prove liars. To
portray the African states as strongly united within the OAU,
and uniformly hostile to Britain because of its reluctance to endorse extreme measures against South Africa, is to portray a
phantom. Africa is far from united; its multiple interests are a
great deal wider than the particular aim (however strongly desired) of trying to overthrow European rule in South Africa; and
relations with the west are both good and bad according to the
context in which they are examined. Nor are the African states
likely to be so well placed in the future to make demands on the
west. Nearly all of them are economically dependent still—and
for as far ahead as one can see—on western markets and aid;
many, by their abandonment of free institutions, have disappointed the once high hopes (in the west) of the anti-colonialists. They may also have to adjust their demands to their strength
on more general grounds. For it seems doubtful whether they
will continue to receive the attention that was brought to their
first appearance as sovereign states. There are many other claims

on the world's concern for the primary issues of war and peace—
above all in Asia, where China's overriding interests must surely
be held to lie, and where bloodier conflicts than anything that
has happened in South Africa are in danger of renewal.

III

Basutoland, Bechuanaland, Swaziland

THE three Southern African Territories are a problem within a problem. They have survived as small communities under British rule, each of them numbering less than a million people, embedded in southern Africa yet legally distinct from the Republic which overshadows them. They pose a problem not only of 'smallness', but of smallness in relation to a very large neighbour; yet the direction in which they are now moving is familiar. In different parts of the world, states are beginning to appear whose *de facto* independence must always be in doubt once anomalies of history and geography, formerly obscured by the protective covering of a powerful empire, are exposed. The three Territories examined in this chapter are likely to be in the same uneasy situation as a number of economically backward, politically divided communities have found themselves when deprived of Imperial control. At present, the United Kingdom is still responsible for their safety, but the pace of constitutional advance is quickening even among these small groups of people, and 'sovereign status' is likely to be attained by all three within the next few years.

It is difficult to over-emphasize their weakness, whether in terms of income or political structure. True, there are other land-locked states which have survived in circumstances comparable to those of Bechuanaland and Swaziland by virtue of their treaty relationship with much larger neighbours—like the Himalayan states of Bhutan and Sikkim.[1] Others have gone under— absorbed, engulfed, almost obliterated, as the Baltic states were by the USSR after 1946. But even the most fortunate of them

[1]

	Area (sq. miles)	Population
Bechuanaland	220,000	540,000 (1964 census; provis. figures)
Swaziland	6,704	280,300 (1962 official est.)
Basutoland	11,716	461,674 (1956 census)
Bhutan	18,000	700,000–800,000 (est.)
Sikkim	2,818	161,080 (1961 census)

have to learn to live in some form of practical dependence on the states that overshadow them, and there are surely few parallels to the totally enclosed position of Basutoland—a tiny state within a state.[2] A peaceful coexistence (between unequals) may be maintained in southern Africa if the party leaders of the three Territories and the Republic of South Africa are prepared to try and live amicably together: it is worth recalling that all four have lived for over fifty years within a single labour market, a currency and customs union, and the joint use of road and rail communications. Yet it would be mischievous in the present situation in southern Africa to pretend that the omens are good. And one may easily list the dangers.

Many of them spring from the primary fact that British responsibility for all three Territories will soon come to an end. They will then be isolated not only from Britain but from each other, and open to a great deal more influence from Pretoria than when Britain stood between them and the Republic.[3] For over fifty years the South African government pressed openly for the transfer of the then Protectorates to the Union—and had good grounds for doing so. The preamble to the South Africa Act of 1909 envisaged 'the eventual admission into the Union of such parts of South Africa as are not originally included therein'; Section 151 laid down the procedure for transfer.[4] It was the United Kingdom's insistence on the need 'to consult the inhabitants of the Territories' before any change was made that first delayed and then ruled out the possibility of transfer.[5] Nevertheless, what cannot now be gained by agreement may still

[2] There are remote parallels perhaps: San Marino (38 sq. miles, 17,000 pop.) and the Vatican City (108·7 acres, *c*.900 pop.) in Italy.

[3] Relations between the three Territories have never been very close, and have become markedly less so as each moves (at a different pace) towards self-government; e.g. the overall responsibility of the office of High Commissioner (who was High Commissioner, later Ambassador, in Pretoria) has disappeared. The one obvious link—at present—is the University College of Basutoland, Bechuanaland, and Swaziland, opened at Roma, Basutoland, on 1 Jan. 1964.

[4] It empowered the King in Council, on an address from both Houses of the Union Parliament, to transfer the administration of the Territories to the Union, subject to conditions designed to protect 'Native rights'. The 1961 South African republican constitution incorporated these provisions.

[5] For an account of the debate over transfer, see Lord Hailey, *The Republic of S. Africa and the High Commission Territories* (1963), chs 4–6; G. V. Doxey, *H. C. Territories and the Republic of S. Africa* (1963), pp. 28 ff; and J. E. Spence, 'British Policy towards the High Commission Territories', *J. Modern African Studies* ii/2(1964).

be thought obtainable by stealth. In 1950 the Tomlinson Commission was appointed 'to conduct exhaustive enquiry into and report on a comprehensive scheme for the rehabilitation of the Native Areas'. When the *Report* was made public,[6] it was found to include all three Protectorates in its examination of the proposal to establish seven Bantustans, and it would be naïve to assume that the South African government has finally abandoned its earlier hopes, although it may well be that more subtle methods than that of formal integration will be used. As late as September 1963 Dr Verwoerd declared that if the choice were put to the Territories he was sure they would choose South Africa to be their 'guardian' on the road to independence.[7] The immediate effect of the pronouncement was nil: yet it was of a piece with earlier and—one may assume—future 'declarations of intent' by the South African government towards the Protectorates. As a minor irritant in the situation there are muffled counter-claims by the Territories themselves. Each has an irredentist area across its borders. Basutoland has its 'conquered territory' which it lost in 1870. There are many Swazi living across the border of their own kingdom. Bechuanaland lost part of its tribal lands in 1895 when the Protectorate border was shifted north of the Molopo river; it has also cast eyes from time to time on the Caprivi Strip, the 275-mile-long finger of South West African territory (administered from Pretoria) which gives the Republic direct access to the Zambesi and Chobe rivers.[8]

After independence, new dangers may appear. In each of the Territories there are rival groups among the handful of politicians who, having no large source of local funds, may be tempted by offers of help from interested parties outside, whether in the Republic or farther north, or beyond the continent. Basutoland

---

[6] The Commission submitted its findings at great length on 1 October 1954 but the report was never printed in full, an abbreviated version appearing in March 1956.

[7] 3 Sept. 1963, speech at a National Party Congress in Pretoria (*Annual Register 1963*).

[8] In December 1963 Mr T. T. Tsheko was reported as saying that the Caprivi Strip and its 17,000 people should become part of Bechuanaland. He was outvoted in the legislative council by the official majority, but his followers announced that they would renew the claim after independence (*Africa Research Bull.*, Jan. 1964). Other, rival, interests are affected: e.g. the Caprivi African National Union, and the South West African People's Organization.

and Swaziland are particularly vulnerable in this sense. Rival party groups in Basutoland are sharply opposed to each other throughout the country. Swaziland has to face not only the familiar quarrel between traditional authorities and party leaders but problems arising from the presence of European settlers to whom over 40 per cent of the country has been ceded on a freehold basis. Furthermore, once the Territories have become independent, embassies may be opened belonging to governments which are openly hostile to the Republic, although their representatives will have to obtain permission from Pretoria to cross or overfly South African territory even to reach Maseru in Basutoland. The OAU may see the three countries as 'forward bases' of a pan-African advance against the Republic. So may the leaders of nationalist movements within the Republic itself, many of whose colleagues have already used the Territories as bolt holes or escape channels to the outside world. So, indeed, may the South African government, which is hardly likely to tolerate three Trojan Horses within, or bordering, its own territory. In sum, relations between Pretoria and the three capitals—Maseru, Gaberones, and Mbabane—will require very delicate handling if the existing position is to be maintained in anything like its present form.

What are British interests in the matter? Of a material kind, very little. Those who like to interpret colonialism in economic terms must be puzzled to understand why Britain should have maintained its protection over these small communities. Trade with all three was minimal; and they are now a charge on the United Kingdom exchequer.[9] Moreover, Britain had every opportunity of ridding itself of the burden, for had the Protectorates been handed over in the inter-war years to the Union government (which wanted them), the problem would have been absorbed today in the larger issue of white minority rule throughout southern Africa. Instead, Labour and Conservative leaders alike resisted attempts by the South African government to shift the responsibility. It is possible to argue that the Territories suffered in consequence—neglect may have been born of uncertainty over the future—but they were also preserved as separate dependencies. In recent years a new possibility appeared—

---

[9] Swaziland is something of an exception: it is now an important source of asbestos, iron ore, and timber (see below, p. 78).

self-government, a line of advance which would hardly have been thought relevant a decade ago when the United Kingdom seemed likely to have to face the prospect of an indefinite involvement in southern Africa. Now, in the second half of the 1960s, it may be able to end its formal responsibility for the Territories by the transfer of power to locally elected governments.

Whether in practice Britain will then be free of all its obligations is much less certain. In other parts of the world relations between Britain and its former colonies have not ceased at independence. They have been recast in a Commonwealth setting, and in a number of African countries Britain's interests have been involved much more closely than the formal ending of colonial rule was once thought to imply. Since the Southern African Territories are particularly frail and poor, they are all the more likely to look for external help over a wide range of problems, and (one may suppose) they will look first to the United Kingdom. What are the implications if they do? The question is central to the argument. But something should first be said of the present stage of constitutional advance in all three countries, and the extent to which each is still dependent—economically and financially—on South Africa and Britain.

Basutoland

It is in keeping perhaps with the element of fantasy in the present situation that the country which is most dependent on South Africa should have taken the first steps along the road to self-government. There are more rational explanations, however, why Basutoland should have taken the lead. Its contacts with South Africa have been close, the result being a greater sophistication among those who had worked in the Republic; education has also been more widely spread than in Swaziland or Bechuanaland. Despite current political differences among the leaders, there is also an underlying unity about the Basotho in language and history stretching back to the early nineteenth century when Moshesh (1831–70) gathered together the remnants of various clans that had been scattered by Zulu and Matabele raids. Subsequent wars against the Boers of the Orange Free State in the 1850s and 1860s deepened this sense of unity. Then, when Moshesh was defeated by the Boers and forced to sign the treaty of Thaba Bosiu in April 1866, he renewed his earlier requests for British protection and, eventually, it was granted although no formal act of annexation was proclaimed until March 1868. This declared that: 'The tribe of the Basuto shall be and shall be taken to be for all intents and purposes British subjects, and the territory of the said tribe shall be, and shall be taken to be, British territory.' From 1868–71 the territory was under Imperial rule, from 1871 to 1873 under the Cape Colony, and it was not until 1883 that the Imperial government, again with reluctance, agreed to take over its administration, and not until March the following year that a final proclamation brought the Basuto under the direct rule of the Queen.

Thereafter, the triangular relationship of Basuto, Boer, and Briton was a minor irritant in the larger problem of British-South African relations. The Basuto disliked the Boers; the British stood between them and their former enemies. The territory slumbered under a colonial administration; the economy stagnated on a weak agricultural base, without industry and with few natural resources. The most active element in the country were the missions, who developed a broad base of primary education throughout Basutoland. Politics consisted of a struggle for power, within a hierarchical, traditional structure of authority, among the 'Sons of Moshesh' who were hereditary chiefs 'placed' in control of local areas by the Paramount. In later years, the administration was concerned primarily with the problems involved in establishing a form of indirect rule. The Territory was also troubled by medicine murders, of great ferocity, arising out of unrest among the reformed native authorities and the problem of the accession to the paramountcy after the death of Seeiso in 1940.[10] It seemed doubtful, even as late as the 1950s, that Basotho society would provide the base for a nationalist movement comparable with the new party organizations which were beginning to be formed elsewhere in the continent. The influence of the chiefs was very great. Where were the leaders of a nationalist movement to come from? The Territory had no money; how could any appeal to the commoners be financed, and party officials paid? It was also dwarfed by a South Africa under Nationalist rule. Who would protect it if Britain did not?

It was easy to pose these questions. Yet by 1960 there were at least three party groups in the country, and the chiefs had joined

[10] H. Ashton, *The Basuto* (1952), pp. 307 ff.

in the struggle between them.[11] There were other signs that the times were changing. A new Paramount Chief was installed in March 1960—Motlotlehi Constantine Bereng Seeiso, Moshoeshoe II; he was only 28 years old and had been educated at Ampleforth and Corpus Christi, Oxford. There was also a Basutoland National Council (operating as a legislative body) of 80 members, of whom half were elected by local district councils from among their own number, the remaining 40 consisting of 22 chiefs, 14 nominees of the Paramount Chief, and 4 colonial officials.[12] Elections had been held in January 1960, when the 40 elective seats were divided among the Basutoland Congress Party under Ntsu Mokhehle—29 seats; the Marema 'Tlou Party led by B. M. Khaketla—5 seats; the Basutoland National Party led by Chief Leabua Jonathan—1 seat; and 5 independents. In broad terms, they represented a range of political opinion from 'left socialist' (Congress) to 'right traditional' (National Party). The Congress split in 1961 and a breakaway Basutoland Freedom Party was formed. The following year a Communist Party was formed by John Motloheloa, who had been deported from South Africa some years earlier. Each of these warring groups corresponded more perhaps to the local factionalism with which earlier traditional disputes had been associated than to pan-African or world movements, but the effect of party competition hastened the process of constitutional change which the administration was now prepared to sponsor. For the reluctance with which the United Kingdom had once approached the problems of self-government for so poor and small a community virtually disappeared in the 1960s under the pressure of local demands. In September 1961 the Basutoland National Council called for the setting up of a body to work out proposals for full internal cabinet government; the following year a Commission consisting of representatives of local political groups was estab-

[11] There was an embryonic political movement in the 1940s—the *Lekhotla la bafo*—which was anti the colonial administration and anti-European, but it could hardly be seen then as a 'nationalist movement'.

[12] Basutoland (Constitution) Order in Council 1959. The terms of the constitution were approved unanimously by the Basutoland Council in July 1958. The Council had been instituted as early as 1903 and given statutory form in 1910; it was then consultative and advisory, presided over by the Resident Commissioner and the Paramount Chief as Chief Councillor. A popular element was introduced in 1944 when members of local advisory councils elected some of their members to the Council.

lished. Its recommendations were submitted to the Council and, after a number of amendments, were accepted unanimously on 11 February 1964. The scene then shifted to London in April–May, where agreement was reached between the United Kingdom government and the Basuto representatives on 15 May. The salient points were:

1. The Paramount Chief—Motlotlehi Moshoeshoe II—to be a constitutional figurehead with powers approximating to those of a Governor-General; after independence he will be Head of State.

2. A two-chamber legislature. (*a*) A National Assembly of 60 members elected from single-member constituencies on universal adult suffrage. (*b*) A Senate of 22 principal chiefs or their nominees, and 11 others appointed by Motlotlehi, with powers of reference back to the National Assembly.

3. A cabinet consisting of a prime minister and not less than seven ministers.

4. Responsibility for external affairs, defence, and internal security to be retained by the Resident Commissioner who also has certain powers of financial control, interim responsibility for the public service (pending the appointment of an executive public service commission), and the power to secure legislation necessary for the exercise of his responsibilities.

5. A privy council composed of the Resident Commissioner, the prime minister, and one other, to advise Motlotlehi in the discharge of his duties.[13]

The Secretary of State also undertook to give effect as quickly as possible to a request for independence (if made through a joint resolution of both houses of the Basuto parliament) a year after the holding of elections under the new constitution. The elections were held in May 1965 and resulted in a slender majority for the Basutoland National Party over its two rivals. (See table on p. 66.)

The results were a remarkable victory for the BNP over the radical pan-Africanism of the Congress Party: in 1960 it had won only a single seat, now it formed the government of a quasi-independent state. Its success may have been due to a new awareness among a well-educated electorate of the need for moderate leadership after independence, more probably to the

[13] *Basutoland Constitutional Conference 1964*, Cmnd 2371 (Apr./May 1964).

	Votes	*Per cent*	*Seats*
National Party	108,162	41·6	31
Congress Party	103,050	39·7	25
Marema 'Tlou Party	42,837	16·5	4
Others	5,776	2·2	—
TOTAL	259,825	100·0	60

Source: Information supplied by the CRO.

Chief Leabua Jonathan was defeated in the general election but successful in a by-election on 1 July and was appointed prime minister (in succession to Chief Maseribane) on 7 July.

latent power of conservatism in a traditionally based society.[14] But there were ominous features to the election as well, notably the attempt by foreign interests to influence the voting. Money was sent from Peking and Accra to the Congress Party; from the Christian Democrats in West Germany (and local business interests in South Africa) to the National Party. The outside world and its dogmas—communism, pan-Africanism, Catholicism—had arrived in Maseru, although it was difficult to see what tune these distant pipers would call. It was clear, however, that Basutoland was now on its way to joining the Commonwealth, the OAU, and the United Nations.

None of the external links that Basutoland may be able to forge with the world at large will affect its economic dependence on the Republic. Indeed, the reverse is true, in the sense that almost all forms of development (other than the enlargement of subsistence agriculture) are likely to add to the Territory's need to find markets for its goods, and sources of supply for its needs, in the Republic. The facts are plain. Basutoland exports labour to South Africa. It imports food from South Africa. It relies for most of its communications on South Africa. It uses South African money. It draws from South Africa a fixed percentage of the customs revenue collected by the South African govern-

[14] The Congress Party might have done better had Basotho working in the Republic been allowed to vote. There was a general agreement among the parties, however, that electors had to return to Basutoland; some were assisted financially (mainly in the form of payment for transport, or the provision of free transport) by European interests in the Republic, almost certainly to the benefit of the BNP.

ment. It benefits by remittances earned by Basotho in South Africa to the extent of nearly £1 million a year. When not dependent on South Africa, it relies on Britain. In 1963–4, the budgetary position was:

	£	*Per cent*
Revenue	2,095,245	
Expenditure	3,503,750	
British grant-in-aid	1,534,000	73
Main Sources of Revenue		
Customs & excise		
(collected by South Africa)	974,272	46
Taxes	496,483	21
Wool/mohair export duty	90,110	4

Source: UK, Central Office of Information, *Basutoland* (Fact Sheet 1964).

To be sure, Basutoland has not always been so poorly placed. Periods of doubt have alternated with moments of optimism. In 1935, for example, Sir Alan Pim placed the larger share of blame for the absence of development not on the Basotho, or their lack of resources, but on the frustration of a dual system of administration by officials and chiefs. Similar judgements were passed by Professor Hancock nearly ten years later: the Territory (it was argued) had 'suffered from a lack of governance which was sometimes dignified with the title of "indirect rule" '. But Professor Hancock also believed that by 1938 a very different picture could be drawn, more favourable to Basutoland than to its sister Territories. There had been progress 'in education, health, public works, and the rest'; there was now 'an administration which combines the efforts of European officials and Native institutions towards the achievement of a single end'. And the end? 'By every strict test that can be applied Basutoland is today financially self-supporting.' Nor was this the only achievement that could be recorded. There was evidence of 'far-reaching changes in the outlook and agricultural technique of the Natives', and 'an indication that something more than an agricultural revolution is taking place.' It seemed reasonable to hope that a 'new era [had] opened.'[15]

[15] Sir Alan Pim, *Report on the Financial and Economic Position of Basutoland*, Cmd 4907, 1935; W. K. Hancock, *Survey of British Commonwealth Affairs*, vol. 2, pt 2 (1942). Certainly a great deal of progress was recorded both in the *Annual Report on the Social and Economic Progress of the People of Basutoland, 1938*, and later accounts. 'By the end of 1959 nearly half a million acres had been ter-

It is possible, therefore, that independence will give a new impetus to energies that were released in the latter half of the 1930s. Yet one may doubt whether it will alter substantially the Territory's need for external aid or its dependence on the Republic. Moreover, pessimism has returned. The report of an Economic Survey Mission in 1960 was in sharp contrast to the glowing account given by Professor Hancock. It had a melancholy tale to unfold. Basutoland was now marked out as needing special treatment, although the Mission also concluded that each Territory was 'in the situation of a patient confronted with a choice between having an expensive operation, which would entail a long period of recuperation but offer a high chance of full recovery, and the alternative of lapsing into a state of chronic illness'.[16] What will a future survey of an independent 'Lesotho' have to report when another generation has elapsed? Will there be fresh evidence of major economic change? Or renewed advocacy of the risk of an 'expensive operation'? Will there still be a belief in the possibility of a cure? Who will offer to pay for it? There can be no answer to these questions. Yet one must raise them, for many of the recommendations of the Morse Mission in the 1950s would have made familiar reading in the unreformed 1930s: soil conservation, improved cattle breeding, water supplies, communications, education, 'and the rest'. Nor can one live for ever in the hope that fortunes will turn once again for the better. For the truth of the matter seems to be that the relation between population and agricultural production has worsened, the pull of the South African labour market is growing. In 1954 nearly 9,000 tons of maize had to be imported; by 1962 the figure had increased to 19,000 tons.[17] In 1962 over 120,000 Basotho were

---

raced, 688,000 acres of buffer strips had been formed, and large-scale dam-building and tree-planting programmes had been completed.' See Doxey; and *Basutoland, 1962, Annual Report.*

[16] CRO, *Basutoland, Bechuanaland Protectorate and Swaziland: Report of an Economic Survey Mission* (1960), p. 14. The chairman was Professor Chandler Morse of Cornell University. The estimated capital cost of the Mission's recommendations was in the region of £7 m.; Basutoland—£2·7 m.; Bechuanaland—£1·5 m.; Swaziland—£2·7 m. There would be an annual recurrent cost of about £500,000 for the first five years.

[17] *Annual Reports*, 1954–62. Poor farming methods and soil erosion have reduced the area of arable land to 930,000 acres—about 12·4 per cent of the total land area. Even cattle imports exceed exports: in 1962, some 8,800 cattle valued at £185,300 were exported, and 19,900 head of cattle costing £370,000 imported.

issued with passes to take up employment in the Republic; in 1950 the figure had been 50,000.[18] The trend is clear and shows no signs of diminishing. Basutoland is an agricultural country that is now unable to grow enough food to feed itself. But is it truly an 'agricultural country'? There are those who doubt it. 'It is true that there is nothing there besides agriculture. It has an agricultural economy because it has no industries and not because of any marked agricultural potential.'[19] It is for this reason, of greater significance than the attraction of city lights, that migrant workers cross the border, until the point has been reached when 'Basutoland might be described as a dormitory suburb of peasants who commute back and forth over the South African border'.[20] There are many also who are living permanently in the Republic (though liable to repatriation), with the result that nearly half the adult male population is absent from the Territory at any one time. A number of them in the Republic perform skilled, responsible jobs such as shaft sinking; they are highly valued no doubt by the mining companies, which might find it difficult to replace them. Yet the overriding fact remains that, while the mines might be hard hit by a withdrawal of Basotho labour, the effect on the Basotho—and Basutoland— would be catastrophic.

One further example of the underlying economic reality must suffice. It illustrates the fact that Pretoria has the power both to harm and help the Territory—by curtailing imports of Basuto wool and labour, or by offering money and technical assistance. Basutoland's one great natural resource is water.[21] Its mountains are the source of the Orange as well as of the principal tributaries of the Caledon river. In theory, Basutoland could exercise control of the headwaters; it could harness them for hydro-electric power and use the power to develop local industries. In reality, it is inconceivable that these developments could take place in isolation. Power would have to be sold to South Africa, and the

[18] *Annual Reports;* Ashton, p. 162. In 1875 it was estimated that the numbers working in the Republic were 15,000 out of a total population of 130,000; by 1908 it was thought to be 39,000; by 1946 the number was 58,634 men and 12,144 women.
[19] Unpublished seminar paper on Basutoland by Miss Sandra Wallman, Inst. of Commonwealth Studies, London Univ.
[20] Ibid.
[21] Other than scenery: but a tourist industry also means dependence on South African holiday makers.

amount of capital needed on the scale of operations required to justify the undertaking would almost certainly lead to a controlling interest being exercised from Pretoria—beneficial control no doubt, but control none the less.[22]

If, therefore, one considers the pattern of migration, and a trading relationship whereby South Africa takes 90 per cent of Basutoland's exports, and supplies a substantial proportion of its imports—plus the dependence by Basutoland on the road and rail facilities, and the capital and technical resources, of the Republic—the conclusion is inescapable. It is that Basutoland is vulnerable at every point in its national life to pressure by the South African government.

Bechuanaland

In one respect at least Bechuanaland is different from Basutoland and Swaziland: it is very large—as large 'almost as Texas', as American writers remind us.[23] It is also less circumscribed by the Republic since it has a northern frontier with Rhodesia.[24] It has easier access to the outside world, as numerous refugees from the Republic have discovered. On the other hand, the Tswana (or 'Bechuana') are small in number, divided into tribal communities[25] and no more able than the Basotho to earn their living independently of South Africa. A familiar process has been at work: on the one hand, a slowly rising standard of living; on the other, the unfolding of a political relationship with Pretoria which seeks to combine sovereignty with practical recognition of the Republic's wealth and power. Self-government is now almost within reach, but whatever may be the scale of international aid to the Territory, it is unlikely to affect the basic need of the

[22] For an examination of the Orange river development scheme see *Optima*, Mar. 1963.

[23] e.g. Edwin S. Munger, *Bechuanaland* (1965), on which the writer has drawn freely; or 'about the size of France, England and Wales together' (Doxey, p. 13).

[24] It also has a common 'frontier'—at one point in the middle of the Chobe river—with Zambia.

[25] There are eight major communities of which the largest are the Bamangwato numbering about a third of the total population of 540,000. The Bakgatla spill over into the Transvaal; the Barolong actually have more of their people in the Republic than in Bechuanaland. There are aboriginal Bushmen in the Kalahari, and a number of non-Bechuana immigrants like the Herero from South West Africa, the Koba from Zambia, and a little over 3,000 Europeans (English and Afrikaners), many of them from South West or South Africa.

Tswana government to live as amicably with its apartheid neighbour as the circumstances allow. It is true that to live thus is to live dangerously; but since no other pattern of national life is conceivable, the reality of the situation may itself be an asset. Nor will the Tswana government have been plunged suddenly into dependence on the Republic: the leaders have grown up in the shadow of South Africa, and have learned (painfully from time to time) something of the art of political manœuvre *vis-à-vis* London, Mafeking, and Pretoria.

Consider, for example, Seretse Khama's bid for leadership. He is the nephew of Tshekedi Khama, the Bamangwato Regent who had tried in his own way—on the memorable occasion of the trial of an Afrikaner youth in 1933—to assert his will against the colonial and South African governments.[26] In 1949 Seretse Khama ran into trouble on his own account following his marriage to an English girl; he was exiled in London until 1956, and obliged to forswear his right to the Paramountcy. But if the first steps in this 'very disreputable transaction'[27] were dictated by the colonial administration, the final stages were wholly to Seretse Khama's benefit; he was able to retain a great deal of the traditional authority that was his by birth while remaining free of the practical limitations that being a Chief would have imposed on him. The long-term advantages were soon evident. In May 1961 elections were held, and a new constitution introduced, based on the recommendations of a Constitutional Committee of the 'Joint Advisory Council'.[28] As in Basutoland the previous year, a legislative council was established with an unofficial majority: 3 *ex officio* members, 7 nominated officials, 21 elected members, plus 4 unofficial members nominated at the Resident Commissioner's discretion. The contrast with Basutoland was seen in the composition of the elected membership—divided equally between Africans and Europeans (10:10), and 1 Asian. But the election of Seretse Khama to the Council and the emergence of African parties were portents which the administration recognized in good time, for in 1964–5 the constitution was again amended. In place of the indirect elections of 1961, the lower

[26] Hailey, p. 66; Munger, p. 14.
[27] Winston Churchill's phrase (see Munger, p. 15).
[28] Consisting of members drawn from the separate African and European Advisory Councils, given statutory recognition in 1920.

F

house of a bicameral legislature was now based on universal suffrage from single-member constituencies; a consultative House of Chiefs was also established, consisting of the 8 tribal heads of the territory (plus 4 others chosen by them). The executive council became a quasi-cabinet, responsibility being divided between the Commissioner, an *ex officio* finance minister, and representative ministers drawn from the elected members of the legislature. Seretse Khama was thus able to avoid the House of Chiefs and to take his place as prime minister under the new constitution. When elections were held in March 1965, the Bechuanaland Democratic Party carried the day with 28 seats out of the total of 31 in the new Legislative Assembly; and Seretse Khama was summoned to the new capital at Gaberones and asked to form a government.

Parties	Date of origin	Votes	Seats
Bech. Democratic Party	1961	113,168	28* Led by Seretse Khama and Quett Masire
Bech. People's Party	1960	19,964	3 Led by K. T. Motsete and P. Matante
Botswana Independence Party	1964	6,491	0 Led by M. K. Mpho as breakaway movement from the BPP
Others		1,166	
		150,789	31

* Incl. B. Steinberg, a European candidate.

Dr Verwoerd sent his 'personal congratulations' to the BDP leader, saying that the former ban on Seretse Khama's entry into the Republic had been lifted as early as October 1964 'when it became clear that Bechuanaland had been placed on the road to independence and after [he] had indicated on behalf of the South African Government that since this was in accordance with the policy of separate development, the Republic would desire friendly relations with such a neighbour state'.[29] During the same month the South African government also announced its inten-

[29] *The Times*, 5 Mar. 1965.

tion of establishing a 'Bantustan' for the Tswana in the Mafeking district of the Republic. No date was appointed for its inauguration, and the additional status to be given the existing Territorial Authority is hardly likely to exceed the limited self-government now exercised by the Transkei Legislative Assembly; yet it may provide an interesting link between an independent Bechuanaland and the Republic. On that issue, as on matters of general policy, Seretse Khama has been circumspect, paying sensible regard to the frontier position occupied by Bechuanaland between tropical and southern Africa. At the end of December 1964 he was able to assure President Nkrumah that his government would join the OAU.[30] Earlier he was reported as saying in New York in August that Bechuanaland would be unable to participate in any form of economic sanctions against South Africa since 60 per cent of its income was derived from cattle exports to the Republic.

I think South Africa knows very well they stand for one thing—apartheid, while we stand for the exact opposite. . . . But they have not tried to intervene in our affairs or seriously influence us in any way and we have no reason to expect that they will try to do so in the future.[31]

If this proves a reasonable prophecy it may well be because of South Africa's willingness to continue to provide a market for Bechuanaland's exports. Once again we have a familiar picture: dependence on a trading relationship with the Republic within a common monetary and customs union, and financial dependence on external help from the United Kingdom and the United Nations, as the following budgetary figures show.

	(£) *1963/4*
Revenue	1,934,000
Expenditure	3,257,000
UK grant	1,592,000
Customs collected by S. Africa	280,000

> *Note:* UK financial assistance 1945/6–1962/3 totalled £12,420,000. The UN is expected to allocate £1,500,000 between 1963 and 1968.
>
> *Source:* COI, *Fact Sheet on the Commonwealth, The Bechuanaland Protectorate, July 1964.*

---

[30] *Ghanaian Times*, 30 Dec. 1964.   [31] *Africa Digest,* Oct. 1964.

In 1963 a Five-Year Development Plan was formulated. It envisaged a total expenditure of £10 million for 1963–8, the bulk
of which was to come from external sources. Britain will undoubtedly help; agencies of the United Nations may be persuaded to increase their contributions. It is possible, though
hardly likely, that the OAU may make a token offer. What of
South Africa? There are ambitious schemes devised for the
Territory, such as those which propose to develop the mineral
resources which many believe lie below the scrub land of the
Kalahari, or to use the immense flood waters of the Okavango
delta to irrigate the flat, barren plains of the hinterland. Such
schemes demand skill and experience, as well as capital. And, as
Professor Munger has argued, the most likely sources of enthus-
iasm, capital, and technical expertise are South Africa and,
secondly, Rhodesia.[32] In the past, the colonial administration
was reluctant to enlist the direct financial aid of the South
African government—such an invitation might well have been
open to a great deal of criticism—and it remains to be seen
whether Seretse Khama and the other BDP leaders will ask for
help, and what the response will be from Pretoria if they do. But
the South African government can claim that it is already helping in the development of the Territory, not only by buying its
cattle and employing its labour but (for example) in veterinary
research and the supply of vaccines. And, again, Professor
Munger has drawn the moral. Bechuanaland (he points out) has
the advantage of

physical proximity to South Africa, and especially to the booming
Witwatersrand. Few undeveloped countries are as accessible to[33]
highly developed countries as Bechuanaland. . . . A short distance
away, inside the same financial system and customs wall lie great
monetary institutions, advanced educational facilities, and enormously complex and diversified skills. . . . It is hard to realise the
savings in money, time, and general efficiency of having nearby
specialists and research stations.[34]

---

[32] Munger, p. 59.   [33] i.e. 'have such easy access to'.
[34] Munger, pp. 38–39. In 1963–4, a bad crop year, between 13,000 and 14,000
sought work in the Republic, in addition to 'about 23,000 Bechuanas normally
resident and working in South Africa' (*Africa Digest*, Oct. 1964). The airfield
at Francistown is controlled by Wenela—the company which recruits labour
for the Rand and Free State goldfields.

One must recognize that there is a reverse side to this close relationship. South Africa can as easily withdraw as proffer its friendship. Restrictions on the sale of cattle in the Republic— whether on political grounds to exert pressure on the Bechuana- land administration, or on grounds of public health to check the spread of foot-and-mouth disease[35]—could do great harm to the Territory precisely because of the disparity in wealth and power between the two states. And there would be little that the Tswana government could do about it. Revenue drawn from a slowly developing economy and spent on education might do something to lessen its dependence on South Africa for admini- strative and technical assistance.[36] If copper and other minerals were found on a larger scale, or if the output of chilled beef were to be increased from the abbatoir and cold storage plant at Lobatsi, Bechuanaland might be able to spread its trading inter- ests more widely in Africa and Europe: nearly two-thirds of the export of chilled beef now goes to the United Kingdom and Central Africa, a little over one-third to the Republic.[37] But these distant markets are auxiliary, not an alternative, to South Africa. Moreover, the line of rail, on which the Territory depends for the greater part of its exports, passes south through Mafeking to Cape Town, or north to Bulawayo in Rhodesia, and the con- struction of an alternative route through South West Africa (even assuming that South West Africa were no longer admini- stered by the Republic and that the capital required would be forthcoming) would be a very long-term venture.

The conclusion, therefore, in respect of Bechuanaland and its relations with South Africa is not substantially different from that reached earlier for Basutoland. There are differences of degree, in some contexts favourable to Bechuanaland, in others

---

[35] In 1964–5 there were a number of ugly incidents on the borders of Swaziland and Basutoland arising from cattle raiding and defiance of the regulations imposed by the Republic on the movement of cattle in the areas of foot- and-mouth disease.

[36] 'Approximately half the civil servants, and many of those acknowledged the most capable, are South African born' (Munger, p. 46).

[37] Asbestos, manganese, and small quantities of gold, silver, and kyanite (silicate of aluminium) are produced. Deposits of copper, coal, and nickel are known to exist, but (in Professor Munger's view) there is unlikely to be 'a bonanza on the scale of B.P.'s neighbours'. The Lobatsi abbatoir was opened in 1954; it is financed and managed by the Colonial Development Corporation. By 1962 the value of cattle carcases (including those exported to Britain) had risen to £2,046,058.

to Basutoland, but not of kind. In both countries nationalist sentiment has struggled to find expression in political demands for
independence. National interests, on the other hand, point to the
economic necessity—and one must stress the word—of maintaining good relations with South Africa.

Swaziland

The history of Swaziland, at first sight, is not very different from
that of its sister Territories. Many of the familiar characteristics
were present—a tribal community in the process of becoming a
state, a reluctant Imperial power, the conflict of interests among
local Europeans, and the appeal from harassed tribal chiefs for
British protection. By the turn of the century, there were the
beginnings of a colonial administration; there followed long
years of quiet stagnation under British rule until external forces
once more disturbed the scene. Nationalist sentiment grew to the
point when self-government (formerly canvassed only among the
European settler minority) became an African demand shaped
to local needs, and independence—once ruled out as impracticable—was accepted as inescapable. In broad terms, therefore,
Swaziland has followed a well-trodden road; it is now approach-
ing the final stages in the transfer of power. But there are unfamiliar aspects also, and the end may see a government in
Mbabane which is very different from the nationalist regimes in
other African capitals.

Swaziland owes its origins as a separate state to Mswati, chief
of the Nkosi-Dhlamini clan among the Ngoni, who turned for
help against the Zulus to the Boers in the Transvaal and the
British in Natal. Both were drawn into Swazi affairs, a Boer
commando entering the territory in 1875 to give support to
Mbandzeni—the successful contender for the position of paramount chief. The Swazi were then tossed from one side to the
other in the dispute between the Boer Republics and Britain. In
1894 they were placed under the Transvaal Republic. At the end
of the Anglo–Boer War they were put under the British Governor
of the Transvaal (under the Foreign Jurisdiction Act of 1890)
until 1906, when they were brought under the authority of the
High Commissioner for South Africa.[38]

[38] Hailey, pp. 10–14, and Noel Garson, 'The Swaziland Question and the Road to
the Sea 1887–1895', *Archives Year Book for S. African History*, 1957, pt 2.

By this time the chiefs had sold land and trading concessions to European interests on such a scale that very large tracts of territory were lost. Mswati had conceded land in the 1880s in what is today the Lydenburg area of the Transvaal; Mbandzeni granted further concessions 'of the most amazing scope, variety and intricacy'[39]—selling grazing, timber concessions, mineral rights, trading and tax monopolies—until, in 1906, the British Administrator undertook what was virtually a rescue operation. Each concession was scrutinized, rejected, or regulated, with the result that a third of the territory was recovered and preserved for African occupation. Subsequent land purchases by the Swazi nation and the local administration (financed out of Colonial Development & Welfare funds) raised the total acreage to a little over half the present area of Swaziland. One per cent is Crown Land, the balance—a little over 40 per cent—remaining in European hands, much of it on a freehold basis.[40] But despite the efforts of the chiefs and the colonial administration, landownership still bears little relation to the relative size of the African and European populations:

	1962 Population est.
Africans	270,000
Europeans	8,040
Mixed race	2,260

Source: COI, *The High Commission Territories*, Jan. 1965.

Swaziland is thus differently placed from the other Territories. The patchwork of African- and European-owned land has no parallel in Basutoland, and is of much greater complexity than the European settlement in the Ghanzi district and Tati Concessions in Bechuanaland. But although it can be argued that Swaziland has been held back politically by the need to accommodate African and European interests, it must be acknowledged that the Territory has not suffered financially. On the contrary, its economy is in advance of both Basutoland and Bechuanaland. It is paradoxical that the only one of the three Territories which might be thought to have reached a level of development suffi-

---

[39] Hailey, p.12.
[40] Figures are: total 4·3 m. acres; Swazi occupation 55 per cent, European 42 per cent.

cient to enable it to maintain something of an independent
posture is precisely the least likely to pursue radical policies. If its
economy is progressive, its politics are conservative. Moreover,
although development may free Swaziland from some of its
earlier dependence on the Republic, it will also tie the Territory
more closely to the need for cordial relations with its other neighbour—Portuguese Moçambique.

Pastoralists by tradition who numbered their wealth in cattle,
the Swazi have now begun to enter a modern economy. Cattle
are slaughtered and sold under quota to South Africa; cash
crops—cotton and tobacco—are grown by African and European farmers, and are also sold to South Africa on a quota basis.
Since January 1965 sugar has been exported to the United Kingdom under the Commonwealth Sugar Agreement. Some 10,000
Swazis are employed in South Africa, and about twice that number in industry and government service in Swaziland itself.[41] The
distinctive feature, however, of the Swazi economy is its relatively large extractive industry—timber, asbestos, and iron ore.
Its principal source of wealth is the big Havelock asbestos mine
in the Pigg's Peak area from which shipments in 1960 amounted
to over 60 per cent of the value of total exports: R5·4 million out
of R12·1 million. More recently, extraction of the immense iron
ore deposits at Ngwenya, some thirteen miles north-west of
Mbabane, has begun. It has meant the construction of a new
140-mile railway from Bomvu Ridge to Goba on the Swazi–
Moçambique border, and a contract with Japanese companies
for 12 million tons of ore, to be shipped through Lourenço
Marques over a period of ten years from 1964. Lastly, there
have been the remarkably successful ventures undertaken by the
Colonial Development Corporation, the Department of Agriculture, and private interests, whereby some 200,000 acres of
forests now clothe the formerly bare hillsides of the highveld.
There are three major enterprises—Usutu forests, with 119,000
acres of conifers and eucalyptus, Peak Timbers Ltd, with 75,000
acres, and Swaziland Plantations Ltd, with 11,000 acres. In 1959
the CDC and Courtaulds Ltd joined forces to form the Usutu

---

[41] At the end of 1960 1,585 Swazi were employed in mining, 3,092 in forestry, 7,506
    on sugar estates and in manufacturing (COI, *H.C. Territories*, p. 32). Migrant
    labour to the Republic represents about 15 per cent of the adult population, and
    contributes approximately £200,000 to the Swazi economy.

Pulp Company; a £5 million mill was established and now produces 100,000 tons of unbleached sulphate pulp a year for export (also through Lourenço Marques) to the United Kingdom. There are a number of other enterprises—fruit canneries, a printing works, a creamery, a bonemeal factory, a clothing factory, and the like.

In each of these schemes the network of communications linking Swaziland with South Africa and Moçambique has drawn the territory into closer association with its neighbours. For example, the Department of Agriculture in Mbabane is helped by its counterpart in Pretoria; the pulp mill at Usutu depends on lubricants and machine parts bought in the Republic. Iron ore and wood pulp have to be shipped abroad through Portuguese territory. Similarly the injection of about £40 million of private capital over the past twenty years has linked companies in Swaziland with parent concerns in South Africa.[42] One must add, too, the effect of a sizeable European community, many of whom farm in the Territory and live in the Republic.[43] In sum, Swaziland has been very successful in exploring new markets overseas; but it cannot escape its geography. Indeed, if one wished to free the Swazi economy of its need for good-neighbourly relations with South Africa and Moçambique, it would have to be reduced to a subsistence level of maize growers and cattle owners; a *reductio ad absurdum*. Its greater scale of industrial activity has created a broader economic base than exists in Basutoland or Bechuanaland, but (like its sister Territories) it remains part of the economic unity of the whole of southern Africa.[44]

---

[42] Hailey, p. 122; see too the article by L. P. Green and T. S. Fair, 'Preparing for Swaziland's Economic Growth', *Optima*, Dec. 1960.

[43] African farmers produce about 18 per cent of the cotton grown and 40 per cent of the tobacco; but (as J. E. Spence has pointed out) their contribution 'should not be exaggerated. White farmers were credited in 1959 with a cash crop production worth £730,000; while only 1,000 of the 27,000 acres under irrigation are in the African areas' (seminar paper given at the Inst. of Commonwealth Studies, London University, on 'The High Commisssion Territories, with special reference to Swaziland', 1964).

[44] The main sources of ordinary revenue in 1963–4 were:

Income tax (including mining tax)	£1,017,672
Customs and excise (collected by S. Africa)	304,285
Posts and telegraphs	167,569

The budgetary position 1963–4 was:

Revenue	Expenditure
£2,053,112	£2,929,140

Nor is it so very different from them in its politics.[45] In June 1964 the Imbokodvo Party and the United Swaziland Association made a clean sweep of the first elections to the newly constituted legislative council. Imbokodvo was a new movement launched by royal edict of the Ngwenyama Sobhuza II as a political arm of the traditionally constituted Swazi National Council; the United Swaziland Association was an offshoot of the European Advisory Council led by Mr Carl Todd. In the four multi-member constituencies, Imbokodvo won all eight open seats on a non-racial, taxpayers-plus-senior-wives' franchise. The United Swaziland Association, helped by Imbokodvo, won the four seats (elected on the same franchise) which were reserved for European or 'Eurafrican' candidates. Eight Imbokodvo members were also elected by 'traditional methods'. And the United Swaziland Association won all four seats of a single multi-member constituency in which electors were restricted to Europeans (and Eurafricans) resident in Swaziland or South Africa. The overall position was:

> Speaker—non-elected, no vote
> 4 officials
> 16 Imbokodvo
> 8 USA
> 1 nominated member

Note: The picture has been simplified a little. Mr Todd of the United Swaziland Association was elected on an Imbokodvo ticket in the reserved seat of the Lubombo (4-member) constituency. Mr Fitzpatrick was returned unopposed on a joint Imbokodvo–USA ticket for the reserved seat in Shisalweni. The eight Imbokodvo traditional seats included P. L. Dhlamini (a member of the executive council); Prince Makhosini Dhlamini, Imbokodvo leader in leg. co.; Dr Misibi, general secretary of Imbokodvo; and a Eurafrican.

The opposition parties were totally defeated. They were a confused mixture of several groups: the Ngwane National Liberatory Congress (NNLC) formed out of Dr Zwane's Swaziland Progressive Party; a splinter section of the SPP under Mr Nquku; the Mbandzeni National Convention; a Swaziland

---

[45] The following account draws on Michael Laschinger's 'Roads to Independence: the Case of Swaziland', *World Today*, Nov. 1965.

Democratic Party; a Eurafrican Welfare Association. In general, their members wanted a greater emphasis on one man, one vote, and a constitution which played down the element of communal representation. The parties they formed were very new—it was not until July 1960 that Swaziland could be said to have a recognizable 'political party', when Mr Nquku turned the Swaziland Progressive Association into the SPP; their appeal was largely among teachers' groups, clerical associations, and the small though growing number of workers in the main 'industrial centres'.

The colonial administration in Mbabane tried to stand between the conservative alliance of Swazi traditional leaders plus the European farming and business community on the one hand, and the more radical party groups on the other. It resisted European claims for parity of representation on the legislative council —a demand supported from time to time, though in ambivalent terms, by the Swazi National Council. It resisted counter demands by the party leaders for one man, one vote, and a constitution on the Basutoland model. Eventually, after numerous meetings and a full-scale constitutional conference in London, a point of deadlock was reached between the quarrelling leaders. The British government then imposed its own views, set out in a White Paper early in 1963: it provided for a legislative council based on a minority of reserved seats for Europeans, near-adult suffrage in multi-member constituencies, and a traditional right of selection by the Ngwenyama. This satisfied nobody—until the 1964 elections when Imbokodvo and its European allies entered the legislative council.

The opposition parties were defeated by the strength of the conservative alliance, their own internal weakness, and by the peculiar form of the constitution with its large multi-member constituencies.[46] During the election, earlier disputes between Sobhuza and the European Advisory Council had been set aside.

---

[46] 'If the Lubombo constituency, for instance, had consisted of three single-member divisions, the NNLC, which gained 21 per cent of the vote there, would probably have carried one division. Size also placed a premium on organization. The NNLC's organization was poor, it was short of money, and donations from the OAU came very late. Imbokodvo, on the other hand, had money and assistance from substantial white sources, and used organization and ceremonial proper to the SNC, the statutorily recognized traditional authority, for electoral purposes' (ibid, p. 489).

And if Imbokodvo was strengthened by money and advice from friendly allies in the Republic, the United Swaziland Association was also given full support by the Ngwenyama and his representatives in a predominantly conservative society. There was little that the small splinter groups of radicals could do to challenge them within the terms of the new constitution, and they turned instead to 'positive action'. Rejecting the White Paper and the 1963 constitution as 'racialist', they encouraged the trade unions to take a militant stand, not only over the demand for higher wages and better working conditions but for a more democratic legislature. Early in 1963 there was a well organized strike at the Big Bend sugar plantation; in June a major stoppage occurred at the Havelock Mine, followed by a general strike in Mbabane. The main opposition party (NNLC) certainly had a hand in these illegal strikes,[47] basing its appeal on economic grievances of long standing among the workers. The leaders were successful in one respect, for the colonial administration found it increasingly difficult to maintain law and order until a battalion of British troops arrived from Nairobi to assist the local police. It was under these conditions that elections were held some ten months later, and the new constitution introduced.

Politically, therefore, Swaziland is some distance behind Basutoland and Bechuanaland. The constitution is to be reviewed not later than 1968, and independence is unlikely before 1968–9. If fresh elections are held by the administration, on the basis of adult suffrage in single-member constituencies, the NNLC (or whatever form the opposition takes in future) may strengthen its hold in the townships. Yet it is difficult to see how it can gain anything more than a minor foothold in a newly elected legislature, and Swaziland is likely to enter independence under an Imbokodvo government of African and European ministers. It will be a multi-racial government—a curious anomaly in the context of apartheid and African nationalist rule; it will also be a traditional-conservative regime drawing a great deal of its authority from the power of the Ngwenyama, and in this respect parallels can be drawn with the success of the Bechuanaland Democratic Party and the Basutoland National

[47] 'Illegal' because the ordinance requirement of 21 days' notice had not been met. The NNLC has also tried to turn to its advantage rural discontent with measures adopted to control foot-and-mouth disease.

Party. There are, to be sure, differences in outlook among the leaders of Imbokodvo, the Democratic Party, and the BNP, as there are between the three traditional leaders, Sobhuza, Seretse Khama, and Constantine Seeiso. Yet in all three Territories the elections were won, and control has been maintained, through a pattern of organization (based on traditional ties) which has been eclipsed over a large part of tropical Africa by new parties of a more radical appeal. Whether moderation and tradition can hold their own after independence remains to be seen: perhaps they can in the particular context of southern Africa. But the uneasiness which prompts such a question is one more element of doubt in the total picture, since it is difficult to be wholly confident that the political situation in Swaziland, or its two companion territories, will remain set in its present conservative pattern.

The picture that emerges from this quick sketch of the three Territories is clear. The United Kingdom is committed to the transfer of power to territories, two of which are dependent primarily on South Africa and the third on South Africa and Moçambique. With the possible exception of Swaziland, they are opposed to control from the Republic: they will be 'sovereign and dependent'. Is Britain sensible to encourage them along such a road, or should it reverse its decision and stop short of a full surrender of sovereignty. Would there be any advantage in doing so? When Lord Hailey reached the final pages of his own account of the Territories he had little sympathy for the notion of self-government. He believed it could not be entertained 'without a grievous loss of self-respect' on the part of the United Kingdom.

And as for the Territories, it would be well for them to realize that liberties once lost are not easily regained by the small peoples of the world. What would it profit the small peoples of the Territories if they now loose their hold on the solid fact of liberty under British rule, in order that they may grasp at the fantasy of Independence?[48]

Lord Hailey's plea was for the retention of an 'ultimate control over the Territories' by Britain while devolving a substantial measure of responsibility on the local legislatures. Eventually, perhaps, on this basis they might attain the position reached by Samoa in its relations with New Zealand; they would become

[48] Hailey, p. 128.

near-sovereign states whose external relations are managed by a friendly power. One might argue that the Samoan example is hardly applicable to the three Southern African Territories, which are border states having to face problems arising not from their isolation but involvement in a conflict transcending their own powers of control. But such a reservation would add force to Lord Hailey's contention. It is precisely on these grounds (it can be argued) that Britain should retain control, since it is more likely to be able to deal with a delicate relationship of this kind than any nationalist government in one of the three Territorial capitals. It can mediate in Pretoria should relations between South Africa and the Territories become strained; it can stand between them and the Republic should Pretoria threaten them. It can impose its own authority if there is a serious breakdown in public order, or if the problem of control of the border becomes excessive. It could check any tendency on the part of the Basotho or Tswana or Swazi leaders to exercise power to the detriment of 'the solid fact of liberty under British rule'. Not for the first time in the history of southern Africa the Imperial factor would provide a useful—an indispensable—reserve of power on the side of law, order, and liberty.

Yet the case for withdrawal is also very strong. Indeed, it can be supported by what many would think an incontrovertible argument: that, although the British government may persuade themselves that they should stay, no one else is asking them to do so, either abroad, or in the Territories, or even in the Republic. No substantial section of the African population in any of the Territories has expressed a preference for continued British protection in place of the uncertainties of independence. It is possible that the party leaders may be wrong to choose the uncertainties; they may even come to regret the decision. But how are they now to be persuaded otherwise? Moreover, if the United Kingdom were to refuse to surrender control, it might have to face a widening area of hostility in all three Territories, thus making its own position less tenable, and precipitating under worse conditions the situation it was hoped to avoid. If independence were now to be withheld, it would almost certainly lead to a less co-operative attitude towards Britain on the part of local political groups. The result would be a restless discontent, which would be at best an unsatisfactory, at worst an impossible, basis for a sensible long-term relationship with the Republic. Meanwhile, the anti-colonial states in the United Nations would have new grounds for criticism. The OAU would be hostile; the Commonwealth unsympathetic. And the South African government would have every opportunity for ironic comment in terms of adverse comparisons (however unmerited) with its own Bantustan policy. In short, Britain would be isolated in defence of a situation which she alone was prepared to justify. Where would be the gain in those circumstances?

From the United Kingdom's point of view, the basic need is to be free of any formal commitment in southern Africa, and one should not only accept but on balance welcome the decision by Britain to move towards independence for all three Territories. One must also assume that all three countries will remain within the Commonwealth; they are virtually certain to apply for membership, and no other Commonwealth government is likely to oppose them. They will be members also of the United Nations and, presumably, of the OAU, although one cannot be sure that the OAU will still be in existence as a single organization by the time Swaziland is independent.[49] In addition, embassies and consulates may be opened in Maseru, Gaberones, and Mbabane. But, whatever range of contacts the newly independent governments may make, their relations with South Africa and Britain are certain to remain by far the most important. And the extent of British involvement is likely to turn on the nature of the relationship between the Territories and Pretoria.

If, as one may hope it will, the disparity of wealth and power between the two sides imposes its own restraint, the United Kingdom may have no grounds for disquiet at having surrendered control. There is some evidence for this in the shifts of attitude on both sides. In June 1964, for example, Dr Verwoerd told the Senate that he was opposed to the incorporation of the Territories into the Republic; nor did he object to their being given their independence since it was in keeping with South Africa's policy in its own 'Native areas'. 'We do not mind their freedom. The independence of the protectorates is in line with apartheid. If Basutoland becomes free, then it has passed

---

[49] In September 1964 the Basutoland Congress Party actually opened an office in Dar es Salaam and appointed Mr Litsebea Matooane as their representative there, to maintain contact with the OAU Liberation Committee.

through a phase which corresponds with apartheid.'[50] The Basotho leaders are unlikely to endorse Dr Verwoerd's description of their path to independence: they use strong words to condemn apartheid. Nevertheless, there is a detectable substratum of caution to their criticism which is easy to understand against the background of their dependence on the Republic. Having surrendered control, therefore, Britain may be able to note with satisfaction the formal end of a triple strand of colonial rule— thus bringing nearer the day of its total disengagement from empire. It is true that the Territories will still depend on the United Kingdom for financial help, and on many of the ties which continue to link Britain with its former colonies. But they will be no different in this respect from a number of other Commonwealth countries. In sum, the three Territories may continue to adjust their local needs to regional interests; South Africa may continue to treat them as separate though subordinate entities within its own economy; and Britain may at last escape involvement in South Africa.

Certainly one may hope that a peaceful *modus vivendi* will be worked out. Yet the worst must be considered alongside the best. For the caution tending to limit extremism—on both sides—can only lessen the chances of conflict between the Territories and South Africa; it can hardly eliminate them. The areas of danger noted earlier in the chapter will still remain, and might usefully be reconsidered here by way of conclusion. In so far as one can look ahead to the immediate future, they may be said to centre on a particular problem in each Territory—party rivalry in Basutoland, the question of refugees in Bechuanaland, and of militant strike action in Swaziland—although the danger in each instance is certainly not exclusive to the Territory concerned. In more general terms, the weakness of the Territories lies in the absence of any reserve of power on which the newly independent governments will be able to draw. All three are virtually certain to enter independence without an army. They—and the Gambia —will be the first African states to do so. And although the local police forces were strengthened by the inclusion of mobile units after the riots in Swaziland in 1963, they may find themselves hard pressed to maintain even a minimum of order should serious rioting occur.

[50] *The Times*, 6 June 1964.

Suppose, for example, riots break out in Maseru between rival political factions, as happened in the latter part of October 1964 when followers of the Basutoland Congress Party were murdered? A police raid on the hostel for members of the legislative council led to the confiscation of firearms, ammunition, and 'other weapons including pangas and battle-axes', and twelve members of the Marema 'Tlou Party were arrested.[51] The Resident Commissioner was quick to act, and announced a Public Order Proclamation to strengthen his authority. But will the order be issued so easily after independence? And will the South African government wait patiently until it is? Or suppose terrorists from the Republic cross the border into Basutoland in search of a base for subversion? It happened in the early part of October 1964 when *Poqo* organizers were arrested 'in a series of raids in Maseru'; more than twenty were arrested as part of 'an anti-*Poqo* campaign' and to 'enforce the conditions of entry and residence laid down by Basutoland's immigration laws'.[52] Will they be arrested as promptly after independence? And how tolerant is the South African government likely to be in such a situation?

A year earlier, Bechuanaland had held the stage. According to the Police Commissioner in Pretoria, some 200 political refugees passed through the Territory during June and July 1963;[53] according to Amnesty International (also in 1963) some 1,200 Africans and Europeans had sought asylum there (and a passage farther north) since the emergency in 1960.[54] It was said that '491 persons had applied for temporary residence permits . . . and there were 711 refugees there'.[55] Individual cases dramatized the danger. Arthur Goldreich and Harold Wolpe, fleeing from the impending Rivonia Trial, succeeded after a number of mishaps in escaping via Swaziland and Bechuanaland to Dar es Salaam and London; Kenneth Abrahams, a Cape Town doctor practising in Rehoboth among the Baster community in South West Africa, was seized on the Ghanzi–Lobatsi road while

---

[51] *Africa Digest*, Dec. 1964.
[52] 'There have been unconfirmed reports that the *Poqo* organization's youth wing is planning terrorist raids on South Africa' (ibid). For an account of the *Poqo* movement, see SAIRR, *Survey of Race Relations in S. Africa 1963* (1964), pp. 13–21, 46–48.
[53] *Star* (Johannesburg), 18 Aug. 1963.   [54] *Rand Daily Mail*, 18 Aug. 1963.
[55] *Survey of Race Relations 1963*, p. 58.

G

attempting to escape through Bechuanaland, and forcibly taken into the Republic.[56] In both instances—as over the problem of refugees generally—the Resident Commissioner maintained a delicate balance between too great a tolerance of subversive movements aimed at South Africa and too harsh an attitude towards political refugees.[57] It has been a careful exercise of judgement and restraint, which would have been still more difficult but for the influence that the United Kingdom government can exercise not only on the Tswana leaders, but also (it is fair to assume) in Pretoria. The Tswana government has announced that it will continue after independence to be guided by the same considerations as the former colonial administration; and it is surely right to do so. But it will be a difficult task for the newly independent government to face unaided.

The particular danger of Swaziland lies in the possibility that the 1963 strikes will be repeated after independence. It is true that the newly formed trade unions are isolated centres of radicalism amidst the general conservatism of the population: hence the Imbokodvo victory in the 1964 elections. Yet they have been able to provoke unrest on a scale out of proportion to their numbers. British troops were still there in 1965, and had been used by the administration more than once in the strike areas. If a similar crisis arose after independence, who would send troops? Britain? on the analogy of the action taken in East Africa? But an appeal from a traditionalist government for soldiers to suppress a strike may be viewed very differently—by other African states and by Britain—from action taken to quell army mutineers. An appeal may go to Pretoria from Mbabane and be met, thus completing a full cycle of Swazi history since 1885 when the Boer commando helped to restore order during the election of Mbandzeni. Once invited in, the South African troops or police might stay, against insistent demands from outside critics in the OAU and the United Nations for their withdrawal. It would not be a specifically British problem; yet it might raise awkward

[56] Abrahams was eventually returned to Bechuanaland by order of the Minister of Justice in South Africa after representations had been made by the UK Ambassador in Pretoria, despite a Supreme Court ruling that Abraham's arrest in South West Africa, prior to his escape, was still lawful.
[57] Cf. the comment, by a writer in the *Round Table*, Dec. 1963, that in all three Territories Britain has had 'to tread a tightrope between appeasement and provocation of the Republic'.

questions in respect of Swaziland's membership of the Commonwealth.

It is easy to note these dangers, far more difficult to know what Britain should try and do to minimize them, now or after power has been transferred. Certainly, it should go on helping the Territories with development aid, technical assistance, and budgetary grants. In the post-war years some £30–40 millions have been spent in the three Territories, the greater part since the mid-1950s.[58] The Morse Mission in 1960 called for a further injection of £7 million, and it would be helpful to associate the United States and United Nations agencies in joint schemes of aid. Yet it would be idle to pretend that help of this kind, however generous, could do more than strengthen the base of authority of each government among its own people. This is important. But it cannot alter the Territories' dependence on the goodwill of the Republic within the South African monetary and customs union. And, in these circumstances, it is pointless to talk of a defence agreement between Britain and the Territories, or of a United Nations guarantee of the frontiers, or the placing of an 'international presence' in the three capitals. Responsibility without power has never been a satisfactory basis for keeping the peace, and power in southern Africa rests with Pretoria. There is little that the United Nations or Britain or any outside force could do if South Africa wished to harm the new states. There is a wide range of pressures that Pretoria can exert—by imposing controls at the border, or checking the flow of trade and labour, or withholding its services, all of which would be within the legal competence of the Republic. Nor could United Nations officials stationed in the Territory do more than protest against violations of the frontiers by South African police. The existence of such officials in the various disputed areas of the world has been primarily the result of mutual agreement among the states concerned—a position unlikely to be reached at present in southern

[58] Grants and loans were made as follows:

Treasury grants	1956–63	£9,132,236
CD and W	1940–63	£11,674,569
Treasury Assist. up to	1964	£3,477,712
CDC	1949–63	£21,317,000 (committed, £16,223,000 spent)

Included in these amounts are special grants for the University College of Basutoland, Bechuanaland, and Swaziland at Roma in Basutoland.

(*Source:* Hailey, p. 122)

Africa. Certainly the United Kingdom would be unwise to attempt to play a 'protective role' by means of a defence treaty or the formal underwriting of Commonwealth ties: as independent states, the three Territories will have as much (and as little) protection through their membership of the United Nations as Britain or any other power could provide. Nor is it clear why the Territories should be singled out for particular attention. There are many troubled areas of the world already in need of international supervision, while the dangers that may arise in relation to the former High Commission Territories would be of very minor consequence to the world at large. The verdict may sound harsh: but what would it profit Basutoland, Bechuanaland, or Swaziland if they lost the goodwill of the Republic and gained only an international guarantee of doubtful worth in exchange?

It would be wrong perhaps to conclude this chapter on a note of unqualified pessimism. If one looks at the Southern African Territories in the context of the total situation in South Africa, there are hopeful signs. In the first place, it will surely be of advantage to the United Kingdom to have independent voices from southern Africa speaking in the Commonwealth, the OAU, and the United Nations on developments in that part of the continent. Hitherto, Britain (and the United States) have tried to counsel restraint and caution in respect of South Africa. In the words of a former High Commissioner for the Territories: 'Britain's concern for the Territories must always mean concern for good relations between them and the Republic: must always weight the balance on the side of neighbourly respect, however much the other scale may be depressed by hatred of *apartheid* policies.'[59] The concern may continue after independence, but once power has been transferred Britain will be spared the formal embarrassment of control; its place will have been taken by the Basuto. Tswana, and Swazi governments, and it is difficult to believe that they will want to alter the balance. Indeed, there are the clear statements by African leaders (quoted earlier) expressing the same view. The OAU has already been obliged to listen to a plea for greater economic realism from Malawi, and it will be interesting to see what effect the views of representatives from the Southern African Territories will have on the demand for sanctions. Similarly, opposition, or abstention, on the part of Basuto,

[59] *Round Table*, Dec. 1963.

Tswana, and Swazi representatives at the United Nations to a resolution calling for sanctions may have a sobering influence on those who, in revulsion against the policy of apartheid, are prepared to vote for punitive measures against South Africa with little thought given to the consequences.

Secondly, there is the effect of independence for the three Territories on South Africa itself, with whose fate the future of these very small communities will now be linked inseparably. If catastrophe overwhelms the Republic, it is difficult to see how they can escape injury, and membership of the Commonwealth or the OAU or the United Nations will not help them; but if, against all present forebodings, South Africa continues to confront but not to be overwhelmed by its racial problems, the Territories may be able to play their own minor part in the drama. Within the next few years South Africa may have to recognize the existence of sovereign African states within and on its own frontiers; and if the Territories can do nothing to change the situation in the Republic by their own efforts, they may perhaps, in a very small way, influence policy in Pretoria by their example. African rule in Basutoland may do something to help the Transkei to secure a greater measure of local autonomy since, if apartheid is to be followed to its logical end, it is difficult to see why Umtata should have less power than Maseru. Similarly, a working partnership between African and European leaders in Swaziland, and the knitting together of Tswana society under an independent government in Gaberones, might provide a practical example of co-operation across racial and tribal barriers. There are few signs at present that the example of multi-racial government, or stable African rule, in one or other of the Territories will affect the racialism of the National Party: the odds are heavily against so hopeful a conclusion. Yet the possibility is there—faint on the horizon—that an independent Basutoland, Bechuanaland, and Swaziland may provide the first steps towards 'a loose confederation of autonomous states'[60] within a wider South African society.

[60] Sir John Maud's phrase: 'The Challenge of the High Commission Territories', *African Affairs*, Apr. 1964.

IV

Britain, South Africa, and the
United Nations

THE case for keeping a watchful but waiting brief on South
Africa rests largely on the immense difficulties involved in
attempting to change the situation from outside, but it is reinforced by the present position of the organization which is cast
as the principal actor in the play—the United Nations. Again,
Britain is directly affected, as a permanent member of the
Security Council and the chief target of attack by the Afro-Asian
representatives. The debate between them and the United
Kingdom delegation has occupied a great deal of time. It has
often seemed little more than a hollow warfare, not least because
—being conducted in terms of the Charter—it is difficult to
grasp by those who are unused to the subtleties of legal conflict.
Yet behind the arguments over apartheid, and the feasibility of
United Nations action in South West Africa, are aspects of international law fundamental to the hope that the world may one
day manage its affairs on the basis of consent rather than power.
The importance of the debate over South Africa is that it raises
many of the problems concerned with the legitimacy of collective
action by the United Nations in a particular setting—including
the limits which at present exist to the range of measures authorized by the Charter. These problems are embodied in the two
principal themes examined in this chapter—the attack on apartheid, and the case brought against South Africa by Ethiopia and
Liberia before the International Court: but something must also
be said, by way of introduction, of the general difficulties facing
the United Nations.

They stem from a mood of almost universal disappointment
among the member states, so much so that early in 1965 a sympathetic observer of the Organization was obliged to recognize
that 'the commonest attitude towards the United Nations is,
today, disenchantment'.[1] It was the beginning of a year devoted

[1] 'The UN at Twenty', survey by Andrew Boyd, *The Economist*, 3 Apr. 1965.

to International Co-operation, an unhappy dedication, since it was clear that the organization which had been created twenty years earlier 'to be a centre for harmonizing the actions of nations'[2] was in serious difficulties. The prevailing note during the brief opening—and closing—scenes of the nineteenth session of the General Assembly had been one of confusion. In order to avoid a decision on Article 19 (the loss of voting rights by states two years behind in their payment of their financial contributions), the delegates agreed to a number of interim arrangements 'on the basis of consensus and no-vote' before going into recess on 1 September.[3] The uncertainty which underlay the debate came from a discernible source—a doubt among many of the delegates not only about the particular problem of financial responsibility but the nature of the Organization as a whole. As Mr Andrew Boyd observed: 'the procedural deadlock over peacekeeping costs is not itself the real crisis which does, indeed, threaten the United Nations' whole existence. The real crisis arises because ... the nations still have only a hazy idea of what it is for; and, therefore, whether they really need it.'

These were harsh words after two decades of the United Nations existence. Yet one must quote them here, at the beginning of a survey of the particular issue of South Africa, for by 1965 it was clear that the combination of political manœuvre and legal argument which governed the deliberations often had little effect on the major issues confronting the world. In the excitement of debate, or arguments over interpretations of the Charter, it was easy for many of the smaller member states, which played such part as they could in international affairs through the United Nations, to forget not only that they lacked the power to act otherwise but even that there were states who were under no such handicap. The election of an African as President of the Assembly, and an Asian as Secretary-General, helped to increase the illusion: it added weight to the argument

[2] Charter, Ch. I, Art. 1(4). Special years are always fickle. 1960 was designated Africa's Year, and so it proved, if the attention paid by the rest of the world to events in the Congo after 1 July were taken as a measure of the interest aroused; but that was hardly what was intended.

[3] GA, 18 Feb. 1965. The normal conduct of business would have raised the question of whether a member state which had fallen two years in arrears in its contributions to the UN budget (among them the USSR and France) was entitled to vote in the General Assembly.

that the uncommitted members could mediate, and even affect the balance of power, between the giants. Hence the 'illusory voting victories' when

by huge majorities, the Assembly will condemn Dr Verwoerd's policies, or call for economic concessions to underdeveloped countries; but the actual effect is as hard to discern as it was in those first years, when the Assembly used to urge Russia to allow elections in Korea, or to accept international control of nuclear armaments.[4]

By 1965 the reality was beginning to show through the illusion. Communist China was still outside the Organization, and had rejected the United Nations right to concern itself with Vietnam; Indonesia had withdrawn its membership. The Soviet Union was still a member but it could hardly be regarded as a fervent supporter of its aims. There were also signs that the United States was no longer so concerned even to appear to use its immense power through collective rather than unilateral action; it was increasingly difficult to believe that the United States would be greatly influenced over South Africa by the African states, however active or numerous their delegations might be in New York, and inconceivable that it could be forced to take action that it did not want to take.[5] In sum, the sombre truth persisted that the *pax oecumenica* which kept (most of) mankind free from 'the scourge of war' still depended on mutual restraint, induced by mutual fear, on the part of the two major powers. Collective security through the United Nations was still a dream, and the time when 'a new security system can be made to rise slowly out of the ashes of the old'[6] was still remote.

Any weakening of the position of the United Nations must be a serious blow to the hopes of the African states. It is hardly an exaggeration to say that it is only at the United Nations that they have been able to find ground for concerted action, through

---

[4] Andrew Boyd, 'The UN at Twenty', *Economist*, 3 Apr. 1965.
[5] In May 1965, when the US landed troops in the Dominican Republic, the *Observer* (9 May), noted with dismay that the 'assertion of American power and of a Super-Power's right to intervene in the affairs of small neighbour States betrays a misunderstanding of the realities of the world situation. . . . How can one build a world society if any Power simply ignores the need for rules?' How indeed? But the truth may be that the world still has to accommodate itself to the fact not only that overwhelming power lies in the hands of the 'super-powers' but that there are no rules save those made by the principal antagonists.
[6] Younger, p. 68.

which by skilful campaigning they have pressed hard to bring Britain and the United States to the point where at least they have been prepared to examine coercive measures against South Africa. Numbering thirty-six of the 114 states, they have joined with other countries on the particular issue of apartheid to embarrass those who resisted their demands. In August 1963 they secured the resolution in the Security Council calling on states to deny arms to South Africa; they also succeeded in establishing a number of committees to advance their case—on non-self-governing territories,[7] on apartheid,[8] on conditions in South Africa,[9] on sanctions,[10] and so forth. They have used the wording of the Charter to widen the scope of United Nations inquiry into questions of self-determination and human rights.[11] Ethiopia and Liberia have brought South Africa before the International Court at The Hague over South West Africa. There has been no lack of ingenuity or want of resolution in their attack. The effect may have been to achieve little more than 'a concentration of international attention on the situation in the colonial territories' and 'the growing isolation of South Africa and Portugal in the world community';[12] but they can pride themselves at least on

[7] The 'Committee of 17' consisting of representatives of African, Asian, and colonial powers plus Russia and the US, set up in January 1962 after protracted arguments over the question of a time-limit for the formal ending of colonial rule. The USSR had suggested 1962; Nigeria and Liberia 1970. It proved impossible to agree on a date, quite apart from the refusal of the colonial powers to accept the idea of a time-table and of Portugal to admit that she had colonies.

[8] Established in November 1962 (Resolution 1761 [XVII]) by 67 votes to 16 with 23 abstentions). It consists of Algeria, Costa Rica, Malaysia, Ghana, Guinea, Haiti, Hungary, Nepal, Nigeria, Philippines, Somalia. M. Diallo Telli (of Guinea —later to be the first General Secretary of the OAU) was appointed chairman.

[9] The 'Group of Experts' appointed in December 1963—Mrs Myrdal (Sweden), Sir Edward Asafu Adjaye (Ghana), Josip Djerdja (Yugoslavia), Sir Hugh Foot (UK), and Dey Ould Sidi Baba (Mauritania). It submitted its report in April 1964 after Mr Djerdja had resigned in March in protest over its failure to agree to a proposal that an 'ultimatum' be issued to South Africa should it fail to take part in the 'National Convention' recommended by the committee.

[10] Appointed in 1964 (on a proposal by Norway) to examine the feasibility and implications of economic sanctions against South Africa.

[11] 'One of the most obvious of the achievements of the African states has undoubtedly been to accelerate discussion on and feeling over questions of human rights and self-determination, and the contrast between 1958, when a very mild resolution on Algeria was defeated in the General Assembly, and 1963, when the Security Council adopted unanimously a call for an arms boycott against South Africa, is striking' (C. Hoskyns, 'The African States and the United Nations, 1959–64', *International Affairs*, July 1964).

[12] Ibid.

having done that, and it has always been possible to argue that greater ingenuity and further effort might do a great deal more. The International Court has yet to deliver its judgment on the question whether South Africa is in default of the terms of its mandate over South West Africa. Fresh resolutions in the Security Council on apartheid, whether based on the judgment or more general grounds, may (it is hoped) 'bring nearer the day of mandatory economic sanctions against South Africa'.[13] Hope may have been born of illusion, but it was sustained by constant activity in New York.

The uncertainty that haunts the United Nations is bound therefore to reduce the 'special pressures' which are seen as 'essential to get the Governments of the United Kingdom, the United States of America, and France to change the direction of their policies on the South African question'.[14] And since Britain has been particularly affected, a weakening of Afro-Asian pressure may be a welcome relief. Yet the long-term prospect of an enfeebled world organization—or even of a long period of inactivity by the United Nations—can hardly be thought to be to Britain's advantage. Precisely because it has global interests, and now lacks the power to safeguard them, the United Kingdom has reason to encourage co-operation across international frontiers —whether through the United Nations and the Commonwealth, or through regional bodies like the OAU. The South African and Rhodesian issues apart, the United Kingdom might be thought well placed within an international organization in which there are twenty-one Commonwealth countries linked by their membership of a number of other associations. There are familiar faces in the Assembly from the former British dependencies, and only a particularly obtuse observer of the United Nations would suppose that past colonial ties were a disadvantage in relations between Britain and many of the newly independent states. It is true that opinion in Britain has tended to swing between too sanguine a view of what can be achieved through the United Nations and an exaggerated suspicion of the attitude of the newly independent countries, but party leaders on both sides have

[13] 'Findings and Recommendations of Commission IV and V', Internat. Conference on Econ. Sanctions against S. Africa, *Economic Sanctions Against S. Africa*, ed. R. Segal (1964), p. 271.
[14] Ibid.

steered a cautious path between theory and practice.[15] Certainly neither party, nor any substantial section of British opinion, would suppose that Britain and the world would be better placed *without* the United Nations.[16]

Apartheid

The intention of the Afro-Asian states is clear. Unable to alter the racial situation in South Africa directly—and who can doubt that they would do so if they had the power?—they have combined to exert pressure on Britain and the United States through the United Nations. In an attempt to keep within the terms of the Charter, they have developed two main lines of argument: that acts of the South African government have infringed basic human rights; and that these infringements are of such a kind as to constitute a 'threat to the peace'. South Africa's defence has been, primarily, that the United Nations has no *locus standi* in disputes of this nature since apartheid is a domestic issue, and thus beyond its jurisdiction. The Nationalist government has also denied any infringement of human rights, claiming that apartheid is a just solution of South Africa's racial problems, and that if indeed a threat to the peace exists in southern Africa the fault lies on the side of the OAU and those who support its policies.

At first sight, it might be thought that South Africa had a clear

---

[15] The following extracts from the Commons debate on the government's Defence White Paper on 3–4 March 1965 are representative of a broad stratum of belief in the Labour and Conservative parties:

'*Denis Healey:* It must . . . remain our main aim to enable the United Nations to take these responsibilities over from individual Western Governments or combinations of Governments. A major element in the foreign and defence policies of the Government is to ensure that responsibility for peace-keeping outside Europe falls increasingly on the United Nations.' Mr Healey was careful, however, to add: 'that is obviously a long and difficult road, especially at the present time' (HC Deb., vol. 707, col. 1339).

'*Sir Alec Douglas Home:* There is no fault that can be laid on the Charter, if it is examined closely. The fault lies in the member States, who have such differing standards of values and such mixed motives. It is the Communist Powers' abuse of the veto which has paralysed the United Nations over the years, and some of the newer and smaller countries who, short-sightedly and against their own interests, are using the Assembly . . . for selfish and not collective purposes' (ibid. cols. 1550–1).

[16] For a sober American assessment of the practical advantages of the UN in its numerous activities throughout the world, see Richard N. Gardner, *In Pursuit of World Order* (New York, 1964).

case. The United Nations is an international body designed 'to maintain international peace and security', and the Charter expressly forbids it to intervene in matters of domestic jurisdiction:

> Nothing contained in the present Charter shall authorize the United Nations to intervene in matters which are essentially within the domestic jurisdiction of any State or shall require the Members to submit such matters to settlement under the present Charter. . . . (Art. 2 (7)).

The only exception is:

> this principle shall not prejudice the application of enforcement measures under Chapter VII

whereby the Organization is empowered to take action 'with respect to threats to the peace, breaches of the peace, and acts of aggression'.

On a closer view, the problem of 'domestic jurisdiction' becomes a great deal more complicated. It has troubled the United Nations for a very long time, well before the arrival of the African representatives in New York. It was raised, for example, in the attack on South Africa from 1947 onwards over its treatment of persons of Indian and Pakistani origin, when South Africa protested on the grounds that questions of citizenship and voting rights were clearly protected by Article 2(7). Since there existed the Cape Town agreements of 1927–32 between the South African and Indian governments, it was possible to argue that the problem had something of the nature of an international dispute; but the Indian government also raised the particular issue of the Asiatic Land Tenure and Indian Representation Act of 1946, and argued that it was not only a violation of the Cape Town agreements and the general provisions of the United Nations Charter, but came within the scope of Article 14:

> . . . the General Assembly may recommend measures for the peaceful adjustment of any situation regardless of origin, which it deems likely to impair the general welfare or friendly relations among nations . . .

In these early years of the United Nations, the General Assembly was uncertain what to do, and it referred the matter jointly to the First Committee (Political) and the Sixth Committee (Legal) in October 1946. It thus set 'the pattern for mixed political and juridical treatment of the South African question'[17] —a pattern that was to continue down to the present controversy over South West Africa. The Assembly agreed that discussion of the problem of the Indian population of South Africa was an 'important matter' (under Article 18) and, therefore, a two-thirds majority vote would be necessary on any resolution. It also declared that there was no infringement of the domestic jurisdiction reservation of Article 2(7), although it refused to accept South Africa's offer to ask the International Court to pronounce on the issue. Thereafter the matter wound its way by debate and resolution through successive Assembly sessions—the United Nations urging and South Africa denying the need for joint discussions between the South African, Indian, and Pakistani governments—until 1961, when it became merged with the question of apartheid in general.

It was argued first that the case against apartheid was open to inquiry under Article 55 (c): 'The United Nations shall promote . . . universal respect for, and observance of, human rights and fundamental freedom for all without distinction as to race, sex, language, or religion.'[18] There was room for debate over the question of interpretation here too, but by 1957 the General Assembly was calling on South Africa in specific terms to revise its policies. When nothing came of successive appeals to the Nationalist government to mend its ways, the Assembly turned to the recommendation of measures. In April 1961—three months after Hammarskjöld had met representatives of the South African government in Pretoria—the Assembly asked member states to consider such separate and collective action as was open to them to induce South Africa to abandon its racial policies. In November 1962 members were asked to break off diplomatic relations with South Africa, close their harbours to its shipping, forbid their own ships to use its ports, boycott its goods, and cease the sale of arms to the Nationalist government. The November resolution also brought into being the Special Committee of eleven states to keep South Africa's racial policies under review. By these means the Afro-Asian states sustained their attack through the General Assembly, and gradually per-

---

[17] Rosalyn Higgins, 'South Africa at the United Nations', unpublished paper given at the Inst. of Commonwealth Studies, Mar. 1965.

[18] Reinforced by Arts. 56 and 1(3). See below, App. 1.

suaded a growing majority of members of their right to do so. On the general issue whether the Assembly was within its powers to include resolutions against apartheid on its agenda, the United States moved from abstention to concurrence, and in April 1961 the United Kingdom representative announced that:

> While the importance attached by the United Kingdom to Article 2, paragraph 7, of the Charter remained undiminished, it regarded apartheid as being now so exceptional as to be *sui generis*, and his delegation felt able to consider the [draft resolution under discussion] on its merits.[19]

On the basis of this somewhat cryptic assessment, the United Kingdom (and by 1964, every member state of the United Nations except South Africa and Portugal) voted in condemnation of apartheid.

From the Afro-Asian point of view, there were two difficulties about this attack. One was the fact that the General Assembly has no power to pass binding resolutions on these issues: it can only recommend a course of action to its members.[20] Only the Security Council may order enforcement actions binding on all member states—and then only if there is a majority vote which includes the unanimous approval, or at least abstention, of the Permanent Members. The other was that it was doubtful whether a breach of the Charter provisions on human rights, however grievous, could be made the basis of a demand for economic or military sanctions unless it could also be shown that a threat to the peace existed. The states which sought coercive measures against South Africa had to shift their attack, therefore, to the Security Council, and find more substantial grounds for complaint. Protected by a remarkable degree of self-assurance, the South African government was hardly likely to be moved by resolutions and appeals, however many United Nations members might vote for them. Thus the question which confronted those who were urging sanctions was whether they could persuade Britain and the United States of the need for measures which only the Security Council could authorize and undertake.

[19] *GAOR*, 15th sess., Special Political Committee, 5 Apr. 1961.
[20] Under the terms of the Uniting for Peace Resolution, the General Assembly may recommend action when it finds that an act of aggression or a breach of the peace has occurred, but not where there exists a 'threat to the peace'. Moreover, it may only *recommend* enforcement action: it has no mandatory power; its resolutions cannot compel states to participate.

The authority for enforcement measures is given in Chapter VII, Article 39:

The Security Council shall determine the existence of any threat to the peace, breach of the peace, or act of aggression, and shall make recommendations, or decide what measures shall be taken in accordance with Articles 41 and 42 to maintain or restore international peace and security.

Article 41 is concerned with action not involving the use of armed force, such as a severance of trade or communications, including diplomatic representation. Article 42 provides for a second stage when 'action by air, sea, or land forces . . . may be necessary to maintain or restore international peace and security'.

The first attempt to widen the attack on apartheid came in 1960, immediately after the Sharpeville shootings, when emotions ran high and South Africa appeared to be on the edge of revolt. The Afro-Asian states on the Security Council sponsored a resolution describing the situation in the Republic as one which had 'led to international friction and if continued might endanger international peace and security.'[21] The resolution used the language of Chapter VI—'the pacific settlement of disputes' —not Chapter VII and coercion,[22] and a peculiar verbal battle developed between the Afro-Asian members supported by the USSR on one side, and Britain, the United States, and France, plus Nationalist China, on the other. The conflict came to a head on 7 August 1963—three months after the inauguration of the OAU—over the wording of a further resolution. This called upon South Africa to 'abandon the policies of apartheid and discrimination', and on all states 'to cease forthwith the sale and shipment of arms, ammunition of all types and military vehicles' to the Republic, on the grounds that 'the situation in South Africa is seriously disturbing international peace and security'. The Afro-Asian states had sought to use the words 'threat to the peace'. Britain and the United States objected, and a compromise was reached.

[21] S/4300, 1 Apr. 1960. There was an earlier use of similar phrases in the report of the Commission on the Racial Situation in South Africa in 1954, which expressed its 'profound conviction that the policy of apartheid constitutes a grave threat to the peaceful relations between ethnic groups in the world'.
[22] Art. 34 (Ch. VI). See below, App. 1.

The African states were reasonably encouraged. Mr Mongi Slim, the Tunisian Foreign Minister, was to tell the OAU meeting in Dakar that:

the Security Council while refusing to admit that this situation constituted a threat to international peace and security—which would have compelled it to apply Chapter VII of the Charter—nevertheless accepted that the present situation disturbs international peace and security, and with the words 'disturb' we already have an expression stronger than 'endangers'. It was compelled to take a decision constituting a compromise between Chapter VI and Chapter VII. . . .[23]

But, as Dr Higgins noted:

A semantic ritual is now observed whereby the Western nations resist the use of phraseology 'threat to the peace' in Security Council resolutions on South Africa; and the representatives of the Afro-Asian group on that body eventually accept a phraseology referring to 'grave friction' or a 'serious disturbance of the peace'. In this way honour is served—but sanctions are not achieved.[24]

The 1963 debate was a remarkable example of the warfare conducted at the United Nations. The western governments conceded, on paper, a great deal more than they had earlier been prepared to do. (In December 1963 they also agreed to cease the sale of arms, although the Conservative government insisted on drawing the distinction between arms for internal and external use.) But one must not be deceived by words. Ritual is important not for what it is but for what it represents; and it was precisely because the phrase 'threat to the peace' carried the implications set out in Article 39—and the possibility of the measures described in Articles 41 and 42—that Britain and the United States insisted on a different form of words. In a paper given at the London Conference on Sanctions in May 1964, Mr Calvocoressi was critical of these verbal manœuvres. He believed that:

the Security Council had got itself into the position of acknowledging a threat to peace but evading the consequences of its own resolution by calling it something else. There is therefore a conflict between the

---

[23] Address to the Council of Foreign Ministers at the OAU conference in Dakar, 2–11 Aug. 1963. Verbatim Report of Plenary Session (restricted pub., Lagos, n.d.), p. 84.
[24] Rosalyn Higgins, in unpublished paper referred to in n. 17 above.

facts which set the law of the Charter in motion and the political will of states which have the power to implement it.[25]

Mr Calvocoressi's solution was to unite 'the facts' with 'the political will', and accept the consequences of sanctions under Article 39 because 'Good cases make good law, and the South African case is a good occasion to test the meaning of Article 39 and to define and extend the rule of law in human affairs.' Those who look forward hopefully to an era of collective security, under a common system of international law, must feel a sympathetic response to this appeal: but was it really a question of uniting the facts with the political will? There was disagreement on the facts. For neither the United States nor Britain was prepared to admit that the situation in South Africa constituted a threat to peace. Mr Adlai Stevenson and Sir Patrick Dean condemned the policy of apartheid in harsh terms, as 'abhorrent, evil, impracticable and leading to disaster',[26] but they also insisted that 'the application of sanctions under Chapter VII in the situation now before us would be both bad law and bad policy'; Chapter VII was intended to apply (said Stevenson) 'where there was an actuality of international violence or such a clear threat to the peace as to leave no reasonable alternative but resort to coercion'.[27] Sir Patrick Dean was even more explicit: there was 'no evidence before us that the actions of the South African Republic, however repellent they may be for all of us, are actions which threaten the territorial integrity or political independence of any member country'.[28] On the basis of these arguments, therefore, one may turn Mr Calvocoressi's criticisms the other way round and argue that a more logical course would have been for Britain and the United States not only to contest the relevance of Chapter VII to the problem of apartheid but to oppose any notion that even suggested it. 'Juggling with synonyms'[29] is a

[25] *Economic Sanctions against S. Africa* (1964), p. 61.
[26] On balance, Britain has been more outspoken than the United States. 'Abhorrent' was Stevenson's phrase. Sir Patrick Dean declared that apartheid was 'evil—it is also impracticable and will lead eventually to disaster in South Africa itself . . .' Its policies were 'entirely repugnant to the feelings and traditions of our people' (UN Doc. S/PV 1052, 2 Aug. 1963).
[27] Ibid.
[28] Ibid. The phrase 'territorial integrity or political independence' is taken from Art. 2(4) of the Charter (see below, App. 1).
[29] Mr Calvocoressi's phrase.

H

poor way to conduct an argument, and if Britain or the United
States one day have to veto a resolution which describes the
South African situation in terms of Article 39, their stand will be
none the better for having conceded so much already.

Would the United Kingdom be justified in using its veto? The
question is one of interpretation of the words 'threat to the
peace'. If the domestic policies of the South African government
can be construed as constituting a 'threat to peace', then Article
39 can be held to apply, since the domestic jurisdiction safeguard
of Article 2(7) 'shall not prejudice the application of enforcement measures under Chapter VII'. The emphasis throughout
the Charter, however, is on relations between states, its signa-
tories are called upon to 'maintain international peace and
security' and the measures authorized under Article 39 are
directed to the same end—'to maintain or restore international
peace and security'. A reasonable interpretation of the phrase
'threat to peace', therefore, might well be thought to lie in Sir
Patrick Dean's words, as meaning a threat to the 'territorial
integrity or political independence of a member country'. The
situation envisaged is familiar—the threat of invasion of a state,
or of intervention by outside powers in the domestic affairs of a
state, there being clear evidence that action of this kind is
imminent. They are threats which the African states themselves
have been concerned to minimize by the 'territorial integrity
clauses' of the OAU Charter. However odious, therefore, one
may think the domestic policies of the South African government
are, they can hardly be said to fall within these definitions of a
threat to the peace.

Such is the gist of the argument developed by the western
powers in the Security Council, and one might suppose that it
had good sense as well as good law on its side. Whether it can
stand as a definitive interpretation of the Charter is another
question. If the world grows more orderly and its sovereign states
less hostile to restraint, it is possible that the Charter may be
widened to allow a more general interpretation of what constitutes a 'threat to peace'. Certainly it is possible to imagine a situation in which the policies of a government, though domestic in
scope, would have a critical effect beyond its own borders. Suppose, for example, treatment of a racial or religious group in a
particular country, as by the Nazi government of the Jews in

Germany, aroused widespread compassion and anger abroad on behalf of the victims, of a nature likely to lead to hostilities: could such a government be accused of pursuing policies which constituted a threat to the peace? And might it be brought to book by collective international action? The African states' plea is that this is precisely what they mean when they describe apartheid in these terms. And although one may argue that it is an unreal exaggeration of the actual situation, one cannot be sure that events in South Africa, or developments at the United Nations, will not be held to justify intervention. It is possible perhaps in the future that gross and continued infringement of human rights may be held so intolerable by the rest of the world as to lead to United Nations action to put a stop to it, or that prolonged civil war in a particular state may be said to constitute a threat to the peace, and thus warrant intervention by the United Nations.

Perhaps that will be possible—in the future; but it is, at best, a very distant prospect—no more than a candle gleam of hope—that the world may one day put its house in order. Such a hope can hardly be sustained by the present position of the United Nations or the requirements generally accepted as necessary to justify collective action under the Charter. Intervention in South Africa, or even in situations of the kind sketched in the previous paragraph, would be an immense departure both from past practice and current interpretations of the Charter. It would mean the assumption by the United Nations of a right to resort to force not simply in self-defence during peace-keeping operations, or to remedy a clear *breach* of the peace or act of aggression, but to bring about a change of domestic policy within a state. It would be difficult to find any student of the United Nations to argue that this was possible.[30] There is U Thant's own opinion that 'the idea that conventional military methods—or, put bluntly, war—can be used by or on behalf of the United Nations,

---

[30] The Afro-Asian states themselves have been indignant at times when attempts have been made to exert pressure on a particular government to make it change its policies. 'The Conference, considering that foreign pressure and intervention to impose changes in the political, economic and social systems chosen by a country are contrary to the principles of international law and peaceful co-existence, requests the Government of the United States of America to lift the commercial and economic blockade against Cuba' (Conference of Heads of State or Government of Non-Aligned Countries, Cairo, Oct. 1964, *Proceedings*).

to counter aggression and secure the peace, seems now to be impractical'.[31] Yet to intervene in South Africa on the grounds that its domestic policies constitute a threat to peace would be to go far beyond the countering of aggression. As the report of the Council of Churches noted, it would 'represent an unprecedented increase in the legal claims of the world community upon sovereign states',[32] and the United Nations would have to find a much wider measure of support among its members than it has hitherto been able to do, whether in respect of the costs of such an operation or the ends it proposed to achieve. In all its operations so far, the United Nations has been very careful not to infringe the domestic jurisdiction clause of the Charter; they have been undertaken either at the invitation of a government (or governments), or because of international involvements. In the Congo, for example, both Hammarskjöld and U Thant insisted that the action being taken by the Organization did not infringe Article 2(7). That is to say, the United Nations acted because it was invited into the country and, once there, did what it could to claim a position of non-intervention in the internal affairs of the Congo, however much practice may have belied theory. Moreover the only occasion when the United Nations has used force, other than when claiming the right of self-defence, was on the finding of a clear breach of the peace when North Korea invaded South Korea. There is little comfort here for those who urge sanctions and an enforcement blockade against South Africa. It is true that the United Kingdom, having conceded that the problem of apartheid is *sui generis*, voted in condemnation of the internal policies of the Nationalist government and for an embargo on arms to South Africa: but there is a very great gap between these decisions, whatever gloss is given

[31] U Thant, 'United Nations Peace Force', address to Harvard Alumni Ass., 13 June 1963, in L. P. Bloomfield, ed., *International Military Forces* (Boston, 1963), p. 260. The simplest course open to the African states might be for them to attack South Africa. They would be quickly defeated; but they would have succeeded in causing a breach of the peace. True, they would be the aggressors, but it can be argued that the only concern of the UN is 'to restore international peace and security', not to punish. They would also be acting contrary to Art. 2(4) of the Charter (see p. 129) unless, by a gross distortion of the Charter, they were able to plead that they were exercising a right of collective self-defence under Art. 51. But the reader might well conclude that there is an air of fantasy about such arguments. Moreover, at least at present, the African states lack not only the power but the will to provoke the crisis.

[32] *The Future of S. Africa*, ed. T. Beetham and Noel H. Salter (1965), p. 75.

them in terms of 'intervention', and readiness to concede the legitimacy of coercive measures.

There are clearly arguable, factual grounds, therefore, for opposing any attempt to describe the situation in South Africa in terms of Article 39 of the Charter. Apartheid is 'evil and abhorrent', but it cannot reasonably be described as 'a threat to the peace' within the present context of United Nations practice—even if (as indeed is far from being true) the Organization were in a strong position to take action under the Charter. One must hope that argument and persuasion will enable Britain and the United States to escape the formal embarrassment of a veto; they must wish to avoid a situation in which a small group of western countries are on one side, and the newly independent countries, plus the communist states, are on the other. There can be no guarantee, however, that this will not happen. The African governments pressed home their demands over Rhodesia during the dissolution of the Central African Federation in 1963, and Britain used its veto for the third time. It is unpleasant to have to resort to the formal machinery of dissent, but there is a case for not treating apartheid as a 'threat to the peace', and both Britain and the United States have to argue it as plainly as they can.

South West Africa

The other line of attack on South Africa has been over the mandated territory of South West Africa. The African states have conducted a long campaign at The Hague and in New York in an attempt to show that the South African government is in default of its original Mandate and, therefore, open to inquiry and correction by the United Nations. The stages in this campaign may be illuminated by a simple chronology:

1919, June: Para. 6 of Art. 22 of the Treaty of Versailles established the category of Class C Mandates under the Covenant of the League of Nations. They were 'territories, such as South West Africa . . . which . . . can be best administered under the laws of the Mandatory as integral portions of its territory'.

1920, December: Under Art. 2 of the Mandate South Africa has: 'full power of administration and legislation over the territory subject to the present Mandate, as an integral portion of the Union of South Africa, and may apply the laws of the Union of South Africa to the territory, subject to such local modifications as circumstances may require' (para. 1).

But the next paragraph added:

'The Mandatory shall promote to the utmost the material and moral well-being and the social progress of the inhabitants of the territory subject to the present Mandate.'

1946: South Africa failed to obtain recognition for the integration of South West Africa into the Union. Other mandated territories became trust territories.

1949: The International Court of Justice, on a request by the General Assembly, advised that:

(*a*) South West Africa was still a Mandated Territory.

(*b*) South Africa was under a duty to transmit petitions and annual reports to the UN General Assembly.

(*c*) South Africa was not legally bound to place South West Africa under trusteeship.

(*d*) South Africa could not unilaterally alter the international status of the Territory.

1954/5: The ICJ, on a request by the General Assembly, advised that decisions on petitions and reports from South West Africa should be by a two-thirds majority of the General Assembly present and voting. (This was in contrast to the supervisory body of the League whose unanimous vote was required.)

1956: The Court advised that the UN Committee on South West Africa could grant oral hearings to petitioners.

1960, 4 November: Ethiopia and Liberia instituted contentious proceedings, asking the Court to declare (*inter alia*):

(*a*) that South West Africa is still a Mandated Territory;

(*b*) that the 1920 Mandate is still a treaty in force under the ICJ;

(*c*) that South Africa is still under the obligations imposed under Art. 22 of the Covenant;

(*d*) that South Africa has practised apartheid in the territory and that this is contrary to Art. 2 of the Mandate and Art. 22 of the League of Nations Covenant;

(*e*) that South Africa has failed to promote the well-being of the peoples of South West Africa and has impeded opportunities for self-determination;

(f) that South Africa must cease these violations and meet its obligations.

1962, 21 December: The ICJ decided by 8 votes to 7 that it had jurisdiction in the case.

The turning-point in the chronology came in 1960 when Ethiopia and Liberia, members of the former League of Nations, began contentious proceedings against South Africa. Whereas earlier hearings before the Court had been to elicit advisory opinions, there was now the possibility of a binding judgment against the Republic to provide a legal base to the demand for sanctions. The dilemma facing the western powers over South West Africa is thus of a different order from the more general problem of apartheid: it has behind it a concern for the upholding of law, and both Britain and the United States are bound to consider very carefully the case for sanctions once it is grounded on a clear breach of an international treaty—and a breach which the International Court says should be remedied. Hence the argument put forward by Mr Gross, the American lawyer briefed by the applicants, that the 1920 Mandate is still a treaty in force which the South African government has violated by its failure to comply with Article 2—the promotion 'to the utmost [of] the material and moral well-being . . . of the inhabitants of the territory'. Moreover, there is provision in the Charter for moving the legal argument from the International Court to the Security Council once a judgment has been handed down. Article 94(2) states that:

If any party to a case fails to perform the obligations incumbent upon it under a judgment rendered by the Court, the other party may have recourse to the Security Council, which may, if it deems necessary, make recommendations or decide upon measures to be taken to give effect to the judgment.

Admittedly, if one of the parties 'has recourse to the Security Council', there is no obligation on its members to take action: they may or may not act; or they may merely 'recommend a course of action'. One may be sure, however, that if the Court's ruling over South West Africa goes against the Republic, the Afro-Asian members of the Council, urged on by their supporters in the General Assembly, will demand coercive measures.

The Afro-Asian states might then be thought to be very near

the end they have struggled so hard to reach, for it can be argued that the United Nations will have no alternative but to act to enforce the Court's decision, should South Africa reject its findings. Either the Nationalist government will have to comply with the judgment, thus opening a breach in the 'granite walls' of apartheid, or South West Africa will be removed from its authority. So it may be argued. Nor is it only Afro-Asian opinion which finds comfort in the range of possibilities open to the United Nations over South West Africa. The careful assessment by the British Council of Churches of 'the future of South Africa' reached the conclusion that 'Britain should . . . vote in favour of such measures as the Security Council may determine to uphold the rule of law in respect of the judgment of the International Court'. The Working Party was in favour of action by the Organization 'if it were based on a clear legal decision'. It thought that 'in certain circumstances South-West Africa [might] provide a unique opportunity for concerted United Nations action for limited ends', which should include the possibility of 'the flying in of United Nations officials to confer with the administration in South-West Africa, and later take over [the territory]; South-West Africa would then become a trust territory under direct UN administration pending her early independence'.[33]

The recommendations of the Council—for which many thoughtful groups in Britain to whom apartheid is a cruel and dangerous form of rule are bound to have some sympathy—are bold, since they envisage the possibility not only of economic sanctions but, presumably, force should the South African government resist any attempt by the United Nations to impose its authority. Are they clearly in line with the Charter, or is there room, again, for genuine differences of interpretation? The Court has yet to reach its findings, and one cannot be sure of the verdict; but, even assuming that there is a majority ruling in favour of Ethiopia and Liberia, there are a number of uncertainties about what may follow. Will there, for example, be a 'clear legal decision'? One must remember what it is the Court has been asked to decide. The applicants have not sought that the Mandate be terminated, the legal position for such a step being very obscure, but for a ruling that South Africa 'has the

[33] *Future of S. Africa*, pp. 85–86.

duty forthwith to cease and desist from any action which thwarts the orderly development of self-government in the Territory; and . . . to refrain from acts of administration and legislation which are inconsistent with the international status of the Territory'.[34] On this basis, there can be no ruling that South Africa's right to administer the territory has lapsed. As Mr Gross has said:

It was decided that we would ask the Court to make findings of fact, drawing conclusions of law respecting the violations and the obligations of the mandatory power and enter a judgement which would resemble a 'cease and desist' order. . . . That is to say, the Court would be asked to judge and declare that the Mandatory was under a duty forthwith to cease the practice of apartheid in the Territory.[35]

Thus the judgment—assuming that it is in favour of the applicants—is likely to be in the nature of a ruling that South Africa is still under an obligation to meet the terms of the Mandate and that, in certain respects, it has acted contrary to its provisions.

What may follow? If the Court delivers such a judgment the Security Council is bound, in fairness to South Africa, to agree to an interim period to allow the South African government to comply. There are no clear grounds for believing that the Nationalist government would reject an adverse verdict, and it might modify its administration in such a way as to enable it to assert its compliance. The Security Council would then have to assess the significance of the reforms introduced; but, although the South African government might be able to buy time, it is unlikely to buy acquiescence, since the Afro-Asian states would surely refuse to accept any changes introduced by the Nationalist government as justifying its continued administration of the territory. At some time in the future, therefore, they would be bound to demand enforcement measures under Article 94(2) on the grounds that South Africa has defied or evaded the judgment. Then Britain and the United States would have to decide whether the charge was valid. If they did, they would have to face the further problem of what was meant by 'measures to give effect to the judgment'.

[34] *ICJ Reports 1962.* Mr Gross has admitted that 'African delegations felt we should ask the Court to order the Mandate terminated. This raised a number of thorny questions . . .' (Ernest A. Gross, 'The South West African Case: On the Threshold of Decision', *Columbia J. of Transnational Law,* iii/i (1964).
[35] Ibid.

Unfortunately there are no precedents to guide them; Article 94(2) has never been expressly invoked by the Security Council.[36] It is sometimes suggested that the measures which may be employed 'to give effect to the judgment' must fall short of coercion because the article does not form part of the coercive measures authorized in Chapter VII of the Charter—being grouped (logically) with other articles relating to the International Court in Chapter XIV. The argument has been discussed by a number of distinguished commentators, and the weight of legal opinion is on the side of a generous interpretation of Article 94, by which the Security Council could, if it wished, employ a wide range of the measures outlined in Chapter VII. None the less, there is a general hesitation over the question whether the Council members can authorize the use of the 'air, sea, and land forces' described in Article 42 *unless it can also be shown that the consequences arising from a failure to comply with a judgment of the Court constitute 'a threat to peace, breach of the peace or act of aggression'* (Article 39).[37] If U Thant's warning is heeded, it is doubtful whether the United Nations, certainly in its present state, can employ force in any circumstances other than self-defence. On a longer and more optimistic view, one may argue that the Organization has a clear right under the Charter to employ force to check the use of force—to kill to stop the killing—where there exists a breach of (or an unambiguous threat to) the peace and security of any part of the world; but it is also reasonable to oppose coercion under Article 94(2) in respect of South West Africa unless South Africa's failure to comply with an adverse judgment could also be brought within the meaning of Article 39.

On a more mundane level, it is not easy to see the benefit to Britain, even if it were to agree to coercive action by the United Nations over South West Africa. Respect for international law would have been enforced; but where would be the immediate, practical benefit to those primarily engaged in the operation? The writer has no wish to argue that the problems should be decided on the basis of advantage to Britain, or even that Britain should work towards such a goal, but there is no harm in

[36] Though the Security Council has been faced with the applicability of Art. 94(2) to an interim award of the Court (see *SCOR*, 6th yr, 561st mtg, and *Anglo Iranian Oil Co.* case, ICJ *Reports*, 93).

[37] See Oscar Schachter, 'Enforcement of International Judicial and Arbitral Decisions', *American J. Internat. Law*, Jan. 1960.

looking at the question in these terms. Suppose, for example, that the threat of sanctions, and the degree of force that would almost certainly be necessary to implement them successfully,[38] proved sufficient to persuade the South African government to yield. It might agree to the territory's becoming a trust territory, and the appointment of a United Nations inspectorate, or that it should be partitioned between the Republic and a new United Nations territory (though these concessions would hardly satisfy African opinion); it might agree to 'give up' the Mandate and withdraw inside the frontiers of the Republic. *Cui bono?*

If South Africa were to cease to administer the territory, the United Nations would have to decide what to do with it, amidst conflicting advice from its members. The simplest course might be to agree to a rapid transition to independence, although massive United Nations financial and technical assistance would be needed not only in the preparatory stages of self-government but to provide a minimum base for independence. The report of the Odendaal Commission, for example, included the recommendation of a two-stage development plan for the territory for which the capital cost was estimated at £72 million: £57 million for the first five years and £15 million for the subsequent period.[39] The United Nations could hardly be less generous than the South African government, though it would be spared the £8½ million allocated in the Odendaal report for compensation to white farmers whose lands are to be incorporated in the new homelands. If South Africa withdrew its capital and technical skills, however, and offered resettlement grants to induce the

---

[38] One cannot be sure that force would or would not be needed: it would be necessary, therefore, to be prepared to employ it.

[39] Commission of Enquiry [Odendaal Commission] into South West African Affairs, 1962–3, *Report* (1964). The Commission concluded that 'one central authority, with all groups represented therein, must be ruled out and that as far as practicable a homeland must be created for each population group, in which it alone would have residential, political and language rights to the exclusion of other population groups so that each group would be able to develop towards self-determination without any group dominating or being dominated by another' (para 190). It divided the territory, therefore, into twelve separate 'homelands'. See the excellent commentary by Gordon Lawrie, *New Light on South West Africa* (Johannesburg, 1964), and J. H. Wellington, in *Optima*, Mar. 1965. The figures given in the text do not include estimated South African government grants in aid or the capital cost of expenditure on new roads. This would add £70 m. over the ten-year period.

70,000 Europeans to leave the 'police zone'[40] and move to the Republic, a great deal more money would be needed. One may doubt whether it would be readily forthcoming. One may also question how competently the United Nations could administer so vast a country. There would be the added anomaly that South Africa would still control Walvis Bay, the one major port in the territory. One must remember that South West Africa is very large—almost the size of Tanzania or Nigeria; and its population —although fewer in number than the Gambia or Malta— divided among several groups:

	Southern sector	Northern sector	Total
Ovambo	8,804	230,559	239,363
Okavango	169	27,702	27,871
Berg-Damara	44,044	309	44,353
Nama	34,606	200	34,806
Herero	35,354	—	35,354
Rehobother	11,257	—	11,257
Bushmen	9,484	2,278	11,762
East Caprivians	—	15,840	15,840
Kaokovelders	9,638	354	9,992
Tswana and others	—	9,234	9,234
Coloured	12,699	9	12,708
European	73,106	358	73,464
Total	239,161	286,843	526,004

Source: 1960 census.

Even if South West Africa were given independence, the boundaries separating the new state from South Africa would be largely meaningless except on a map; the land is for the most part empty, arid, barren. It may have 'great economic potentialities'[41] in terms of the diamonds and copper mined by overseas and South African companies, the pilchard canning industry based on Walvis Bay, or the small Karakul sheep raised by European farmers; but the capital and skills necessary to develop

---

[40] S.W. Africa is divided administratively into two: a northern sector (97,788 sq. miles) which includes the Caprivi Strip, and a southern sector (220,463 sq. miles) formerly known as the 'police zone'. Walvis Bay is legally part of South Africa.
[41] British Council of Churches, *Future of S. Africa*, p. 154.

its resources must come from outside the territory. Were South Africa to surrender its formal, mandatory control, the result is likely to be simply to add South West Africa to Bechuanaland and Basutoland as politically sovereign, economically dependent neighbours of the Republic. To the north would lie the Portuguese-controlled territory of Angola; to the east, the great Kalahari desert area of western Bechuanaland; to the south the wealth and power of South Africa.[42]

Where would be the gain? Presumably it would accrue to the political leaders of the territory, though they are divided by rival factions;[43] independence might also benefit the general run of the African population since they would be free from the insecurity and indignity of apartheid legislation and would have access to the richer grazing areas now in European hands. These would be substantial gains—provided the present rate of growth of the economy were maintained. But how would it affect the total South African situation or advance the aims of those whose primary objective is to overthrow white supremacy in the Republic? It is argued that resolute action by the Security Council over South West Africa might produce 'a wholly new position . . . concerning *apartheid* in South Africa':

> even the brief application of sanctions—or the threat so to do by the Security Council—might well be sufficient to convince the South African Government that South-West Africa was not worth the economic disruption which sanctions would cause in South Africa herself, with all the wider implications of internal disorder. . . .
>
> Such an event could provide an element of shock necessary to bring a sense of reality in the cocoon-like nature of present South African politics, as it would constitute a considerable blow to the prestige of those who seek to implement a policy of *apartheid*, and a decisive blow to the belief that South Africa can act permanently in defiance of the rest of the world. . . .[44]

But the argument rests on a number of uncertainties. What would happen if 'the brief application of sanctions' were not sufficient? Would the United Nations retire defeated, or would it enforce its authority regardless of the 'economic disruption'

---

[42] See Chapter III.
[43] SWAPO (South West Africa People's Organization); SWANO (South West Africa National Organization).
[44] *Future of S. Africa*, pp. 85 and 87.

and 'internal disorder' that it might evoke in the Republic? It is also difficult to see the immediate object of a decision to employ sanctions. The United Nations cannot deprive South Africa of the Mandate, since it would then be guilty itself of acting without clear legal authority: it can only enforce the Court's judgment and this (as Mr Gross has said) is likely to be in the nature of a 'cease and desist' ruling. The Organization would thus be in the very difficult position of trying, by force, to compel South Africa to administer the territory in accordance with the terms of the Mandate. If, on the other hand, South Africa *were* prepared to 'give up' the Mandate—although there is very little evidence that it is—the decision would presumably be because the territory was not considered essential to the Republic, or perhaps because the Nationalists wished to embarrass the United Nations by off-loading on it the enormous area of South West Africa: in either case the decision would have been taken precisely because the loss of South West Africa would have little or no bearing on the Nationalists' hold on South Africa itself. Similarly, if after unsuccessful attempts by the South African government to evade the judgment, it was somehow to be deprived of its authority in the territory, the effect would surely be to harden its determination to control the 'true homeland' of the Afrikaner Republic: that is to say, the shock would have the reverse effect from what was intended. Nor is there any reason to suppose that the United Kingdom would benefit from the action taken. The likelihood is that it would be subjected to increased pressure, the African states arguing that the western powers, having gone so far as to force South Africa to respect the Court's ruling on apartheid, should now go farther and act against apartheid in South Africa itself.[45]

These difficulties have to be faced if the problem is to be measured realistically. It is one thing to propose solutions based on the need to uphold the concept of law, quite another to translate them into practice. No doubt the sensible outcome to the case, if the decision is in favour of the applicants, would be for South Africa to reform its administration of the territory, and it

---

[45] 'South Africa, by its decision not only to join issue on the merits of the case but to use the occasion for a detailed defense of its racial policy, has helped make the South West Africa case indirectly a trial before the world community of the doctrine of apartheid' (W. Nielson, *African Battleline*, p. 116).

is possible that British and American persuasion along these lines might be effective. Suppose it refused to listen to such advice? Direct defiance of an adverse judgment might perhaps force the western governments to withdraw or reduce the level of their diplomatic representation in Pretoria, and such a step would undoubtedly disturb the Nationalist government, part of whose case for support among its followers rests on the assumption that the west, though critical, is 'on South Africa's side'. It would not satisfy the demand for militant action; but those who call for coercive measures are in no danger of being called upon to give effect to them, or to cope with what may follow their application. Britain and the United States cannot escape the issue so easily. They will have to decide, knowing that they must bear the full weight of the consequences, how far they are prepared to go in support of the demand that the judgment be enforced against South Africa, or whether to oppose a resolution to that effect introduced by the Afro-Asian states and supported by the Soviet Union.[46] They are hardly likely to agree to the drastic steps authorized by the Charter in situations of 'a threat to the peace, breach of peace, or act of aggression'. Nor is it clear who would apply the force that would be needed, even if agreement to intervene were reached in the Security Council. Undoubtedly the United States, and possibly Britain, have the power in the last resort to impose a decision on South Africa; but even the United States must pause before adding South West and South Africa to its areas of direct responsibility. There is no saying where such a commitment would end; or what conflicts might spring from a clash of policies not simply between South Africa on one side, and Britain and the United States on the other, but among the members—including the permanent members—of the Security Council. For there is no agreement on what should be done about South West Africa, even within the range of the verdicts that the Court may deliver, still less on what should follow the ending of

[46] The Soviet Union would have to shuffle its feet a little to bring itself to support such a motion, since it has always been unenthusiastic about the Court and suspicious of UN actions. France is unsympathetic to racialist attitudes but hostile to the UN and a willing trading partner (including arms) with South Africa. As Dr Karefa Smart, the Sierra Leone Foreign Minister, told his colleagues at the Dakar meeting of the OAU: 'The French Government of course, as you know, have an absolute disdain for the United Nations. What they did at the Security Council was simply to confirm this' (Verbatim Rep. Plen. Sess., p. 89).

apartheid in the Republic itself. There is the very real danger, therefore, that any attempt by the United Nations to apply coercive measures to enforce a judgment of the Court would add a new and fertile ground of controversy to those which have already seriously weakened the central machinery of the Organization.

The conclusions are plain. The legal arguments which seek to justify coercive action by the United Nations over South West Africa are open to question; the practical consequences of doing so are almost certain to be harmful to Britain, the Organization and—in all probability—South West Africa itself. If, on the other hand, the western powers use such diplomatic and political pressures as are open to them to urge the South African government to comply with an adverse judgment of the Court, they may possibly succeed in securing a reform in the territory. The Nationalist government has always argued in legal terms in defence of its position over apartheid and other contentious issues. It has been careful to avoid illegal and unconstitutional action in its domestic policy (although it came close to sharp practice on the Senate Act of 1955). It has been quick to point to gross violations of the rule of law in other African states, as in the dismissal of the Chief Justice and other judges in Ghana. One may fairly conclude, therefore, that the government is likely to be sensitive to any charge that it is acting illegally and open to pressure along these lines, particularly from those with whom it must wish to remain on good terms. The result would not be dramatic; it would be piecemeal reform in legislative and administrative terms; not total surrender by the South African government. The ultimate beneficiary however would be the African and Coloured peoples of South West Africa whose 'material and moral wellbeing' ought, after all, to be the primary considerations of all parties in the dispute.

In respect of the wider issue of apartheid in the Republic, the United Nations must continue to scrutinize and explore, if only to take full measure of the difficulties. It was suggested in Chapter I that it is possible the time may come when the United Nations will be called upon to act, either by the South African government itself which, frightened by growing violence, may be prepared to accept United Nations mediation, or by agreement among the permanent members in the Security Council that it is necessary to intervene directly. The first is only likely to happen after fundamental changes have begun to take place in the internal struggle for power. A decision by the Security Council—including the United Kingdom and United States— in favour of intervention would have to be based on a finding that the situation in the Republic did in fact constitute a 'threat to peace', and this, too, is only likely to happen in circumstances very different from the existing position in South Africa. Thus the difficulties discussed in this chapter in the way of international action are very real, given the continuance of Nationalist rule in its present form. They add weight to the argument that the United Nations should continue its efforts to measure the problem, for if the time should come when it has to act in South Africa, it will need to be fully aware of the immensity of the task before it.

V
Defence Interests

BRITISH defence interests in South Africa arise from two sources —the strategic position of the Republic in the Indian and South Atlantic Oceans, and the special relationship which formerly linked the two countries. Generations of naval strategists have stressed the importance of South Africa's command of the sea routes to the east, and it remains true today that if the Suez Canal were closed, there would be no practical alternative sea route to Asia and Australia other than that round the Cape of Good Hope. The special relationship was formed during the Botha–Smuts period when South Africa entered both world wars on the side of the allies: over 200,000 troops of all races took part in the First World War and over 5,000 were killed; nearly half a million South Africans fought during the Second World War and over 12,000 died in action. These strong Commonwealth links were broken between 1948 and 1961, and the ties linking the two countries are now frayed. Yet Britain continues to use the naval base at Simonstown, and to co-operate with South African naval and air forces. One may ask, therefore, how important these defence arrangements are today, and what would be the consequences if they were interrupted. These are the primary questions examined in this chapter. They are not new, and other writers have concluded that the sensible view of the defence facilities made available to Britain by the South African government is that they are now 'useful though not indispensable'.[1] The difficulty, however, about such phrases is that they are very broad; they require elaboration, and the following pages are an attempt to examine the evidence which might be thought to support their conclusion.

There is also a wider aspect to consider: defence interests in South Africa are part of the general problem of British defence policy in the 1960s. The use of Simonstown, for example, cannot

---

[1] Mr W. F. Gutteridge's phrase in a letter to the author. See, too, British Council of Churches, *Future of S. Africa*, p. 133: 'The criterion of judgment is that Simonstown is useful but not of irreplaceable strategic importance'.

be assessed in isolation, but only in terms of a number of overseas commitments, and while there may be excellent political or
financial reasons why Britain should cease to use a particular
base—or many of the existing bases when each is examined
separately—the picture is different when looked at as a whole.
Nor can defence be divorced from external policy. The need for
bases and overflying rights (whether in South Africa or elsewhere) arises from considerations of foreign policy, and in 1966
it is still necessary to start from the premise that neither the Conservative nor the Labour Party is prepared to see the United
Kingdom as a 'regional power'. Both insist that there are global
interests which require the maintenance of defence forces at
different points throughout the world, and the concept of empire still overshadows British policy. One is tempted to substitute
the words 'illusion of empire'; but simply as a matter of practical
policy, quite apart from what may be desired, it would be impossible by a single effort of will to escape the post-Imperial
obligations of an empire that once covered so large an area of
the globe. There are also Commonwealth ties which raise problems of military assistance by Britain, at least for the next few
years. The scale of help may diminish as the newer members of
the Commonwealth become more firmly established or turn to
other sources for aid; but it cannot be suddenly withdrawn without making worse the already unsettled pattern of international
relations.[2] The extent to which these views are held by political
leaders (whether on the left or right of party politics) may be seen
from Mr Wilson's first speech on foreign affairs as Prime Minister:

> The problem we are facing derives from the fact that alone in the
> world—apart from the United States and the USSR—we are trying
> to maintain three rôles. There is the strategic nuclear rôle. There is
> our conventional rôle within NATO . . . to which we are committed
> by interest and by treaty. And there is our world rôle, one which no
> one in this House or indeed in the country, will want us to give up or
> call in question.
>   . . . We have a major rôle in the Middle East, defending interests
> which are not exclusively ours, at a cost of about £125 million a year.

---

[2] 'The emergence of many newly independent countries, especially in Africa, has
been accompanied by unrest and armed conflict. These countries are rightly
determined not to accept foreign domination; but if our friends turn to us for help
we must be ready to give it where we can . . .' (Cmnd 2592).

We have numerous other contractual commitments in the Middle East and in Asia. We have to be ready at a moment's notice . . . to respond to the needs of our Commonwealth partners. . . .

I want to make it quite clear that whatever we do in the field of cost effectiveness, value for money and a stringent review of expenditure, we cannot afford to relinquish our world rôle—our rôle which, for shorthand purposes, is sometimes called our 'east of Suez' rôle, though this particular phrase, however convenient, lacks geographical accuracy.

Once these arguments are accepted—although one may doubt whether they would be universally endorsed—then overseas bases are needed, preferably (as Mr Wilson went on to say) on friendly soil:

Obviously our overseas rôle depends on having adequate bases both for our peace-keeping forces and as an essential link in communications with areas still further afield. . . . If we are to fulfil our overseas rôle . . . we need most, if not all, of the bases we hold, but we need to be accepted in those bases.[3]

The speech was a remarkable exposition of the continuing pattern of British defence needs. And although it is possible to argue that both British and Commonwealth interests (for example, at Aden and Singapore) are limited in time, it is also extremely difficult to define the limits: there are too many areas of uncertainty to justify prediction. There is the threat arising from Chinese activities throughout South and South East Asia; one may have to face continued pressure from the Yemen and Egypt in South Arabia; there is the possibility of armed stalemate between Indonesia and Malaysia, and of further conflict between India and Pakistan. In none of these situations—and others may develop— is Britain likely to be able to escape its military obligations in the immediate future.

The Labour government's emphasis on Britain's overseas role bears directly on its defence interests in South Africa. There is a difficulty however in measuring the scale of their importance, for it is all too easy to be misled. The South African government exaggerates the contribution it is prepared to make 'to the defence of the west' in order to bolster local self-esteem and to try and blunt western criticisms of apartheid. Opponents of the

---

[3] 16 Dec. 1964, HC Deb., vol. 704, cols. 421, 423, 424–5. Similar phrases are used in the *Statement on the Defence Estimates 1965*, Cmnd 2592, p. 6, para. 7.

regime decry the importance of co-operation with the Republic, not because they are concerned with British defence requirements but with the need, as they see it, to break the links between South Africa and Britain in order to deprive Dr Verwoerd of external support. What is required is an assessment of the present defence arrangements between the two countries in terms not of South African but British interests, using Mr Wilson's description of Britain's continuing responsibilities in the 1960s. One may envisage three situations: global war in which nuclear weapons are almost certain to be used; the state of armed peace between east and west in which the world has learned to live since 1945, and limited conventional wars, as in Malaysia. This is the setting within which defence requirements are likely to arise. The facilities provided by the South African government also fall into three broad categories—space satellites and missiles, the Simonstown naval base, and overflying rights across the Republic. They correspond roughly, although not exactly, with Mr Wilson's own divisions, and may usefully be discussed in conjunction with them.

Global war is difficult to imagine, hideous to contemplate. The South African Defence Minister, Mr Fouché, however, when he addressed a party rally in Vereeniging in June 1963, was confident about what would happen in a third world war. Within three weeks of the outbreak of hostilities, there would be some 2,000 ships in the South Atlantic and Indian Ocean seeking the harbour and port facilities that only South Africa could offer; moreover, 'with a nuclear war in progress between East and West, where would Britain train her forces? They would train them here in Africa. And where in Africa would it be safe to do it except in South Africa?'[4] It is unlikely (to be sure) that nuclear powers which are bombarding each other with long-range missiles (even assuming they were able to keep alive for any period of time) would be concerned with South Africa or the advantages of a white government in Pretoria. Yet there may be intermediate stages between conventional hostilities and the unlimited use of nuclear weapons when allied forces are still deployed across the world; and military leaders, who are compelled to mount these grisly calculations, have a right to point out that those who contemplate a 'nuclear role' should also consider the

[4] *Star* (Johannesburg), 17 June 1963.

advantages of distant bases. Simply by virtue of their position at the southern end of the great land mass which separates the South Atlantic and Indian Oceans, South Africa's harbours and airfields might then be of great strategic importance, and one cannot wholly dismiss the argument on the grounds that the likelihood of nuclear war is now mercifully remote. What is difficult to accept, however, is that South Africa can derive any political advantage from its strategic position. It has good cause today not to endanger the forbearance of those who do no more than condemn it; and it is in no position, in its present isolation, to exact terms. Arguments which plead for a tolerant attitude towards South Africa on the grounds of its strategic value to the west ignore the much greater need of the Nationalist government to maintain such ties as it can with Britain and the United States.[5] There is no point in making concessions to the Nationalist regime, whether in moral or material terms, if the facilities which may one day be required are virtually certain to be granted out of white South Africa's own needs. It is also extremely unlikely that South Africa would adopt a 'neutral stand' if a third world war were to begin: on the contrary, it is reasonable to assume that the Nationalist government would eagerly seize its opportunity to join the west in an anti-communist alliance.

Similar considerations can be said to govern the facilities made available in the Republic for space research. They are American rather than British interests, but on the familiar assumption that where the United States leads Britain will follow, they are likely to become of future importance to this country. The South African contribution is acclaimed by the Nationalist government with some justification,[6] but it does not follow that it can extract any major political advantage from its co-operation. By 1965 the position was as follows. The launching of satellites into space to circle the earth, or of giant missiles on their 10,000 mile flight across the world, is done from Cape Kennedy, and their initial flight path lies across the Caribbean, down the long

---

[5] Cf. Viscount Montgomery of Alamein, HL Deb., 22 July 1964.
[6] 'South Africa, by collaborating closely with the United States in the complex work of tracking earth satellites and space probes, is playing a part in the American programe of space research. There have at times been as many as six tracking stations in the Republic. At the moment there are four in operation, and two of these have telemetry capabilities. The largest of these, operated by South African scientists, is tracking the latest Venus probe' (SA Dept of Information, Aug. 1962).

western coast of Africa.[7] At every point the missile is tracked
by radar, cameras, and optical-tracking instruments until it
reaches the empty waters of the Indian Ocean. From the satellite, telemetry systems transmit data concerning pressure, tem-
perature, acceleration and control movements to some dozen
island-based tracking stations and instruments in ships and aircraft. The most critical points in the launching of a satellite, or
of an Atlas, Titan, or Minuteman ICBM, occur immediately
after it leaves the launching pad: it is then that the flight may
have to be ended by destroying the rocket, or corrections made
should it veer from its path. For this reason the United States Air
Force has established a chain of tracking stations across the
islands of the Caribbean to Ascension Island in the South Atlantic and Mauritius in the Indian Ocean. Although the flight path
is across almost unlimited stretches of water, avoiding the coasts
of South America and the southern tip of Africa, the Republic of
South Africa is the one great land mass lying close to its path—
hence the importance of the American tracking station outside
Pretoria, as the only mainland-based station, and the most
southerly station, throughout the whole flight once the missile
or satellite has left Cape Kennedy.[8] 'Space probes' to the moon,
Mars, or Venus, use the two large radio telescopes in South
Africa which are locked on the space craft as it sends its signals
back to earth.[9] There is a close working relationship, therefore,
between American and South African scientists—between (for
example) the Smithsonian Astrophysical Laboratory and the
South African Council for Scientific and Industrial Research—
but although such co-operation is valuable it is clearly not
essential. Similarly, the tracking stations are an important element in the American space programme; but they can hardly be

[7] Space satellites are an American more than a British interest, but Britain is
affected not only because of the nature of the western alliance but by its use of
American rockets for its own limited space programme.

[8] The major tracking stations are: Cape Kennedy, Grand Bahama, Eleuthera, San
Salvador, Mayaguana, Grand Turk, Antigua, Ascension, Pretoria, Mauritius.
See the booklet, *Air Force Missile Test Center*, Office of Information, Patrick Air
Force Base, Florida, 1963. France has also obtained permission to maintain a
missile tracking station in the Republic.

[9] The first 'Minitrack' radio tracking station was established at Elandsfontein, near
Johannesburg; it led to the establishment of the Deep Space Instrument Facility,
and an advanced 'Minitrack' station at Hartebeesthoek, near Krugersdorp. See
D. G. Kingswill, in *Optima*, Mar. 1965.

said to be 'indispensable' in the sense that, if their use were denied the United States, the launching of satellites and missiles would have to cease. It is significant that the South African government has not been able to use the 1960 agreements regulating their operation as a lever to modify criticism of its policies; they have not prevented the United States condemnation of apartheid or its compliance with the United Nations embargo on arms. Admittedly, there is an element of hypocrisy of both sides, in that the United States opposes apartheid yet collaborates with South Africa, and the South African government, though affronted by the criticism, swallows its resentment. The hypocrisy, however, does not affect the underlying reality, that although South Africa has a limited usefulness to the United States, it has very little power to affect the United States—or British—policy towards it.

The second defence responsibility outlined by Mr Wilson was Britain's 'NATO role' and, by implication, its participation in the western alliance against the communist world. In past years South Africa was seen as a useful auxiliary to the alliance. Centuries of naval warfare had confirmed the importance of the Cape sea routes; the Suez crisis of 1956 showed once again the value of South Africa's harbour and dock facilities. There was also the general assumption that the South Atlantic was an essential area of western defence, and it was this which underlay both the Simonstown agreement of 1955 and, until 1964, the sale of arms to South Africa.

The Simonstown agreement was drawn up in an exchange of letters between Mr Selwyn Lloyd as Minister of Defence and Mr Erasmus, the South African Defence Minister.[10] It embodied 'agreements and understandings satisfactory to both Governments' on three main items covering the defence of the South Atlantic and the African mainland. The first discussed 'the need for international discussions with regard to Regional Defence' against external aggression. The second was concerned with 'the defence of the sea routes round southern Africa'. The third dealt with the transfer of the Royal Navy's base at Simonstown and arrangements for its future use. Under the first heading it was agreed that the sea lanes round south Africa and 'the gateways to Africa . . . in the Middle East' needed to be secured against

[10] Cmd 9520 (1955).

'external aggression'. The *internal* security of southern Africa was a matter for the individual countries concerned. It was South African policy to contribute forces to 'keep the potential enemy as far as possible from the borders of South Africa, in other words for the defence of Southern Africa, Africa and the Middle East gateways to Africa'; it was United Kingdom policy to contribute forces for the defence of a large part of Africa and the Middle East. The two countries agreed, therefore, to set up suitable machinery to ensure that 'the lines of communications and logistic support in and around South Africa' were adequately defended. The discussions would involve consideration of base facilities, storage and stockpiling arrangements, airfields and seaplane bases, radar facilities and telecommunications.

In respect of 'the defence of the sea routes round Southern Africa', the two governments agreed to co-operate through their 'respective maritime forces'. To be able to do this adequately, the South African government approved a programme for the expansion of the South African navy spread over eight years between 1955 and 1963; it involved the purchase in the United Kingdom of 6 anti-submarine frigates, 10 coastal minesweepers, and 4 seaward defence boats, at a total cost of about £18 million. At the same time a new maritime strategic zone was demarcated; it corresponded approximately to the former Royal Naval South Atlantic Station, within which it was agreed that there should be a 'South African area' (in peacetime under a Flag Officer appointed by Pretoria) stretching from South West Africa to a line drawn from the Moçambique–South African border to Cap Sainte Marie in Madagascar. A joint war planning committee was envisaged to co-ordinate all maritime facilities within the strategic zone; officers were to be exchanged between the two navies, South African naval officers were to receive part of their training in the United Kingdom, and joint exercises were to continue to be held by South Africa and NATO powers.

The third part of the agreement, relating to the gradual transfer of the Simonstown base to the control of the South African government, allowed the Royal Navy to continue to use the facilities at the base in peace and war; it was also agreed that the base would be available in wartime not only to the United Kingdom but its allies. The United Kingdom was allowed the use of the wireless telegraphy installations known as Slangkop, Klaver, and Cape East, and to store certain strategic reserves of ammunition at Ganspan in addition to the 500 tons of Royal Navy ammunition held at Simonstown. In an interesting enclosure which forms part of the agreement, the South African government agreed to take measures to avoid any difficulty that might arise from the provision that the hundred or so United Kingdom personnel at Simonstown should not be required to learn Afrikaans; it also confirmed that there would be 'no bar to the recruitment and employment at the base of non-Europeans'; there would be 'no discrimination based on colour in the rates of pay for comparable jobs', and non-Europeans, once recruited, would 'have the same security of tenure as Europeans'.[11]

The terms of the agreement were part of what was then a broad working relationship between the two countries. The relationship was reflected, too, in the sale of arms, in which there had been a long established pattern of co-operation. Almost all the heavy equipment used by the South African defence forces was British, since it was on British lines and with British help that the South African army, navy, and airforce had been created. The sale of arms and joint training schemes were also based on the assumption, which Britain and America continued to hold throughout the 1950's, that South Africa would continue to play its part in what had become an anti-communist western alliance, as it had done during the two world wars; the contracts for 'seaward defence boats' and aircraft of the destructive power of the Canberra and Buccaneer reflected this belief, as did the joint naval provisions of the Simonstown agreement. It was not until 1960–1 that relations between Britain and South Africa began to be put on a different footing, and the change in attitude is worth recording—by way of a long parenthesis—since it helps to throw light not only on current controversies over the sale of arms, but on the question 'how useful' or 'how indispensable'—or otiose— the Simonstown agreement is to British interests in the 1960s.

The change was noticeable as apartheid began to be enforced more vigorously in the Republic, and pressure from the newly independent African states was exerted within the Common-

---

[11] The paragraph that followed declared that these terms were 'in accordance with the policy of the Union Government', equal pay for comparable jobs 'being the present practice in the Cape Province', and 'security of tenure' being the present practice in the Union.

wealth and at the United Nations. Gradually ties between Britain and South Africa began to fray. In February 1960 Mr Harold Macmillan, in his 'wind of change' address to a joint session of both Houses of Parliament in Cape Town,[12] explained (bluntly, if courteously) that there were aspects of South African policy which went against the United Kingdom's deep convictions about the political destinies of free men. The Conservative government also began to draw an explicit distinction—it was already there in the Simonstown agreement—between arms for external and domestic use; spokesmen for the Labour Party, in opposition, called for an embargo on the sale of all forms of weapons. The result was that the South African government began to look for additional sources of supply, and to urge forward the domestic manufacture of small arms and army vehicles. There was no lack of potential suppliers. At the end of 1960 orders were placed in West Germany for troop carriers; the following year South Africa began to buy Mirage IIIC jet fighters and Alouette helicopters from France, Lockheed C130 Hercules transport aircraft from America, Sabre jet aircraft from Canada, as well as Wessex Wasp helicopters, Canberra bombers, and the Blackburn Buccaneer naval jet aircraft from Britain. Between 1960 and the end of 1963 it is probable that some 200 aircraft and 100 helicopters arrived or were ordered from abroad—no longer exclusively from Britain. For the first time too jet trainers are to be manufactured locally by the Atlas Aircraft Corporation to replace the SAAF's Harvards.[13] Many of the orders placed abroad were of considerable value. In May 1963 the Parliamentary Secretary to the Minister of Aviation told the House of Commons that South African aircraft orders in Britain amounted to a year's work for 25,000 people in some fifty companies. The sixteen Buccaneer aircraft to be delivered in 1964 were worth about £20 million; others were expected to be ordered. The Bloodhound ground-to-air missiles that the South African government wanted to buy from Britain in 1964–5 were said to have amounted to £20 million, and Mr Fouché claimed that orders worth some £150 million would be lost to Britain over the next year; he was reported to be 'shopping' in

---

[12] Mansergh, pp. 347–51.
[13] The Italian Aermacchi MB 326B, with Bristol Siddeley Viper engines which are built under licence in Italy; production is expected to begin at the end of 1966.

Europe—and especially in France—for aircraft, arms, submarines, and 'a new range of frigates numbering five or six all told'.[14] Meanwhile, within South Africa, French radar equipment and Panhard armoured cars, the Belgian FN weapons, including the $7 \cdot 62$ automatic rifle, and a variety of small arms and explosives, from pistol ammunition to rockets with conventional warheads, began to be manufactured under licence. One does not have to accept every word that Dr Verwoerd says as wholly accurate, but there is no reason to doubt the relevant part of his statement at Pietersburg on 14 November 1964:

> South Africa does not need any weapons to do what the outside world says she wants to do—that is, suppress the black man. We do not suppress the black man and do not even need to buy weapons to maintain internal order. These weapons we make ourselves, and—what is more—we do not even need to use them; . . . should Britain and the United States refuse to sell arms to South Africa she would buy them where she could get them . . . even if these methods are considered to be blackmarketing.[15]

By the end of 1964 both Britain and America had ceased to accept any new orders for arms from South Africa. In August 1963 the United States had announced its intention—subject to an important reservation—of completing by the end of the year existing contracts 'which provide for limited quantities of strategic equipment for defence against external threats, such as air-to-air missiles and torpedoes for submarines'.[16] Britain followed suit at the end of 1964 when the Labour Party came to office. Mr Wilson hesitated at first over the question of the export of the sixteen Buccaneer aircraft already under contract, and then decided that they should be sent. His initial statement had been that:

all outstanding licences for the export of arms to South Africa should

---

[14] *The Times*, 20 Jan. 1965.   [15] *Rand Daily Mail*, 15 Nov. 1964.
[16] Adlai Stevenson, 2 Aug. 1963, statement in the UN Security Council. 'We must honour these contracts', said Stevenson and added: 'The Council should be aware that in announcing this policy the United States, as a nation with many responsibilities in many parts of the world, naturally reserves the right in the future to interpret this policy in the light of requirements for assuring the maintenance of national peace and security. If the interests of the world community require the provision of equipment for use in the common defence effort, we would naturally feel able to do so without violating the spirit and intent of this resolution' (*SCOR*, 18th yr, 1052nd mtg, p. 15).

be revoked except where these are known to relate to current contracts with the South African government. . . . Outstanding commitments by the Ministry of Defence will be fulfilled, but, as from today,
no new contracts will be accepted for the supply of military equipment.[17]

Eight days later, on 25 November, he made a further statement
in the House of Commons: '. . . firm contracts will be honoured.
The shipment of the 16 Buccaneers will, therefore, be sanctioned,
but no further South African contracts will be entered into. Her
Majesty's Government will, of course, allow the shipments of
spares for the 16 Buccaneers as and when required'.[18] The purchase of additional British aircraft by the South African government is thus clearly unlikely; the Buccaneers would presumably
meet the fate of the Bloodhounds.[19] By 1965, therefore, both the
United Kingdom and the United States could claim that they
had 'tidied up their moral position' by complying with resolutions of the United Nations on the sale of arms. The United Kingdom could also point out that, at a difficult period in the country's balance of payments, it had voluntarily denied itself substantial export orders running into many millions of pounds.

Like the Simonstown agreement, the sale of arms to South
Africa had been part of a western view of defence strategy during
the period of the cold war which stressed the need for a South
Atlantic Naval Station based on South Africa as part of a defensive system of which NATO was its primary shield. The arms
sold to South Africa were a logical extension of this belief, since
the Simonstown agreement presupposed the joint use of naval
defence forces equipped with British weapons. It seemed reasonable, therefore, to argue that the base and the sale of arms should
stand or fall by each other, and the Conservative government
recognized the logic which was thought to lie behind it. Mr
Butler, as Foreign Secretary, told the House of Commons in
June 1964 that:

. . . If the Simonstown Agreement is regarded as important . . . and

---

[17] HC Deb., vol. 702, col. 200, 17 Nov. 1964.
[18] The sale also includes provision for the training of South African pilots at the
Royal Naval Air Station at Lossiemouth. Spare parts for the 16 aircraft are likely
to be needed well into the 1970s.
[19] The Conservative Party, if returned to power, might resume the sale of weapons
for 'external defence'. It had not said that it would, or that it would not.

if our view is that the strategic needs for it remain strong, we must obviously continue to be prepared to provide arms which are necessary for the support of Simonstown and for the self-defence of the country. It is unreasonable to think that we can have a total embargo of arms to South Africa and still expect that country to continue with the Simonstown Agreement.[20]

A few months later, following the return of the Labour Party to power, Dr Verwoerd tried to make the same point in connexion with the sale of the Buccaneers.

> If . . . it should happen that the present British Government does not honour or uphold the permission given by the previous Government to the firm concerned for the supply of the Buccaneer aircraft, it is proper for me to say betimes that South Africa would regard such an act in the most serious light. I must state here that, should this indeed happen, it would not be possible for the Simonstown Agreement to be maintained.[21]

When, however, Mr Wilson announced that the aircraft would in fact be delivered, Dr Verwoerd was conciliatory: the issue had been settled, and action in respect of the agreement 'had clearly been avoided'.[22]

The present attitude of the British government was given in the House of Commons on 30 November 1964 when the Secretary of State for Defence was asked:

(1) What steps he is taking to establish an alternative base to that at Simonstown;
(2) what estimate has been made of the cost of establishing in the South Atlantic or the Indian Ocean a naval base to replace the facilities now available at Simonstown?

and Mr Healey replied: 'There is no question of our losing the facilities we enjoy under the Simonstown Agreement. . . . This base is of considerable value to the Royal Navy and, as I said

---

[20] HC Deb., vol. 696, col. 1419, 17 June 1964.

[21] *Rand Daily Mail*, 15 Nov. 1964.

[22] Ibid. 27 Nov. 1964. There is a particular lesson to be drawn from these exchanges between the UK and South African governments, of wider significance than the disagreement over the sale of arms, namely the need to avoid a situation in which hesitation over policy appears to yield to South African pressure. It would have been far better either to have sent the Buccaneers, together with a clear declaration that they were a final consignment, or to have cancelled the order, and to have accepted full responsibility for the penalties attached to their non-delivery—including return of part-payments already made.

before, we have no intention of seeking to abandon it.'[23] Mr Healey's argument rests on the first of the two basic assumptions of this chapter, namely that the South African government, for its own reasons, is unlikely to abrogate or restrict the defence arrangements which still link it with the United Kingdom. The second assumption—that even if the South African government were to threaten to end the agreement, it is unlikely to be able to influence United Kingdom policy since what it has to offer is no longer of fundamental importance to British defence interests—was not made. On the contrary, Mr Healey stressed 'the considerable value' of the base to the Royal Navy, and, again, there is an element of hypocrisy and illogicality in the position. The United Kingdom government denies arms to South Africa on the grounds that its domestic policy is 'evil ... totally impracticable, and will lead eventually, but inevitably to disaster in South Africa',[24] while stressing the value to Britain of the defence facilities made available by the Nationalists on a basis of co-operation between the two countries. Still, morality and logic are not always handmaidens of policy, and Mr Healey may be right in assuming that Britain can uphold the morality of an arms embargo without endangering—in practice—the Royal Navy's use of the Simonstown base. Britain would be in a stronger position, however, if it were really the case that the Simonstown agreement was no longer so valuable as it was thought to be when it was first concluded; and the easiest way to examine whether this is so is to ask: what would be the effect on British defence interests if the navy were no longer able to use the base?

In practice, it has not been used a great deal. Between 1961 and 1964 'five frigates, four submarines, an icebreaker, and a Royal Fleet Auxiliary [used the base]. The frigates each spent 16 weeks at Simonstown for maintenance and repairs. The icebreaker and the RFA also undertook maintenance and repairs there.'[25] None the less, it *is* used, and there would be a number of practical disadvantages if its facilities were no longer available. For example, the Admiralty naval wireless transmitter would have to be re-sited, in Mauritius perhaps, or on one of the

[23] HC Deb., vol. 703, cols 12–13.
[24] Sir Patrick Dean's phrases, 6 Aug. 1963, *SCOR*, 18th yr, 1054th mtg, pp. 18–19.
[25] HC Deb., vol. 703, col. 12, 30 Nov. 1964.

smaller islands of the Indian Ocean; it would also hardly be possible to continue to hold joint naval exercises in the South
Atlantic between the South African navy and British, Portuguese, and other NATO forces.[26] More serious would be the loss
of naval dockyard facilities. The stores and spares kept at
Simonstown are available to Royal Naval ships, and since all the
thirty-two surface ships of the South African navy are of British
design, the equipment is interchangeable. There is no other
comparable dockyard in the vast area of the South Atlantic. St
Helena is too far north; Diego Garcia in the Indian Ocean too
far east; and even if the anchorage and shore facilities of these
small island bases were to be developed, they would lack the
advanced industrial resources of the Republic on which the
dockyard at Simonstown can draw. If the bases were not available, therefore, other means would have to be adopted as a substitute to the services it provides. For example, an aircraft
carrier or frigate which was hampered on its journey round the
Cape to and from the east by an electrical failure, or the need to
replace faulty equipment, would have to rely on supply ships
afloat, or the flying out of equipment, the cost of which would be
very high. In such circumstances, the absence of any right to use
the dockyard at Simonstown might be inconvenient.[27]

The primary advantage of the Simonstown agreement, however, was not in the navy's occasional use of dockyard facilities
but in Britain's having access to a base, despite its transfer to
South African control, which was a part of the global defences of the west against the USSR at that date. In 1955 it was
considered essential to have allied, including South African,
anti-submarine frigates based on Simonstown in order to counter
the possible threat of Soviet submarines operating in the Indian
and South Atlantic Oceans: the cold war was still thought of in
terms of a sudden 'escalation' to all-out war; the Suez escapade
was not far off when South African ports were to be crammed
with the world's shipping. The base was on the friendly mainland
of what was then still a Commonwealth country which com-
manded the historically vital 'sea routes and lines of communi-

---

[26] The 'Cape' exercises were not held in 1964, primarily because the Royal Navy
was too heavily committed in South East Asia.

[27] In normal times, ships would go through the Suez Canal; they are then dependent
on the East African repair facilities: e.g. HMS *Eagle* put in at Mombasa for
generator repairs on its way to the Far East in 1964.

cation round southern Africa'; the Cape of Good Hope was the western end of the immense arc of sea which stretches across the southern half of the Indian Ocean to western Australia. It would have been thought extremely foolish, therefore, in 1955 to consider losing the advantages that the agreement offered, in exchange for the moral but very doubtful political benefit of a public gesture of dissent from the domestic policies of the South African government.

The position is hardly comparable today. True, military advisers who are obliged to take a pessimistic stand about the state of international relations may argue that the cold war (by its very nature) can never wholly be isolated from the danger of a breakdown in relations between east and west, and that distant bases in relatively sheltered areas of the world may suddenly become of critical importance. From a professional point of view, they are right to over-insure, and to argue that all bases in all parts of the world are or may become important. Yet one may doubt whether by 1965 the threat of Soviet power in the South Atlantic is of the same dimension as it was in 1955. Militarily, the development of long-range missiles and nuclear-powered submarines has reduced the need for fixed bases overseas; politically, the easing of tension between Moscow and Washington, though threatened today by the conflict in Vietnam, has enabled a reassessment to be made of the relative importance of these distant theatres of war. If current assumptions are correct, the United States (and Britain) are learning to accept the USSR, and vice versa, as a rational enemy which is unlikely to push its rivalry with the west beyond breaking point, and China rather than the Soviet Union is now the principal source of danger in the state of armed peace in the world. In these circumstances, the Simonstown base is likely to be of much less significance even than it was thought to be a decade ago, since future needs are likely to be assessed in terms of defence not against enemy submarines in the South Atlantic but against the land-based forces of China in South East Asia. In addition to allied support for local armies, the primary line of defence is now the United States nuclear-armed fleet operating off the Chinese mainland: if, however, American or British Polaris submarines,[28] operating in the Indian Ocean, need a forward operating base

[28] The first British Polaris submarine is expected to go on patrol in mid-1970.

K

(comparable say to the Holy Loch in Scotland), a sensible policy would be to use Fremantle or Exmouth Gulf in Australia, or an island base at, say, Diego Garcia in the Chagos Archipelago[29] which is a great deal nearer than Simonstown to the Indian sub-continent and China.

What other dangers are there which may threaten British interests, and for which the co-operation of the South African government might be required? Here we may consider the third element in Mr Wilson's triple role for the United Kingdom—'our east of Suez role'—in the light of the very real dangers of limited 'undeclared war'. The problem may be set down in simple terms as follows. If the United Kingdom government is right to believe (as one may infer it does) that British forces should be active in the vast area of the Indian Ocean, then it will have to get its ships and supplies—including aircraft—there. The obvious routes to points east of Suez are through the Suez Canal or by air across the Middle East, but politics—especially Arab politics—cannot be left out of account. The reinforcement of British troops in the Indian Ocean has strong political over-tones, and in the present conditions of Middle East politics the question arises as to what alternative routes there are, and how important South Africa is in this respect.

One might consider first the carrying of supplies by sea. If heavy military equipment is to be shipped within a reasonable period of time to Aden, or India, or Malaysia, the alternative to the Suez Canal is to go round the Cape. The voyage is long: 10,000 miles from Portsmouth to Colombo compared with 6,500 through the Canal. Yet in recent times the harbour and re-fuelling facilities of South African ports were essential both dur-ing the Second World War and the Suez crisis; and although one may question whether parallel circumstances will arise when Britain will again be obliged to turn to South Africa for help, it is impossible to answer that they will not. At present, the pre-dominant threat to British interests lies in South East Asia, where a state of undeclared war exists between the British and In-donesian forces. If the limited state of hostilities which now exists there were to enter a period of fierce fighting—however unlikely

[29] At present administered from Mauritius. According to the *Sunday Times*, 18 Apr. 1965, the US are using Manus, off New Guinea, as a 'refuelling and refitting base for its atomic submarines'.

it may seem at present—attacks might be made by Indonesian-manned Soviet submarines. Such attacks would be in the approaches to Malaysia rather than in the wide area of the South Atlantic. But Simonstown might be of some importance as a very distant base, and a mobile task force (consisting of an aircraft carrier, commando-carriers, assault ships and escorts of the kind now used increasingly in the Far East) might be glad of the repair facilities there. There are some advantages in having access to a base at the far western end of the Indian Ocean in addition to more permanent bases in Australia, and Simonstown is both convenient and inexpensive.

However, even if the 1955 agreement did not exist, and Simonstown was not available, the United Kingdom could still continue to ship arms and supplies via the normal commercial ports of Cape Town, Port Elizabeth, East London, and Durban. The South African government might threaten to place loading difficulties in the way of military transports wishing to refuel at its ports, but action of this kind would seriously jeopardize ordinary trading relations with Britain, which one would suppose South Africa would be loath to do. The loss of naval facilities at Simonstown, therefore, though inconvenient, would not seriously affect British supply routes to the east; and it is precisely because the agreement has a limited rather than an essential use, that the South African government is unlikely to be able to use it as a lever against Britain (or indirectly against the United States) in the hope of extracting concessions. Similarly, one may doubt whether the African states are particularly incensed by Britain's occasional use of the base. It is true that the sale of arms was hotly opposed, but that was on a different scale of emotion, and carried very different implications in terms of South Africa's domestic policy, despite the not unreasonable distinction drawn by the Conservative government between arms for domestic and external use. The Simonstown base *is* 'useful', therefore, but by no means 'indispensable', and there is much to be said for Britain's continuing to avail itself of the limited benefits under the 1955 agreement without placing too great a dependence on them.

There is a related problem, which is less easy to unravel—that of overflying rights. In the present age of undeclared wars, the great need is to deploy troops and arms swiftly by air; and, on the assumption that South and South East Asia are areas of unrest in which there are British interests to be defended, the question of overflying rights and transit facilities may one day become urgent. The dilemma is simple to explain, though far from easy to resolve. To reach the Indian Ocean there are three or four possible air routes. The most convenient, in terms of distance and transit facilities, is across North Africa via Libya and the Sudan to Aden and Singapore. A second route lies along the more northerly air corridor from Cyprus across the CENTO countries—Turkey, Iran, and Pakistan. A third is the long 'west-about' journey across the Atlantic, North America, and the Pacific. A fourth possibility is to fly 'round Africa' to Mauritius and other points in the Indian Ocean. Each requires some preliminary examination before the position of South Africa is considered.

The Libyan-Sudanese route to Aden and Singapore is still in use; RAF aircraft can also obtain permission to overfly Egypt, but these flights are always subject to political strain. Early in 1956 it was reported that talks between the British and Libyan governments (over the removal of the bulk of the army garrison and the RAF contingent at Tripoli) had left untouched the right to use El Adem airfield;[30] the twenty-year treaty which protects British troops, training missions, and the use of air staging posts should run until 1973, but there are statements from time to time by the Libyan government which raise doubts about the future. In March 1964, for example, it 'solemnly affirmed' that 'foreign bases in Libya will never, whatever the cost to us, be used as sources against our Arab brothers'.[31] The statement was for public consumption but the sentiment behind it may one day raise awkward problems over Aden. Similarly, in the Sudan British military aircraft have the right to pass over Sudanese airspace and to land at airfields, but only under carefully detailed regulations. Permission is not granted for any military or civil aircraft suspected of being used for military purposes against Arab countries; an aircraft must inform the Sudanese government where it is bound for and the load it carries, and may be subject to search if it lands at a Sudanese airfield.[32] Farther south,

---

[30] *The Times*, 13 Jan. 1965.

[31] *Sunday Ghibli*, 1 Feb. 1964, quoted *Africa Research Bull.*, vol. 1, no. 2.

[32] Radio Omdurman, 23 Nov. 1964, quoted ibid., vol. 1, no. 11. In February 1965, however, the Sudanese Minister of Information was said to have 'confirmed that some British military aircraft had been permitted to fly over Sudan and land at

staging and training facilities were retained in Kenya after the withdrawal of British troops from the then recently constructed base at Kahawa; but it is impossible to be confident that these rights will continue unscathed.[33] There is always the danger that they may be withdrawn suddenly at times of crisis when they are most urgently needed, and although one can overfly—regardless—if there are compelling reasons to do so at a particular point in time, it is hardly a satisfactory mode of operation.

The more northerly air route across the CENTO countries—via Turkey to Aden, via Turkey, Iran, and Pakistan to Singapore—may be less subject to immediate political difficulties; but the corridor is narrow and runs close to the Russian border, raising ugly possibilities of Soviet interference with radio aids and an infringement of Soviet airspace. There are more natural hazards, for although pressurized aircraft can now fly with a full payload over the mountain ranges that lie across the route, the northern approaches to Teheran airport are not easy. There are long-term uncertainties too in that allegiances are shifting in the CENTO countries, and may easily affect such delicate matters as the use of local airfields by foreign aircraft and troops.[34]

What are the alternatives? As the range and payloads of aircraft in the service of the RAF increase, other routes will become feasible, notably the long 'west-about' journey to South East Asia across North America and the Pacific. If an 'all-red' route is wanted, it is possible to keep within Commonwealth bounds the whole way, via Winnipeg, Vancouver, south to Christmas Island, Port Moresby in New Guinea (or bases in Australia), and north to Singapore. This has a particular disadvantage, however, arising from the absence of British islands in the north Pacific, in that to fly from Christmas Island via New Guinea or Australia to Singapore is to encounter the 1,000-mile-long coastline of Indonesia—an unfortunate obstacle at present. A more satisfactory route would be to use the American bases at Midway and Guam in the Pacific. The assumption has to be made that there

---

Khartoum since Jan. 12 1965 when the blanket ban was lifted by the Council of Ministers' (*Africa Report*, Apr. 1965).

[33] The triumph of sentiment over material advantage may be seen in the loss of revenue to Kenya. The 24th Infantry Brigade, numbering 6,000 men, was withdrawn at the end of 1964, at an estimated loss to Kenya of £10½ m. a year and some 4,000 Africans thrown out of work.

[34] They may also be affected by British-Turkish relations over Cyprus.

will be no serious differences of policy between Britain and the United States over, say, Malaysia and Indonesia or North and South Vietnam: but suppose differences did arise, there is the alternative Commonwealth route available if necessary.[35] To fly westwards round the world to Singapore is longer than the short Middle East distances, approximately 7,000 nautical miles,[36] compared with 1,000–1,500 miles, and tedious for both crews and troop-passengers despite the coming into service with the RAF of long-distance transport aircraft; but the routes are relatively safe and free from political interference, including the danger of a sudden withdrawal of local facilities.

If the problem were only how to get to Singapore, the westward routes might become an alternative to the political hazards of the Middle East, but there is also Aden and the Gulf.[37] And it is hardly possible to fly 'west-about' round the globe from Britain to Arabia. The distances are immense:

United Kingdom to Aden

Route	Distance (nautical miles)
via Libya/Sudan	3,390
via Cyprus/Turkey	4,430*
via United States/Midway	16,790

* If flights over Saudi Arabia were forbidden one would have to add another 500–600 miles. See table of distances, p. 181 below.

It is precisely in this disturbed part of the world, however, that Britain may find itself in trouble. Looking at the present situation in the Aden Colony and the federated states of the hinterland, it is difficult to feel confident that a stable country will emerge, free from domestic unrest and external pressures. It is possible

[35] Ideally, all routes should be flown as often as possible to familiarize crews with the problems involved, and to accustom local ground staff (and the civilian population) to the sight of regular RAF visits. Cf. Denis Healey, 21 July 1964 (H.C. Deb., vol. 699, col. 1569), in answer to a question: 'The RAF already occasionally makes flights to and from the Far East across the longer North American route. We are currently considering what arrangements might be necessary to enable us, with the agreement of the United States and Canadian governments, to make greater use of such routes if need be, in the future.'

[36] 1 nautical mile = 1·85 statute miles.

[37] At Aden there are army units, a Royal Marine Commando, RAF ground attack and air defence, reconnaissance and transport squadrons. Naval units include escorts, an amphibious warfare squadron, and minesweepers. Base facilities also exist at Bahrain.

that Britain may succeed eventually in quitting South Arabia both peacefully and irrevocably; but it may also (as in Malaysia) find it difficult in the short run to abandon the area to its own defences. Such plans are also long-term, rather than immediate, and if large-scale fighting should break out along the borders of the Federation between British troops and Arab armies, existing overflying rights across the Middle East would certainly be jeopardized. A 'reserve route' therefore would have many advantages, and it is in this context that South Africa's offers of help have to be considered, for although it is possible to fly island by island to southern Africa, overflying rights across the Republic would be essential in the long eastwards flight to Mauritius and north again to Aden.

The argument may be elaborated briefly. When the possibility of a Commonwealth African route via Kano, Kampala, and Nairobi proved impracticable in the face of African insistence on non-alignment, the tendency was to look farther south. It is possible to traverse the broad middle belt of the continent by flying from Ascension Island across the Congo and Tanzania to Mauritius or the Seychelles and Aden; and, even without permission to overfly, it might be a long time before either country knew, or, if someone told them, were able to do anything about it. There might be, however, unpleasant political entanglements. The route then begins to be pushed farther south—across Angola, Rhodesia, and Moçambique. But it is not until the Republic of South Africa is reached that overflying rights—and staging-post facilities—can be obtained with a fair guarantee that they will be available on a reasonably long-term basis.

What alternatives are there to South African airfields? Here one returns to the question of island bases in the South Atlantic and Indian Oceans and the problem of how to get there. The intention is easy to state: to devise 'a costly but more secure alternative to the North African air route' and 'a strategy that rings Africa with a chain of island staging posts'.[38] The requirements are easily listed: an 8,000–9,000-foot runway, radar and radio facilities, workshops, recreational opportunities (if possible) for troops in transit, and reasonable accommodation for a limited permanent force of staff and technicians. In addition, a deep-

[38] This is the usual formulation of the aim (*Venture*, June 1964, p. 4) where such a route is advocated as an 'almost certainly preferable alternative to Aden'.

water anchorage, where dockyard repairs could be carried out, would be needed if both sea and air forces were to be provided for. The search is likely to begin at Ascension Island, 900 miles from the African coast, where an airstrip is available although facilities (including provisions) for troops and ground staff are scanty.[39] There is also St Helena, 1,100 miles from the African coast, 47 square miles, 33 of which are barren rocky ground: Jamestown is a good open roadstead with good anchorages, and suitable for carrying out dockyard repairs, but there is no airstrip and the hard volcanic rock of the island may make the construction of an airfield impracticable. Farther south there is nothing, unless a wide détour is made to the south-west to Tristan da Cunha, where the weather is hazardous and the task of building an adequate landing field formidable. Farther east, there are excellent defence base facilities used by the French in Madagascar; east and north again, at Mauritius, Diego Garcia, and the Seychelles, harbours could be deepened and airstrips extended—if the expense involved was thought to be worth meeting.[40] The particular problem lies between Ascension and, say, Mauritius. It is over 5,000 nautical miles from Ascension Island round the southern end of Africa to Mauritius, still farther to what might become a (British) forward base in the Indian Ocean complementary to the main bases at Singapore and Fremantle; the distances are immense, and beyond the capacity, even at half-pay-load, of the most powerful jet transport aircraft. From Ascension to Luanda, however, and across the Republic of South Africa to Mauritius, is 4,800 miles divided into flying distances of about 1,600 miles;[41] the flights are long but well within flying distance, and there are excellent servicing and transit facilities at a number of South African airfields. If, therefore, a southern air route were required as an alternative to existing routes across the Middle East, the co-operation of the South African government would have to be enlisted. One may add

---

[39] The USA established a base at Wideawake airfield (where the missile tracking station is located) on Ascension in 1942.

[40] It would not be negligible. To construct a limited, forward-operating base equipped with good runways as at Gan costs at least £5 m. It has been estimated that a base at Diego Garcia would require $25 m. (*Cleveland Plain Dealer*, 30 Aug. 1964).

[41] Ascension–Luanda, 1650, Luanda–Johannesburg 1,390, Johannesburg–Mauritius 1,740.

that such a route would not be unfamiliar, but a military counterpart of the well-established civilian airlines which fly from
Johannesburg across the continent to Europe, America, and
Asia. Co-operation of this kind is very different from the established objectives of the Simonstown agreement, and it would be
prudent not to try and secure a formal agreement with South
Africa on the use of its airfields. But although the facilities required are likely to be requested only on an *ad hoc* basis, it would
also be unwise to assume that they will never be needed.

There is a final aspect to consider. The argument in this
chapter has been based on the announcement of the Labour
government, when it came to power in October 1964, of a 'triple
defence rôle' for Britain. By the end of 1965, however, the overriding problem became how to cut defence costs in order to re-
lieve pressure on the economy as a whole. On 27 July 1965 Mr
Callaghan announced in the House of Commons that the defence programme would be reduced by £100 million in 1966,
and £400 million by 1969–70. A week later Mr Healey gave
further details. Defence expenditure was running at about 7 per
cent of the national product and had to be brought down to the
equivalent (at 1964 prices) of £2,000 million by 1970; there
would have to be further economies in the purchase of weapons,
through the redeployment of men, and where possible a reduc-
tion in the scale of Britain's overseas commitments. The annual
cost in foreign exchange of operations 'east of Suez' was high—
the highest after Germany: £63 million in Malaysia, £29 million
in Aden and the Gulf.[42] Mr Healey thought Britain would be
'unwise to look at her overseas commitments simply in economic
terms. The United Kingdom had a general interest in the
stability of the third world'—a statement with which it would be
difficult to quarrel in the light of the troubled state of both Asia
and Africa, but it was also clear that the government was being
forced to count the cost in terms of the overall needs of the
economy. To maintain a very large force in Malaysia against an
enemy which had 'received modern equipment from great
powers'[43] was a heavy drain on national resources even if the

---

[42] Germany £85 m., Cyprus £17 m., Malta £15 m., Hongkong £10 m. (*The Times*,
   5 Aug. 1965; report of a press conference on 4 Aug.).
[43] 'The previous government had not the slightest idea, when they undertook to
   defend Malaysia, that Indonesia would have more modern aircraft and naval
   vessels than Britain' (ibid. 5 Aug. 1965).

arguments for resisting Indonesian aggression against a Commonwealth country were valid at the time and—despite Singapore's break from the Federation—still have some validity today. It was more difficult to justify expenditure on Aden and the Gulf, on behalf of a reluctant Colony and the small shaikhdoms of the Arabian peninsula—except as the temporary price of an orderly withdrawal. The question was how long the withdrawal from either base might take, for it was not easy to see an immediate end to Britain's involvement either in Arabia or the Malaysian situation. Between these strategic outposts lie the immense problems of the Indian subcontinent and the multiple dangers of a widening conflict between India and Pakistan. The run-down of empire is proving hardly less fraught with danger—and more expensive—than its acquisition, not least because it is often difficult to decide where Commonwealth interests end, and western strategic interests begin. If, for example, Britain were to withdraw from Aden, Bahrain, and Singapore, many of the problems raised in this chapter would have been avoided, and such a policy may be an eminently sensible one to adopt in terms of the end of empire. But is it in British and western interests to leave the vast area between East Africa and the Malacca Straits to its own defences and its own wars and quarrels? Admittedly, the nature of the help required, as over the 'undeclared war' between India and Pakistan, may be such that only a United Nations-sponsored force could provide. But one cannot be sure that the United Nations will be able to escape its own troubles, and if it were thought necessary that allied (western) forces should still operate in the western Indian Ocean, the problem of how to get them there would return. Moreover, whatever the long-term answer is to these very difficult questions, it seems clear that a policy of total British withdrawal from the Indian Ocean is hardly feasible within, at best, the next eighteen months or two years, and in the interval of time before new defence policies east of Suez can be adopted it may be that interim measures are the most suitable. If one adds to this the financial difficulties in which Britain is now placed, the arguments in favour of retaining existing facilities in South Africa are greatly strengthened. Lacking the ability of the United States to range widely in the use of mobile defence forces, the United Kingdom must make the best use of what is already available, and since it is possible, if occasion arises, to continue to use Simonstown and South African airfields without great expense, it seems sensible to do so.

It is at this point that the separate threads of the argument need to be brought together. Behind the debate over defence interests lies an uneasy mixture of morality and expediency, and one can easily understand why: for while there has been a long history of co-operation between Britain and South Africa, revulsion from the Nationalist government's domestic policies has come fairly recently. It has not been easy, therefore, for the latter emotion to pull down the structure of co-operation already in existence. Nor are the advantages to be gained from doing so easily stated. Again, the balance sheet is uneven. The practical benefits from collaboration stand out plainly. The disadvantages have to be expressed on moral grounds, or in terms of the general uncertainty which surrounds South African affairs. If, for example, a friendly democratic government were in power in Pretoria, its offers of help would be accepted gladly in all three situations examined in this chapter—as an ally in war, as a partner in the existing balance of armed peace, and as a valuable link between Britain and its interests in the Indian Ocean. Against the background of apartheid, however, it is felt to be wrong to participate in joint defence arrangements with the South African government while disapproving strongly of its racial policies. Alliances, it is argued, carry obligations, and South Africa may exact a heavy price. The fears are understandable, but the writer believes them to be groundless, given the two primary assumptions on which the argument of this chapter has been based: that the defence facilities granted by South Africa, though useful, are far from being indispensable, and that the Nationalist government has every reason not to offend Britain or the United States by trying to exact concessions. On the other hand the facilities granted, though hardly capable of yielding a price in political terms, *are* useful. There is little harm, and some advantage, therefore, in maintaining these links with South Africa provided they are kept at a minimum level of use.

VI

Trade, Investment, and Gold

BRITISH economic interests in the Republic, noted in passing in earlier chapters, are set out in greater detail in the following pages, where it may be seen that they reflect the general pattern of the South African economy. Exports to South Africa have benefited from the rapid expansion of the domestic market in the Republic, which has traditionally been favourable to British goods; investment has followed the shift from mining to industry without diminishing its stake in the immensely rich mineral resources of the country. It is true that South Africa is far more dependent on Britain than Britain is on South Africa. It has always looked to the United Kingdom as its chief market and source of supply, whereas the size and nature of the British economy, with its enormous variety of interests overseas, reduces its dependence on any one market. Thirty per cent of South Africa's exports go to Britain, where they are no more than 2–3 per cent of total imports; by contrast, imports into South Africa from Britain constitute a third of the total volume of goods entering the country, but only a twentieth of British exports. None the less, South Africa is an important single market. At the end of 1964 it ranked only after the United States, Australia, and West Germany as a principal buyer of British goods.[1] It is the world's largest producer of gold, the bulk of which is handled by London bullion brokers. And the amount of British investment in the Republic (though falling) is still very great, exceeded only by holdings in Canada, the United States, and Australia.[2] These are the

---

[1] 1964 UK exports to USA £383 m., Australia £257 m., W. Germany £264 m., S. Africa £225 m., Sweden £204 m. (Commonwealth Economic Committee, *Commonwealth Trade 1958/9–1963* (1964), table 16.)

[2] *British Companies' Direct Investment Overseas (at book values) 1962 (£ m.)*

Canada	607·0
Australia	401·3
USA	276·1
South Africa	269·3
Estimated world total	3,500·0

Note: Overseas direct investment holdings of British banks, insurance companies, and oil interests are excluded. See above, p. 42.

Source: Board of Trade Overseas Direct Investment Inquiry, 1962.

principal interests examined in this chapter—trade, investment, and gold—and to take their full measure something must first be said of the structure of the South African economy.

Despite the poverty of many of the non-whites, South Africa belongs to the relatively small number of advanced countries in the world—the United States, Canada, Australia, New Zealand, Britain, western Europe, the USSR, Japan. It has shared in the increase in trade between these industrial states; its national income has more than kept pace with the rise in prices and the growth of population. If, as unhappily seems likely, the gap between the rich and poor nations of the world is widening, South Africa is on the prosperous side of the divide. Indeed, it is one of the few countries to have crossed the gap in recent years. Its economy has moved away from an early dependence on the export of raw materials—gold, diamonds, wool, fruit, and cereals—to a measure of local industrialization; it has a growing capacity to raise living standards throughout the country, despite the obstacles imposed by the nature of white rule to a rational distribution of wealth. There have been several reasons for this shift towards a more advanced economy. The increase in gold production from 11·9 million to 27·4 million ounces between 1946 and 1963 has covered the imbalance in South Africa's external trade—the current annual output, valued at some £340 million, is equal to about 56 per cent of the cost of the Republic's yearly imports—and has generated growth in other sectors of the economy. Controls have been imposed when required, as under the Customs Tariff Acts of 1925 and 1948, and the restraint on capital transfers in 1961. There has been a heavy government expenditure on services and defence, the injection of large amounts of foreign capital and skills, and—in recent years—the infusion of a new Afrikaner business enterprise supported by government capital. The rate of economic growth has reflected these advantages. The national income rose from £693 million in 1946–7 to £2,535 million in 1962–3, representing an increase in real income per head during these decades of about 2·1 per cent per annum.[3] The statistics are not in doubt and are set out plainly in the tables below.

[3] *South Africa Year Book 1965*, ch. 32; and Netherlands Bank of SA, *Business Guide to South Africa* (1965), p. 12.

National Accounts, 1950–63
(Rand millions)

	1950	1955	1960	1963		1950	1955	1960	196
Net national income at factor cost	2,149	3,358	4,502	5,640	Personal consumption expenditure	1,686	2,648	3,604	4,28
Depreciation	169	334	489	595	Purchases of goods and services by public authorities	270	421	590	85(
Indirect taxes less subsidies	137	233	264	432	Gross domestic capital formation	546	980	1,135	1,41(
Gross national product at market prices	2,455	3,925	5,355	6,667	Export of goods and non-factor services	801	1,210	1,532	1,84.
					Less imports of goods and non-factor services	722	1,150	1,312	1,524
					Gross domestic expenditure	2,581	4,109	5,549	6,86'
					Less net factor income from abroad	−126	−184	−194	−196
					Gross national expenditure at market prices	2,455	3,925	5,355	6,667

Source: SA Reserve Bank, 1964.

Balance of Payments, 1946–63
(Rand millions)

	1946	1951	1957	1961	1963
Merchandise:					
Imports f.o.b.	−433	−937	−1,112	−1,018	−1,296
Exports f.o.b.	156	580	903	931	1,017
Trade balance	−277	−357	−209	−87	−279
Net gold output	203	300	429	576	688
Investment income	−51	−121	−153	−178	−158
Total current account (net)	−179	−271	−11	−203	−148

Source: SA Reserve Bank.

A longer perspective confirms this picture of a steadily expanding economy. Professor Hobart Houghton has argued that there
was 'more than a doubling of the real *per capita* income during the
last fifty years' despite periods of recession in the 1930s and the

financial crisis of 1960–1.[4] On the basis of gross national product estimates, the real growth per head was 5·9 per cent in 1962–3 and 6·5 per cent in 1963–4, suggesting that 'the average growth rate over the next few years will reach, and may exceed, the long-term annual average of 2·4 per cent over the past fifty years'.[5] The economic development plan approved by the government in December 1964 is based on the assumption of an annual growth rate of 5½ per cent in the gross national product during its initial five-year period. Whichever way the figures are calculated they reveal the underlying strength of the economy. The current prosperity of white South Africa is immediately apparent to the most casual visitor, in terms of housing, food, motor cars, and travel. Living standards among non-whites are harder to assess, but wages have certainly increased in the towns. The minimum basic wage of R2 a day recently introduced by the Rembrandt group of companies has been adopted by a number of other concerns, and the growing use of Radio Bantu by commercial advertisers points to the increased purchasing power of the African population. The greatest advance has probably been among the Coloured community. As the 1965 *Economist* Survey pointed out:

fifteen years ago probably not more than a dozen Coloureds in the western Cape earned £500 a year, now there are an estimated 17,000 with a further 5,000 earning £1,000 or more. . . . It is becoming rare to see a white man on a western Cape factory floor; frequently only the top managers are white, while at least one factory has a Coloured supervisor with whites working under him.[6]

It is only fair to add that there is also a great deal of uncertainty, partly economic, partly political, about the future. There is a danger of inflation and a further depletion of the reserves to meet the growing demand for imports. There is also the likelihood of a decline in gold exports; production is expected to fall fairly sharply after 1970, despite the discovery of new high-grade mines in the Orange Free State and on the Far West Rand. Its decline may be offset by the mining of uranium—for which there is a rising market—but the shift to manufacturing will have to be

[4] Houghton, p. 205.
[5] Union Acceptances Ltd, *Scope for Investment in South Africa*, Apr. 1964, p. 10.
[6] See too Helgard Muller, *The Role of the Coloured People in the Economic Pattern of the Republic of S. Africa* (1965).

quickened if a new and broader base to the economy is to be found. However, the rate of industrialization has been slower than was once expected. Manufacturing contributed about 20 per cent of the gross national product in 1946 and only 26 per cent in 1964,[7] and if it is to be increased substantially wider issues than economics will have to be faced. The government will have to consider once again the problems of skilled non-white labour for which there is little or no provision in the present policies of the National party. By 1964, for example, it was estimated that 'the building industry was so hard pressed for skilled men that it could handle only about 65 per cent of the work offering'.[8] The government will also have to decide whether or not to remove the financial restrictions imposed in 1961. The present expansion was financed with the help of locally accumulated capital which overseas companies were unable to transfer

[7] Cf. figures given in *Scope for Investment in S. Africa*:

1. *Derivation of National Income*

Productive sector	1946/7		1956/7		1962/3	
	Rm.	Per cent	Rm.	Per cent	Rm.	Per cent
Manufacturing	311	20·8	920	23·4	1,399	25·5
Mining	173	11·6	501	12·7	719	13·1
Agric., forestry, fishing	203	13·6	557	14·2	568	10·4
Commerce & transport	414	27·7	842	21·4	1,123	20·5
Public authorities	393	26·3	1,112	28·3	1,672	30·5
Total domestic prdct	1,494	100	3,932	100	5,481	100

2. *Recent Growth of Secondary Industry**

Year	No. of establishments	'000 of employees	Salaries & wages paid Rm.	Gross value of output	
				Rm.	at 1954/5 prices
1954/5	12,343	732	474·5	2,415·3	2,415
1956/7	12,198	755	527·0	2,540·4	2,403
1958/9	13,530	778	570·3	2,730·9	2,548
1960/1	14,933	796	647·9	3,125·2	2,842
1961/2	15,714	796	684·2	3,317·3	2,982

* Data prior to 1954/5 not comparable with later figures owing to revision of Industrial Census.

[8] *Annual Register 1964*, p. 317.

abroad under the exchange-control regulations. The controls are still there, and they will have to be lifted if further investment is to be attracted into the country. But if they are removed, it is hard to say which would be the greater: the readiness of business enterprises to invest capital in South Africa, or the fears of those who have been waiting to get their money out. In short, the shadow of apartheid lies across the economy, and provides cold comfort for those who try to look very far ahead. The racial policies of the South African government are responsible not only for the restrictions on non-white labour and the movement of capital both within the country[9] and overseas. They also conjure up the fearsome spectre which no boardroom can ignore, and which the policy of 'separate development' (though designed to exorcise) cannot dispel, of large-scale disturbances throughout the main centres of economic life in the country.

This, then, is the nature of the market which now takes over £200 million of British exports a year, more than the whole of the Commonwealth African countries put together. In 1962 the value of exports (excluding re-exports) from Britain to the Republic was £148·4 million; in 1963 it was £198 million, and by the end of 1964 it had grown to £225 million.[10] Not only does South Africa take up to 5 per cent of the United Kingdom's total exports; it is also a growing market for a number of items of central importance to the British economy. Exports of engineering products, for example, were nearly £66 million in 1963; motor vehicle sales (including tractors) to the Republic were £36 million. For some items South Africa was either the principal, or the second, or the third most important market overseas. (See tables on p. 152).

The figures may be expressed in slightly different fashion, in terms of the size of the South African market in relation to the total export from Britain of a particular commodity. Using the Standard International Trade Classification headings, there were over thirty items exported by South Africa in 1963, each of which comprised more than 5 per cent of the total export of the item in question: for example, 8 per cent of motor cars and 9·5

---

[9] Private 'white' capital investment from the Republic is still forbidden, for example, in the Transkei, the government having accepted the minority report of the Tomlinson Commission.

[10] Compare US exports to S. Africa 1963: £276 m., 1·3 per cent of total US exports.

Items for which South Africa was the Principal Customer (by Value)
(£ m.)

	1963	Half 1964
Lorries, trucks	7·66	4·71
Railway vehicles	3·48	1·59
Switches, regulators, &c.	3·94	2·16
Telecom. apparatus	7·61	3·9
Man-made fibres	1·59	0·86*
Cotton fabrics	3·73	1·7

* Fell to second place.

Items for which South Africa was the Second Largest Customer (by Value)
(£ m.)

	1963	Half 1964
Paper & paper manuf.	3·17	1·70*
Agric. tractors	7·87	4·5†
Electrical mach. (general)	22·92	11·02
Transport equip. (general)	52·23	29·69
Motor cars	18·84	11·81
Ships & boats	8·47	1·9*

* Fell to 3rd place.   † Rose to 1st place.

Items for which South Africa was the Third Largest Customer (by Value)
(£ m.)

	1963	Half 1964
Cotton yarn & thread	1·13	0·72
Glass manuf.	1·38	1·08*
Steam engines	0·84	0·58
Mech. handling equip.	2·13	1·45*
Printed matter	2·47	1·49

* Rose to 2nd place.

Source: UN Doc. S/6210 (p. 10).

per cent of all lorries exported from Britain went to South Africa, 16·7 per cent of the total export of railway locomotives, 7·2 per cent of all the electrical machinery exported (including 12 per cent of electrical switches and regulators), 12 per cent of woven cotton fabrics, and 9·8 per cent of man-made fibre fabrics.[11]

These are impressive figures in view of the relatively small size of the South African market. Some of the items are produced especially for South African requirements; others owe their predominance in large measure to a traditionally 'buy-British' sentiment, which has continued unaffected by the victory of the National Party in 1948, or the general loosening of ties between Britain and its Commonwealth (or ex-Commonwealth) members.

A similar picture can be built up of imports (£164·8 million) which entered Britain from the Republic in 1963.[12] They can be subdivided into several main categories, and a list made of the items for which South Africa was the principal or the second or third most important source of supply.

Items for which South Africa was the Principal Supplier (by Value)
(£ m.)

	1963 (£m.)	Half 1964
Fruit & vegetables	33·38	20·93
Pulp & waste paper	5·36	2·51*
Diamonds/precious stones	50·1	25·96

* Fell to 2nd place.

[11] See tables, pp. 182–3 below. The number of new motor cars licensed in 1963 was 144,616, divided by country of origin as follows:

	1961	1962	1963
UK	32,373	39,888	55,526
Germany	31,585	31,315	39,634
USA	10,460	11,646	14,084
France	6,132	5,895	8,831
Italy	6,758	7,526	8,722
Canada	3,355	2,624	2,904
Others	6,127	7,426	14,856

Source: SA Year Book 1965, p. 320.

[12] Cf. S. African imports into USA, 1965—$259 million or 1·5 per cent of total US imports.

Items for which South Africa was the Second Most Important Supplier
(by Value)
(£ m.)

	1963	Half 1964
Maize	14·04	10·25
Groundnuts	1·29	0·9
Animal feeding stuffs	0·71	0·59*
Manganese ore	1·05	0·86†
Ferro-manganese	2·18	1·08
Sheep & lamb skins	1·45	0·88*

* Fell to 3rd place.   † Rose to 1st place.

Items for which South Africa was the Third Most Important Supplier
(by Value)
(£ m.)

	1963	Half 1964
Animal oils & fats	1·28	1·16*

* Rose to 2nd place.

Source: UN Doc. S/6210, p. 109.

Again, one may calculate the relative importance of a number of these items by stating them as a percentage of the total amount imported into Britain. In 1963 South Africa supplied between a fifth and a quarter of the diamonds and precious stones imported, over 10 per cent of Britain's fruit and vegetables, 28 per cent of wood-pulp imports, 15 per cent of the import of asbestos, and 24 per cent of the import of manganese ore.[13]

To this visible trade of nearly £400 million a year must be added other returns. A large part of South Africa's import-export trade is carried in British ships, and much of the banking and insurance covering these transactions is done through British companies. There is also the substantial return in foreign exchange earnings on British investment in the Republic. The Board of Trade figures, totalling a little over £269 million, were given earlier.[14] The more usual estimates are in the neighbourhood of £800–£1,000 million, including those for insurance, banking, and oil. The booklet compiled by Union Acceptances Ltd in April 1964 gave the position as:

[13] See tables, pp. 184–5 below.   [14] See above, p. 42.

Foreign Liabilities of South Africa 1962

United Kingdom	£ m.
A Private sector	
Direct investment	623
Non-direct investment	212
B Official & banking sector	
Direct & non-direct investment	75
	£910

Source: *Scope for Investment*, App. VII.

On the basis of these figures, United Kingdom investment constituted about 60 per cent of the total foreign liabilities of the Republic, compared with 11 per cent for the United States, 6 per cent for France, 5 per cent for international organizations, and 4 per cent for Switzerland. United Kingdom earnings were running at about £60 million per annum. Again, these are impressive figures, although they reflect a pattern which belongs more to the past than the future. South Africa is now an exporter of capital, and, as the United Kingdom representative on the Expert Committee on Sanctions pointed out, the outflow probably exceeds the inflow.

According to the Annual Economic Report of the South African Reserve Bank, the sale of securities on the Johannesburg stock exchange amounted to R 121 million in the fiscal year 1962–63 and R 115 million in 1963–64. It must be remembered, however, that not all the proceeds of those sales were repatriated. South Africa imposed restrictions on the remittances of those funds and substantial sums had to be placed either in special blocked currency and non-resident bonds or kept in blocked accounts with South African banks, where they appeared in the balance of payments as an inflow of capital to the official and banking sectors. That point should be borne in mind, because capital was in fact trying to flee South Africa although it looked as if it were trying to enter the country.[15]

Recently between Britain and South Africa the movement of funds is almost certainly running against the Republic. There has been a 'a sizeable net withdrawal of private British investment funds [taking direct and portfolio investment together]

[15] UN Doc. S/6210, p. 103.

from South Africa in recent years'. The 'average net direct investment in the last five years had been about £14 million per annum, nearly all from ploughed-back profits on operations in South Africa. Average portfolio disinvestment has been about £22 million per annum.'[16]

The scale of investment in the Republic is still very great, however, and may be seen in the interlocking relationship of many British and South African interests. There are close, mutually advantageous ties between a large number of British firms, local subsidiaries, and South African-based companies. The motor industry may be taken as a good example of the general pattern. The market for vehicles has changed considerably over the past few years as the result of government policy which has restricted the importation of complete cars and encouraged the use of South African components in models assembled in the country. The present regulation is that more than 40 per cent of each new motor vehicle sold on the local market should contain locally manufactured components; it is proposed to raise the proportion, on a weight basis, to 90 per cent. The effect has been as intended, namely to bring British (and foreign) motor manufacturers directly into the Republic, where they have established local assembly plants, and factories for engines, chains, front and rear axles, batteries, electrical equipment, and so forth. The British Ford Motor Company, Rover (SA) Manufacturing Ltd—and General Motors from America—have opened assembly plants in Port Elizabeth; the British Motor Corporation—and Chrysler—in Cape Town; Jaguar—and Mercedes Benz—at East London. New companies, based on South Africa, have been formed in Durban and Johannesburg to act as local producers of other models.[17] A similar picture could be drawn of many industries in the Republic to show the spread of business interests between South Africa and Britain—and Britain's main competitors.

Thirdly, there is gold. South African production has risen from 49 to 70 per cent of non-Soviet world output:

---

[16] Ibid. pp. 113–14.

[17] e.g. The Stanley Motors Plant which assembles Rootes Group vehicles, Citroen, Peugeot, and Rambler cars, at Natalspruit. The Leyland Motor Corporation is to set up a £4 million automotive foundry at Elandsfontein for the manufacture of diesel engine blocks (*SA Year Book 1965*, ch. 69).

World Gold Production I

(*'ooo fine oz.*)

	1958	1959	1960	1961	1962	1963	1964
World total exclud. USSR	30,600	32,800	34,300	35,500*	37,700*	39,200*	40,600*
South Africa	17,656	20,066	21,383	22,942	25,492	27,432	29,137
South African percentage	57·7	61·2	62·3	64·6	67·6	69·9	71·8

* Estimated or provisional figure.

Sources: World total and SA percentage, *Annual Bullion Review 1964*, p. 10; SA production, *SA Year Book.*

World Gold Production II

(*'ooo fine oz.*)

	1962	1963
S. Africa	25,492	27,432
Canada	4,158	4,000
USA	1,556	1,500
Australia	1,073	1,050
Ghana	888	921
Rhodesia	555	566
Japan	420	400
Colombia	397	350
Philippines	424	280
Mexico	234	230
Nicaragua	154	200
Brazil	180	180
India	163	160
Peru	125	120
Tanganyika	102	102
Chile	100	100
Sweden	100	100
Others	1,379	1,509
Total	37,500	39,200

Source: SA Year Book, 1965, ch. 32.

In addition, sales of gold by the USSR have averaged between a seventh and a fifth of total world sales, rising from £25 million

in 1953 to £70 million in 1962. At the fixed price of £12.10 ($35)
a fine oz., South African gold constitutes by far the most important source of the annual addition to the gold reserves of the
central banks. Of the total of £343 million mined in the Republic in 1963, a little over £45 million went into South African
reserves, the rest being sold abroad—all but £6 million of it in
London.[18] Over two-thirds of the gold imported into the United
Kingdom came in fact from South Africa and was sold on the
London market. And just about half the total, that is about £215
millions, went into the official reserves of the western countries,
the remainder being bought by speculators.

British interests in gold may be grouped under three headings.
There is the direct gain derived from the actual transactions on
the London gold market, in which the profit margin is small and
confined to the five London firms of bullion brokers in association with the Bank of England. Secondly, there are the numerous
links, comparable to those in the motor industry, between
London and South African mining companies and their allied
banking, insurance, and shipping interests. Again one may take
a single example—the Anglo–American Corporation of South
Africa Ltd—which is the largest of the seven major groups
controlling the gold mining industry of the Republic.[19] The
Corporation was registered in South Africa as a public company
in 1917, and is today responsible for producing 34 per cent of the
Republic's gold, 61 per cent of the copper in Zambia and, in
association with the De Beers group, more than one-third of the
world's diamonds. Its activities extend over an immense range
of interests throughout southern and central Africa, linking the
Johannesburg and London stock exchanges, and providing a
large, profitable area of investment in both countries. Thirdly,

[18] The importance of gold exports to S. Africa may be seen from the following
table (£ m.):

Year	Trade deficit	Gold output	Gold sales	Gold into reserve
1962	46	316	244	72
1963	112	343	298	45

Source: SA Year Book 1965, ch. 32.

[19] Including the recently established Federale Mynbou, an Afrikaans-controlled
group linked with the General Mining and Finance Corp. Ltd.

there are the overall interests of the United Kingdom in the vexed question of international liquidity stemming from the increase in world trade and the diminishing ratio of gold to other holdings in the reserve banks. Between 1953 and 1963 international trade increased by 60 per cent whereas the official gold reserves used to finance it rose by only 15 per cent: here in a single instance is the primary cause of the present preoccupation with reform of the international monetary system. Admittedly, the problem has little to do with the actual sales of gold on the London bullion market, for even if the South African government were to try and carry out the threat (that it occasionally voices) of selling all its gold elsewhere, the practical effect would probably not be very different from the position today: the gold would almost certainly still find its way into official reserves through Beirut, or Zürich, or Johannesburg instead of London.[20] Nevertheless the United Kingdom is very much concerned—as a reserve currency country and in view of the deficit on its own balance of payments—with the need to increase international liquidity, and it is impossible to blink the fact that the problem of reform is still linked inextricably with the further problem of the shortage of gold.[21]

One might now consider briefly the possible effect of sanctions on the United Kingdom economy using this picture of the existing pattern of British-South African interests. There is, firstly, a preliminary general observation which needs to be made. Although the South African market is small in the total spread of the British economy, it is of sufficient importance to add weight to the argument that the loss involved in any United Nations action should not fall disproportionately on any one country. Britain has every right, therefore, to insist that if sanctions are to be imposed, they must be collective, under United Nations scrutiny, and so far as possible universally applicable. An embargo on South Africa might have to last a long time. And one must suppose that the Nationalist government would be busily employed in the meantime in using its gold and diamonds to tempt overseas suppliers to ignore the ban; British industry would then suffer cumulative loss if there

---

[20] Assuming that dealers in these countries were capable of handling the very large amounts of gold.

[21] See below, p. 162.

were widespread evasions, and the government would be under very strong pressure at home to stop the embargo. Approval by the British government of a United Nations resolution on sanctions is likely, therefore, to require assurance that there will be not only a nominal agreement to impose such an embargo, but reasonably adequate machinery to enforce it.

Secondly, one may make some estimate in terms of trade and investment of the effects of a total interruption of commerce between the United Kingdom and the Republic. There would be the immediate loss of a twentieth of Britain's export trade, the disappearance of a traditional source of supply for a number of items, and the sudden drying up of £60 million a year in foreign exchange. It is possible that some of the exports to South Africa would find other outlets, although the most likely effect would be to make it harder for the United Kingdom—because of a general redirection of trade—to sell in other markets. There would also be the loss of plant installations and machinery in the Republic, and of special orders for the South African market. The search for alternative sources of supply is likely to increase the cost of some imports, and there might be some difficulty in finding new sources of diamonds or (at particular times of the year) fresh fruit and vegetables. However, since there is an over-supply of agricultural produce in the world's markets at the present time, it ought not to be too difficult to find supplies of most commodities from other areas.[22] Together, the loss of exports and the price paid for the dislocation of imports might 'worsen the British balance of payments position by something of the order of £300 million in the first year'.[23] This could have lamentable consequences for the economy which is still struggling to cure a chronic balance of payments problem, and is likely to be in the same position for many years to come. It would be roughly the equivalent of the deliberate, financial check imposed by Mr Selwyn Lloyd in 1962, and the multiplying effect of such a shock might be felt for a long time in the home

[22] The removal of South Africa as a competitor might push up the price of some commodities—wool, sugar, fruit, wattle tanning extract, and non-ferrous metal ores—and thus help the economies of some newly independent countries; but it would not help the UK's balance of payments.

[23] UN Doc. S/6210, p. 111. Cf. the figure of—'as a maximum'—£210 m. on the basis of 1959–61 statistics given by G. D. N. Worswick (*Economic Sanctions Against S. Africa*, p. 183).

market, exports, the sterling area, and the rate of growth of the economy as a whole. There would be other consequences: for example, the enforced unemployment of about 150,000 workers, many of whom might, in time, find other jobs although not without hardship during the period of 'redeployment'. There would also be the loss of business to the small number of firms engaged in the bullion and diamond trade, as well as the damage to banking, insurance, and shipping interests.[24]

One would have to add to these domestic difficulties the United Kingdom's obligations to its remaining dependencies. The position of the three Southern African Territories has been examined in an earlier chapter, and one can only repeat here that a total embargo on trade between South Africa and the outside world would be disastrous for Basutoland and near-ruinous for Bechuanaland. They would be thrown on the mercy of the Republic, which would have little to spare from its own carefully husbanded resources. Other very small territories would also be hurt. The closure of the South African market would kill the hemp and tow industry of St Helena, damage the newly started coconut-fibre industry of the Seychelles, and impose further hardships on the island of Tristan da Cunha. These little territories are not of great significance perhaps to the world, but it is easy to overlook the problems of the poor when condemning the vices of the rich.

If the Rhodesia Front were to be overthrown in Salisbury and power assumed by a government which was prepared to enforce a ban on trade with South Africa, damage would also be inflicted on Rhodesia.[25] The trade figures for 1964 were:

Rhodesian–South African Trade

	£ m.	Per cent
Rhodesian total exports	137	
To South Africa	12	9
Rhodesian total imports	110	
From South Africa	27	25

Source: CEC, Commonwealth Trade 1958/9–1964.

---

[24] UK shipping interests in South Africa are worth about £20–£30 m. a year; total investment is about £100 m., half in cargo and half in passenger ships.
[25] See below, Ch. VII.

It would be almost impossible to find adequate alternative suppliers at comparable prices for nearly a quarter of Rhodesia's imports, including 90 per cent of its imports of iron and steel, 80 per cent of its tin, 70 per cent of its motor tyres, and all its imports of maize. Nor would there be comparable export markets for many of Rhodesia's local manufactures, of which a high proportion are sold to the Republic—radios (61 per cent), cigarettes (51 per cent), clothing and footwear (25 per cent). A total embargo on South Africa, therefore, would seriously injure the Rhodesian economy and, by extension, the economies of Zambia and Malawi. There is an economic unity to the whole of southern and central Africa. Communications run south and north, and the three territories of the former Federation would find it extremely difficult to maintain their present level of economic growth—under whatever government may be in power in Salisbury, Lusaka, or Zomba—without the economic co-operation of their southern neighbours, including the Republic.

What could be the effect of a ban on the purchase of gold from South Africa? Here the problem widens into the large and difficult issues of monetary reform now confronting those western governments—notably the United Kingdom's—who wish to reduce the deficit on their balance of payments, and the governments of the underdeveloped countries who are in search of new sources of credit. If the United Kingdom were to impose an embargo on South African gold, and if the ban were to be complied with by the central Reserve Bank, the primary effect would be to reduce the existing level of world liquidity and to weaken the present system of international payments.[26] The problem of how to finance the increase in world trade is already urgent, particularly now that the United Kingdom and the United States are determined to curb the outward flow of pounds and dollars and thus stem the deficit on their balance of payments. The International Monetary Fund has issued a number of warnings of the dangers of the shortage of existing reserves, and the sudden cutting off of South Africa's annual

---

[26] It is difficult to believe that there would not still be a market for S. African gold among private buyers or less than honest governments who ignored the ban in the reasonable expectation of a substantial profit once S. Africa's time of troubles was past.

addition to the ratio of gold to other holdings would make the position still worse. It would not be a major catastrophe, since even the very large amounts of South African gold bought each year by the central banks are only about 1 per cent of their total holdings of gold; but even so small a percentage would diminish still further the ratio of gold to existing currency reserves.

The argument has been put forward that out of further misfortune may come good, that a ban on South African gold might speed the acceptance of reforms which sensible observers have been advocating for many years. It is pointed out that the need for a more intelligent financing of international trade—whether in the form of IMF credits or a new reserve currency—is generally admitted; proposals abound whereby (it is claimed) many of the defects of the present system could be remedied: why not, therefore, make the added difficulty of the loss of South Africa's gold output the occasion and spur of reform? The argument is eminently sensible but, like many arguments seeking to improve the world, it is based more on reason than the present state of international relations. Admittedly, the western governments and the IMF (minus France) were prepared to stretch the present international monetary system in 1965 to provide $3,000 million—the largest currency loan ever made—in order to rescue sterling; but they are a long way from agreement on an alternative system. The Group of Ten industrial nations, on whom the likelihood of any substantial monetary reform depends, are divided not only over the future use of existing reserve currencies, but over the various proposals for a new system of international finance. The present mechanism, therefore, with its use of 'gold and convertible currency reserves', is likely to creak on for some time to come. Only France among the Ten wishes to return to a greater dependence on gold; but none is prepared to abandon it altogether. And the explanation is simple. It is because dollars, pounds, and francs, and any new unit of international currency, are open to suspicion in a way that the value of gold is not. Thus however sensible it might be to demote gold from its present status, there is little chance of its happening. An embargo on South African gold, therefore, would add to the need for reform, but it would not mean that the world was any nearer a solution of its financial problems.

These large issues of monetary reform are a good illustration of the difficulty in taking full measure of the effect of sanctions, and in deciding what should determine British policy. What begins as the examination of a particular question of trade or investment spills over into discussion of a much wider problem involving a whole field of international relations. This is a common feature of the debate over South Africa.[27] It underlines the truth of the general proposition that one cannot assess Britain's relations with the Republic solely on the basis of a limited field of direct interests. If one could, the decisions that might one day have to be taken would be a great deal easier, since none of the interests described in this study is of such overwhelming importance as to dictate British policy towards the Republic. Unfortunately, however, relations between London and Pretoria are now part of an international debate in which the rest of the world has a self-expressed interest, and the argument over defence, trade, the three Southern African Territories, and the United Nations soon passes the point at which it can be settled in terms of the immediate loss or gain to the United Kingdom. These aphorisms may seem self-evident, but it may be useful by way of conclusion not only to the particular theme of this chapter but to the study as a whole to re-examine them briefly.

Consider, for example, the twin problem of trade and investment. Despite the obvious importance of the South African market one might still conclude that Britain could—in time though with difficulty—absorb the shock of a total interruption of trade with the Republic. The losses involved would vary according to the scale of interest taken—disastrous for a few firms, harmful to some, and of marginal importance to others. Nor could the loss of some £60 million investment income be regarded as a threat of such magnitude to the national economy —even at a time of financial strain—as to rule out all possibility of Britain's compliance with a United Nations embargo. Thus although the United Kingdom is right to stress the damage that sanctions would inflict on the economy, and to demand that they should be imposed (if at all) by collective agreement, it cannot do more than underline the hardship which is likely to arise. It would certainly be unwise, in arguing the case at the United Nations or Commonwealth prime ministers' meetings, to make

---

[27] And over Rhodesia; see below, p. 168.

its economic interests in the Republic the principal grounds for
objecting to sanctions. It is true that late in 1964 Britain was
in serious financial difficulties in terms of its own post-war
affluence, but the plea that a loss of 5 per cent of its exports
would make it impossible to take action against South Africa
is hardly likely to convince the indigent governments of the
newly independent states. The fact is that South Africa is a
valuable single market, but still only one of many in the total
range of Britain's overseas trade: it may well inhibit, but it
ought not to determine, in the final assessment, British policy
in respect of sanctions. The same argument may be applied to
many of the ties examined in earlier chapters. To adapt a
phrase from the inquiry into defence, one may describe British
interests in South Africa as 'important'—often very important—
but not 'vital' to the wealth or security of the United Kingdom.[28]
And the explanation why this should be so is plain. It lies in the
nature of the relationship between Britain and South Africa: on
the one hand, a country of world interests and considerable
power still; on the other, a small Republic condemned by almost
the whole world for its racial policies. Thus it was possible to
argue that South Africa's dependence on the tolerance of the
western powers was much greater than the United Kingdom's
need of the defence facilities offered by the Nationalist government, and this comforting conclusion is reinforced by the trade
figures given above. For Britain is by far the largest single
market still for South African goods, accounting for over 30 per
cent of the Republic's total exports and nearly 30 per cent of its
imports.[29] And because it plays so large a part in the South
African economy—to an extent which South Africa cannot hope

[28] The UK's responsibility for the three Southern African Territories imposes specific
obligations at least until independence, but this is now imminent in both Basutoland and Bechuanaland; their fate will then depend on whatever relationship
they can maintain with Pretoria unless it is argued that Commonwealth ties
will re-impose these obligations in a different form. And that is hardly likely.

[29]   *S. Africa's External Trade, 1963*
                            (£ m.)

Total imports:	606·35	Total exports:	452·6 (excluding gold)
from UK	180·7	to UK	136
from EEC	119·95	to EEC	96·5
from USA	102·25	to USA	40·25

Source: SA Year Book, 1965, pp. 232–3.

to do in respect of the United Kingdom—it has little to fear by way of reprisals by the Nationalist government.

Yet here lies the difficulty. For it is precisely because Britain has the power to injure the Republic that it needs to exercise caution. The United Kingdom is embedded so deeply in South Africa's history that it cannot easily turn aside now from the Republic in the hope of escaping from its problems by curtailing its interests. Indeed, it is on these grounds that the Afro-Asian states press home their attack on the United Kingdom government, being fully aware that 'any programme of sanctions [can] never be effective so long as Britain remains aloof'.[30] And it is on these same grounds that the United Kingdom is bound to hesitate. It is an unpleasant position to be in, and one might raise the question again and ask what it is that prevents the United Kingdom from gaining the goodwill of the Afro-Asian world and escaping the opprobrium which clings to it because of its ties with the Republic? The explanation—the writer would argue—does not lie primarily in dislike of having to forfeit its interests in South Africa but fear of the consequences likely to follow United Nations action. It is not simply the loss of British investment and trade, or even the hardship certain to be inflicted on the three Southern African Territories, but apprehension over the effect of the widening area of conflict which sanctions would produce. It is absurd for the Nationalist government to pretend that what happens in the Republic is of concern only to those who live there. But it is also unreal to argue that South Africa's racial problems can be cured by a policy of economic sanctions begun, as it were, in June and ended in December. Here one reaches the point stated earlier: that British policy towards South Africa cannot be reckoned simply 'in terms of the immediate loss or gain to the United Kingdom'. A country less implicated in the Republic, or with narrower interests in the world at large, might be able to take a more detached stand; but Britain is a prime factor in the argument over sanctions, and must weigh the effects of its decisions with anxious care for what may follow—damage to the economies of South Africa's neighbours, hunger and bloody repression in the Republic, the dislocation of world markets, and the intensifying of east-west conflicts not only over the immediate

[30] *Economic Sanctions against S. Africa*, p. 128.

problem of South Africa but at the United Nations and in the numerous disputed areas of the world. In short, in almost every aspect of the argument, as over the particular problem of gold, wider issues are raised which transcend the question of ending apartheid in South or South West Africa.

M

VII

The Rhodesia Parallel

ON 11 November 1965, as the writer was concluding this study, the Rhodesia Front government in Salisbury proclaimed their independence in defiance of the United Kingdom. In reply, the Labour government declared Mr Smith and his colleagues to be rebels, and undertook a number of retaliatory measures, including a policy of economic sanctions. Throughout 1964 and the latter part of 1965, events north of the Limpopo had begun to raise many of the issues discussed in earlier chapters in relation to the Republic: now, in November, it looked as if they were being put to the test in a narrower setting. Here (it could be argued) was virtually a trial run for the larger problems of white supremacy in southern Africa. The Commonwealth was under strain, and many feared that it might founder amidst the angry demonstrations of some African members and resentment in Britain at their strictures. The United Nations was being brought into the quarrel between London and Salisbury: there was talk of oil sanctions, armed intervention, war, and of the danger of a 'Red Army in blue berets'.[1] A colonial rebellion had produced the unusual situation in which the Imperial power was being urged to reassert its control, not indeed out of a love of empire on the part of those who were critical of British intentions, but because the African majority in Rhodesia was unable to stage its own revolt. There were parallels clearly between central and southern Africa, in that the United Kingdom was under attack in both areas because of its reluctance to undertake measures whereby (it was argued) power could be wrested from European hands and transferred to African leaders. It may be helpful, therefore, to look at some of the aspects of the South African problem in a Rhodesian setting—to move from the larger tragedy of apartheid to the Rhodesian sub-plot.

One may note its bearing on the question of sanctions. What

---

[1] Mr Wilson (12 Nov. 1965, HC Deb., vol. 720, cols 635–7) justifying Britain's raising of the Rhodesian issue at the UN on the grounds that it had forestalled more radical appeals.

was formerly in the realm mainly of theory has now been translated into practice, and the crisis over Rhodesia has helped to illustrate many of the difficulties in their application. One can set them out in the form of a number of propositions concerning the nature of sanctions and the lessons that might usefully be drawn from them.

First proposition: that sanctions are likely to be a long-drawn-out affair since, by their nature, they belong to the category of siege warfare rather than assault. The city must be surrounded, the lines of communication cut, supplies blockaded and a period of waiting entered upon by the besieging powers whose patience is then put to the test in equal measure to that of the besieged. The analogy is particularly apt in relation both to the Rhodesian and South African situations in which the aim is not to halt aggression—as by Italy against Abyssinia in 1936–7—but to persuade the inhabitants of the town to parley. The imposition of sanctions against Rhodesia in November 1965 was part of an attempt to apply external, economic pressure in order to achieve a local political end—the redistribution of power within the country. And since what has been sought is the modification by the white minority of policies which they believe are necessary to maintain their privileged position, one ought not to be surprised that they resisted. One major lesson, therefore, to draw from the Rhodesian parallel is that sanctions cannot be expected to produce a dramatic reversal of fortunes: slow to take effect, they are also slow to produce results. It is unwise, therefore, to base one's calculations on, or to raise hopes of, an early end to the enterprise.

Second proposition: sanctions cannot easily be limited to the particular enemy in view. There is the danger of 'overspill' or, in moral terms, the likelihood that the innocent and the guilty will be bound by a common fate, whether it is Zambia, Malawi, and Rhodesia, or Basutoland, Bechuanaland, Swaziland, and the Republic of South Africa. It is another aspect of the clumsy nature of sanctions as a long-range weapon. Hence the need for a careful, prior appraisal of the remedial measures that may be needed to protect—so far as it is possible to do so—the innocent from the guilty. Thus, having imposed sanctions, the United Kingdom government then had to face the problem that the injury inflicted on Rhodesia was bound to damage Zambia and

Malawi. Dr Banda's republic, for example, drew over a third of its imports from, and marketed 15 per cent of its exports in, Rhodesia during 1964–5; if, therefore, unemployment increases among the African population of the towns and white farming areas of Rhodesia, Malawi will lose a substantial part of the remittances sent home by the Nyasa who work there. The scale of the problem is not perhaps very great, since it would well be within the power of the United Kingdom to make good at least the financial loss. But the Copper Belt is in a different category. Zambia exported via Rhodesia £148 million worth of copper in 1964 out of a total of £168 million exports; it bought from Rhodesia £30 million of its £71 million total imports: indeed, virtually all the imports necessary to maintain the country's economy entered by rail from or through Rhodesia. One can understand President Kaunda's reluctance to interfere with the flow of trade between Lusaka and Salisbury, or to add to the tension between his own followers and the 60,000 Europeans on the Copper Belt, many of whom are from Rhodesia or South Africa. Indeed, his primary concern in November was not to hurt Rhodesia by depriving it of the rich Zambian market but to prevent injury to the Zambian copper industry from hostile action taken in Salisbury. It was on these grounds that he appealed to Britain for the dispatch of aircraft and troops. In short, there is an interlocking structure to the economies of central Africa, as there is to those of southern Africa. The ties of the former Central African Federation can still be seen in the flow of trade across the Zambesi, the supply of Rhodesian coal to the northern Copper Belt, the shipment of copper south to Beira, the movement of labour from Malawi to the other two territories, and in arrangements between the Zambian and Rhodesian governments for the allocation of power from the Kariba dam and the joint operation of the railway. If they were to be broken, Rhodesia would suffer but Zambia might collapse.

A third proposition: the danger is always there that the effect of sanctions will exceed what is intended, particularly if the object of the boycott is the overthrow of a regime, or the ending of policies which are held by the regime to be essential to its survival. Resistance is likely to be stubborn, and may lead to the slow crumbling of the economy under siege, privation, hunger, riots, repression, the breakdown of law, and the collapse of orderly society. Indeed the wreckage may be such (as was argued in relation to the problem of sanctions against South Africa) that the sanctioneers may find it difficult to hold aloof from interfering directly in the situation which they themselves have helped to produce.

Fourth proposition: the efficiency of sanctions will depend on the degree of universality with which they can be applied. The particular difficulty which Britain faced in Rhodesia in this respect was the refusal of the South African and Portuguese governments to co-operate in the boycott. (It was not difficult to understand their unwillingness to endorse measures which might one day be urged against them.) When oil sanctions were imposed against Rhodesia, the embargo on supplies to the Umtali refinery was rigorously applied by the major international oil companies: but it was still open to doubt (at the time of writing) whether it was possible to cut off every source of supply. Other interests appeared in Salisbury as soon as trade between Britain and Rhodesia was interrupted: free-booters and agents of unspecified countries. Some of the difficulties in the way of collective sanctions could be seen too in the reservations entered by a number of governments once the prospect of a mandatory resolution at the United Nations began to draw near. A further lesson, therefore, that one could draw from the Rhodesian scene was that the task of achieving effective international action in the subtle, complicated world of international trade was a laborious process which held no promise of easy success.

Fifthly: sanctions being a form of limited warfare, it is wise to give as much attention to the terms of surrender necessary to secure the lifting of the boycott as to the efficiency of the embargo. If no final assault is intended, the hope must exist among the besiegers that a time for parley will come from which a satisfactory settlement can be reached. But the success and length of the siege are likely to be determined in large part by the terms being offered. If they are too mild, they may make the whole operation seem fatuous and unnecessary; if too harsh, they may stiffen resistance, until scenes of ruin and disorder confront those who are applying sanctions. If the terms are muddled, and thus open to a conflict of interpretation, the effect may be even more lamentable: for the parley may begin, the sanctions be lifted, terms agreed to, and a new basis for compromise apparently reached—until a quarrel over interpretation reopens the conflict, sanctions are reimposed, and the whole sorry drama of pressure and resistance is re-enacted.

The sixth proposition follows from the fifth. If one needs to be precise about the terms of surrender, one must also face clearly the task of reconstruction that may be necessary if the sanctions are proved 'successful'. What such a task might be in Rhodesia if Smith is overthrown is not easy to say; but it might require a longer and greater British participation in the administration of the country than is commonly supposed.[2]

A final proposition: sanctions are a trial of strength in terms not only of resources but of the will to resist, and the will on the part of the besiegers to persist in the measures adopted. Siege warfare is arduous warfare, and one must be sure that the will is there to maintain it if a humiliating withdrawal is to be avoided when it may justly be argued that by trying, and failing, one has strengthened and not weakened the enemy. Mr Wilson's use of a quotation from Churchill on the day following Mr Smith's declaration of independence was apt:

Nearly thirty years ago, Winston Churchill, in a debate in the House on Abyssinia, used these words: 'We cannot undo the past, but we are bound to pass it in review in order to draw from it such lessons as may be applicable to the future, and surely the conclusion from this story is that we should not intervene in these matters unless we are in earnest and prepared to carry our intervention to all necessary lengths.'[3]

This is very true. But it was still possible to doubt at the end of January 1966 whether the Labour government under Mr Wilson was indeed 'in earnest and prepared to carry [its] intervention to all necessary lengths'. The writer may be unjust in saying this. It may be when these words are in print that the will and determination (so strongly expressed by Mr Wilson) to bring

---

[2] One should stress here the fundamental difference between Rhodesia and other colonies—Aden and British Guiana—in which rebellion against the colonial government led to the suspension of the constitution and the dispatch of troops. In Rhodesia, there is not and there has never been a colonial government—nor a framework of administration under a Governor and officials responsible to the Secretary of State in London. There is no easy point of entry, therefore, for the 'Imperial government'.

[3] HC Deb., vol. 720, col. 637.

Rhodesia back to legality will still be evident; they may indeed have prevailed, and have succeeded in ending the rebellion. If so, their success will have underlined the moral. But the implication of Churchill's warning needed to be pondered carefully not only by the United Kingdom government which was forced to take action against Rhodesia but by those who call for intervention by way of sanctions in the far graver case of South Africa. In the Rhodesian context, that meant the will to go on hurting the European community for a long time at a level which avoided, if possible, provoking retaliatory action by the Rhodesia Front against Zambia and Malawi, but which would be maintained whatever measures might be necessary in financial or military terms to protect the economy and safety of the two northern republics. It meant sustaining a common front between both major parties in Britain to avoid encouraging the will to resist in Salisbury. It meant continual efforts to dissuade other governments from buying Rhodesia's exports. It meant a determination to resist Commonwealth (and other) African impatience and the demand for immediate military action. It also meant being prepared to intervene directly, with troops, in Rhodesia if violence spilled over beyond Mr Smith's control. In sum, it meant holding resolutely to the course of action begun in November over a period of months and, if need be, for a much longer period, and being prepared to follow the course to the end.

As may be seen, these propositions bear directly on the Rhodesian situation. Once sanctions were imposed in November 1965 many of the problems set out here became apparent. There was the fact that it was impossible to isolate Rhodesia from its neighbours, the difficulty of achieving collective sanctions, whether by voluntary agreement or under the Charter of the United Nations, and the particularly dangerous situation which began to unfold as the result of a conflict between two very different timetables of expectancy—one geared to a course of action plotted by the African states, the other to the much slower pace of change in Rhodesia itself. Thus there was the further danger that the African states would try to widen the conflict between Britain and Rhodesia by direct action on their own part or by involving the United Nations more closely in the crisis than was acceptable to the United Kingdom government.

It was also difficult to see, if sanctions were persisted in, and the Rhodesia Front refused to accept whatever terms were offered, how a satisfactory resolution of the conflict could be achieved— satisfactory, that is, not only to the Commonwealth African states and the United Kingdom, but to the Rhodesia Front government and Britain, and to both the European and African communities in Rhodesia. The Rhodesian problem reinforced, therefore, many of the arguments set out in the introductory chapter in relation to South Africa, and one might usefully consider here in very general terms the relevance of the present crisis in Rhodesia to South Africa.

If, for example, the illegal government in Salisbury is able to defy the British government's attempt to force it to come to terms (or be replaced by others willing to parley) for a considerable period of time, then clearly the case for sanctions against South Africa will be correspondingly weakened. Indeed, disillusionment among some of the African leaders could be detected very early after the beginning of sanctions, in the sense that what was once argued to be easy was now seen to be difficult. In April 1964, for example, M. Mongi Slim, the Tunisian Foreign Minister, told the London Conference on Sanctions that 'economic sanctions are the last possible chance of defeating apartheid peacefully', and the conference agreed with the findings of its first and second Commissions when they reported: 'After detailed consideration, the Commission finds that a policy of total economic sanctions against South Africa is feasible and practicable and can be effective.'[4] By November 1965, however, M. Diallo Telli, secretary-general of the OAU (who attended the London conference), was reported as saying: 'I do not believe British sanctions will work. They did not work when the greatest power in the world applied them against the smallest—Cuba.'[5] Ironically, it was now the United Kingdom which claimed that sanctions would have the desired effect of overthrowing the illegal government.

Even if the Rhodesian leaders were brought to terms, however—and, a more difficult proposition, if the Rhodesian situation were to be resolved in terms of an orderly transfer of power to the African majority—it is far from clear what lessons one could draw from the present crisis for the very much greater

[4] *Economic Sanctions against S. Africa*, p. 270.   [5] *The Times*, 20 Nov. 1965.

problem of South Africa. Certainly the case for sanctions would be reopened. But one could not easily conclude that what had been successful in Rhodesia would also be successful in South Africa. For if there are parallels between the two situations, there are also major differences.

For example, the Rhodesian leaders have defied the Crown[6] and the United Kingdom parliament, putting themselves in the position of an outlaw unrecognized by the world at large. Whereas South Africa is a sovereign state, Rhodesia is under rebel control, in conflict with the British government over the right of political expression among the African majority. Mr Smith and his government have broken the law in pursuit of white supremacy, and the United Kingdom has a clear legal right to act to end the rebellion. The need to do so extends much further than the moral duty to restore constitutional government to Rhodesia. For if the Rhodesia Front were to succeed in defying the United Kingdom, it would be a sad, abject conclusion to the relatively peaceful record of decolonization elsewhere in Africa, Asia, and the Caribbean. It would bring the Commonwealth into jeopardy, in its relations between Britain and the Afro-Asian members, in a manner very different from the argument over South Africa where (as the writer has tried to suggest) there are genuine grounds for disagreement over what can and should be done.[7] Rhodesia is a direct British responsibility: indeed, it is only on this basis that the Labour government originally agreed to take the dispute to the United Nations. South Africa, on the other hand, has been an independent country for over half a century, and is a member of the United Nations. Action against it, therefore, has to be justified in international terms, and this raises particular difficulties, not least (as has been argued) in terms of the meaning of the Charter.

Secondly, even it if were possible to see the Rhodesian situation as a rehearsal in miniature of a far wider crisis to come in South Africa, the very difference in scale is of critical importance. Hence the statement in the paragraph above that one cannot assume that what may be effective against 200,000 Euro-

[6] Represented by the Governor.
[7] Cf. the remark of Dr Obote, Prime Minister of Uganda, in November 1965: 'We have our quarrels with South Africa, but they are different from the situation which has developed in Rhodesia. In this quarrel, South Africa is not the enemy' (*Africa Research Bull.*, Nov. 1965).

peans in Rhodesia would be similarly effective against the 3¼ million whites of the Republic. To the extent that South Africa's economic resources in terms of skills, gold, industrial capacity, and military power are greater than Rhodesia's, so is its ability to withstand a boycott. The difference may be seen in the scale of Britain's financial and trading interests in Rhodesia: £33 million exports, £31 million imports, and some £200 million of investment of which about a quarter is in the form of portfolio investment.[8] In terms of exports Rhodesia is a useful, traditionally pro-British market, but it is comparatively small within the total spread of United Kingdom exports: between a half and three-quarters per cent, that is roughly equal to the size of the British market in Kenya or Ghana—far below the £200 million bought by South Africa.

Thirdly, the determination of the large number of whites in the Republic to resist external pressure is likely to exceed that of the very small European minority in Rhodesia. It rests on a bedrock of Afrikaner nationalism which stems directly from the stubborn pride and determination of the Boer republics which defied the full force of the Empire from 1899 till 1902. Today, flanked by the Portuguese in Angola and Moçambique, the Republic stands as a southern refuge where the white minority in central Africa can join the final laager. Indeed, if the Rhodesia Front were to surrender (or be forced to surrender) power, one must expect that the net movement of Europeans out of the country from 1961 onwards would be accelerated.[9] Nor should it be assumed that an African government in Salisbury, in what may then be a weak, disturbed, and impoverished country, would pose a serious challenge to the Republic. On the contrary, such a situation may accord with white South Africa's readiness to entertain a patron-client relationship with neighbouring

[8] 'The large British companies with interests in Rhodesia give the collective impression that if their operations there were to be written off it would be Rhodesia's loss rather than theirs. . . . A number of British companies have subsidiaries in Rhodesia making goods that are vital to the well-being of the local market whereas the returns to the British principals are only a fraction, usually, of total turnover' (*The Times*, 12 Nov. 1965).

[9] There was a strong inflow during the early years of the Federation, reaching its peak in 1955–6, and a rapid outflow in 1962–3. To this has to be added a high rate of increase of the 4 m. African population at about 2·5 per cent per annum. Thus the proportion of Europeans to Africans is falling—from 6 per cent in 1960 to 5·1 in 1964 (see the migration chart in *The Times*, 17 Nov. 1965).

African countries. It is this perhaps that helps to explain the formally correct position of 'non-alignment' that Dr Verwoerd adopted at the outset of the crisis.

In general, the obstacles encountered by Britain in its attempt to force reform on the Rhodesia Front government are likely to underline the larger problems associated with any comparable move against the Republic. True, sanctions against South Africa, if they are ever imposed, are likely to be mandatory and collective. But the scale of the difficulties involved would also be that much greater, and the hope of a peaceful, settled outcome that much smaller. To the extent, therefore, that Rhodesia is a parallel, it is not a very comforting one to those who look for an early end to apartheid rule.

APPENDIX I

Relevant Articles of the United Nations Charter

GENERAL

Article 2

4. All Members shall refrain in their international relations from the threat or use of force against the territorial integrity or political independence of any state, or in any other manner inconsistent with the Purposes of the United Nations.

7. Nothing contained in the present Charter shall authorize the United Nations to intervene in matters which are essentially within the domestic jurisdiction of any state or shall require the Members to submit such matters to settlement under the present Charter; but this principle shall not prejudice the application of enforcement measures under Chapter VII.

ON HUMAN RIGHTS

Article 1

The purposes of the United Nations are . . .

3. To achieve international cooperation in solving international problems of an economic, social, cultural, or humanitarian character, and in promoting and encouraging respect for human rights and for fundamental freedoms for all without distinction as to race, sex, language, or religion . . .

Article 55

With a view to the creation of conditions of stability and well-being which are necessary for peaceful and friendly relations among nations based on respect for the principle of equal rights and self-determination of peoples, the United Nations shall promote:

a. higher standards of living, full employment, and conditions of economic and social progress and development;

b. solutions of international economic, social, health, and related problems; and international cultural and educational cooperation; and

c. universal respect for, and observance of, human rights and fundamental freedoms for all without distinction as to race, sex, language, or religion.

Article 56

All Members pledge themselves to take joint and separate action in cooperation with the Organization for the achievement of the purposes set forth in Article 55.

ON POWERS OF THE ASSEMBLY

Article 14

Subject to the provisions of Article 12, the General Assembly may recommend measures for the peaceful adjustment of any situation, regardless of origin, which it deems likely to impair the general welfare or friendly relations among nations, including situations resulting from a violation of the provisions of the present Charter setting forth the Purposes and Principles of the United Nations.

ON POWERS OF THE SECURITY COUNCIL

Article 34

The Security Council may investigate any dispute, or any situation which might lead to international friction or give rise to a dispute, in order to determine whether the continuance of the dispute or situation is likely to endanger the maintenance of international peace and security.

Article 39

The Security Council shall determine the existence of any threat to the peace, breach of the peace, or act of aggression and shall make recommendations, or decide what measures shall be taken in accordance with Articles 41 and 42, to maintain or restore international peace and security.

Article 41

The Security Council may decide what measures not involving the use of armed force are to be employed to give effect to its decisions, and it may call upon the Members of the United Nations to apply such measures. These may include complete or partial interruption of economic relations and of rail, sea, air, postal, telegraphic, radio, and other means of communication, and the severance of diplomatic relations.

Article 42

Should the Security Council consider that measures provided for in Article 41 would be inadequate or have proved to be inadequate, it may take such action by air, sea, or land forces as may be necessary to maintain or restore international peace and security. Such action may include demonstrations, blockade, and other operations by air, sea, or land forces of Members of the United Nations.

On the International Court's Decisions

Article 94

1. Each Member of the United Nations undertakes to comply with the decision of the International Court of Justice in any case to which it is a party.

2. If any party to a case fails to perform the obligations incumbent upon it under a judgment rendered by the Court, the other party may have recourse to the Security Council, which may, if it deems necessary, make recommendations or decide upon measures to be taken to give effect to the judgment.

APPENDIX 2

Air Routes London to Singapore : Distances

(*nautical miles*)

London to Singapore—East

London		London		London	
Rome	800	Rome	800	Rome	800
Athens	560	Benghazi	720	Athens	560
Nicosia	500	Khartoum	1,190	Nicosia	500
Tehran	1,030	Aden	680	Teheran	1,030
Bahrein	640	Gan	1,800	Bahrein	640
Karachi	920	Singapore	1,710	Gan	2,080
Delhi	520			Singapore	1,710
Calcutta	710		6,900		
Singapore	1,560				7,220
	7,240				

London to Singapore—West

London		London		London		London	
Reykjavik	1,090	Reykjavik	1,090	Thule	2,180	Thule	2,180
Sondrestrom	715	Sondrestrom	715	Elmendorf	1,750	Elmendorf	1,750
Winnipeg	1,760	Winnipeg	1,760	Midway	2,400	Tokyo	3,000
Vancouver	1,000	Vancouver	1,000	Guam	2,300	Hong Kong	1,560
Honolulu	2,400	Honolulu	2,400	Hong Kong	1,800	Singapore	1,400
Wake	1,990	Midway	1,130	Singapore	1,400		
Guam	1,305	Tokyo	2,225				9,890
Hong Kong	1,800	Hong Kong	1,560		11,830		
Singapore	1,400	Singapore	1,400				
	13,460		13,280				

APPENDIX 3

UK–South African Trade

TABLE I

United Kingdom Exports to the Republic of South Africa (not including Re-exports)

Description of item	1963 A (£ m.)	1963 B %	First half 1964 A (£ m.)	First half 1964 B %	Unit	1963 C	1963 D %	First half 1964 C	First half 1964 D %
Chemical elements and compounds	3·00	3·2	2·01	3·8	—				
Dyeing, tanning, and colouring materials	1·48	3·1	0·93	3·4	—				
Medicinal and pharmaceutical products	1·80	3·3	1·04	3·5	—				
Plastic materials, etc.	3·26	5·1	2·10	5·8	'000 cwt.	285	4·8	173	5·3
Chemicals n.e.s.	1·96	3·3	1·20	3·6	—				
Leather, leather manufactures, etc.	1·07	3·8	0·62	4·1	—				
Rubber manufactures n.e.s.	0·94	1·9	0·63	2·5	—				
Paper, paperboard, and manufactures	3·17	6·8	1·70	7·0	'000 cwt.	362	7·7	201	8·2
Textile yarn, fabrics, etc.	16·00	6·3	8·88	6·4					
of which: wool and animal hair yarn and thread	Z 0·97	4·6	Z 0·59	5·0	}	1,546	4·6	895	5·1
cotton yarn and thread	1·13	8·9	0·72	10·8	'000 lb.	1,183	5·7	705	6·4
man-made fibre yarn and thread	2·43	7·7	1·49	7·5	}	5,324	6·5	3,230	6·7
woven cotton fabrics	X 3·73	12·0	X 1·70	11·1	}	29,195	13·1	12,157	11·8
woven woollen fabrics	0·82	2·3	0·59	3·0	'000 sq. yds.	1,989	3·8	1,254	4·6
woven worsted fabrics	1·13	4·5	0·73	5·9	}	1,575	5·1	932	6·4
woven man-made fibre fabrics	X 1·59	9·8	Y 0·86	9·1		5,881	7·3	3,221	7·2
Non-metallic mineral manufactures n.e.s.	3·93	5·8	2·36	6·2	—				
of which: glass	Z 1·38	10·0	Y 1·08	12·8	—				
Iron and steel	5·79	2·8	3·59	3·3	}	68	1·9	49	2·5
of which: universals, plates and sheets	3·84	4·0	2·12	4·2	'000 tons	52	2·9	32	3·1
Non-ferrous metals	2·35	1·9	1·27	1·9	'000 cwt.	64	2·3	39	2·8
of which: copper	1·08	2·9	0·68	3·4	—				
Manufactures of metal n.e.s.	6·56	4·9	3·89	5·3	—				
of which: tools and parts	Y 1·92	7·3	Z 1·11	7·8	—				
cutlery of base metal	Z 0·86	6·8	X 0·42	5·5	—				
Machinery other than electric									

Item	A	B	A	B	Units	D	C	C	D
agricultural and track-laying tractors	Y 7·87	7·1	X 4·50	7·8	Number	6·8	11,851	6,930	7·5
office machinery	1·66	4·2	0·88	4·2	'000 cwt.	3·8	9	5	4·5
machine tools	2·66	5·9	1·78	7·1	'000 cwt.	9·0	107	57	8·7
textile machinery	3·19	4·8	1·59	4·4	'000 cwt.	7·1	113	35	4·3
construction and mining machinery n.e.s.	2·76	5·2	1·35	4·6	'000 cwt.	4·6	104	52	4·3
heating and cooling equipment	1·16	3·5	Z 0·87	5·3	'000 cwt.	3·7	35	22	4·3
pumps and centrifuges	2·25	5·5	X 1·41	6·1	'000 cwt.	5·3	50	31	5·8
mechanical handling equipment	Z 2·13	6·1	Y 1·45	7·8	'000 cwt.	5·9	86	55	6·9
Electrical machinery, apparatus and appliances	Y 22·92	7·2	Y 11·02	6·8					
of which: generators, motors, etc.	X 4·19	9·1	Z 1·20	5·4	'000 cwt.	8·4	118	33	4·8
switches, voltage regulators, etc.	X 3·94	12·7	X 2·16	12·9	'000 cwt.	12·4	76	41	13·0
telecommunications apparatus	X 7·61	9·7	X 3·90	9·2					
domestic equipment	1·84	5·2	1·03	6·2					
Transport equipment	Y 52·23	8·3	Y 29·69	8·6					
of which: railway vehicles	X 3·48	16·7	X 1·59	16·9	'000 tons	11·6	10	4	11·8
motor cars, new	X 18·84	8·0	Y 11·81	8·6	thousands	9·0	55	37	10·2
lorries, trucks, ambulances, etc.	X 7·66	9·5	X 4·71	10·6	thousands	10·0	12	7	10·6
chassis for goods vehicles	Y 3·37	15·1	Y 2·22	18·5	thousands	13·4	4	2	15·3
bodies, chassis, frames, etc.	6·42	5·1	4·18	5·7	'000 cwt.	3·9	175	119	4·5
aircraft	1·20	2·6	Z 1·97	7·9					
ships and boats	Y 8·47	20·0	Z 1·90	11·7					
Clothing	1·02	2·6	0·68	3·6					
Scientific and photographic goods, clocks, etc.	3·13	4·2	1·73	3·8					
Miscellaneous manufactures n.e.s.	Z 5·77	4·4	Z 3·27	4·8					
of which: printed matter, MSS. typescripts	2·47	5·8	1·49	6·7					
Commodities and transactions not classified according to kind									
of which: firearms of war and ammunition	……	……	……	……					
Total, all merchandise	195·81	4·8	108·99	5·0					
Diamonds and precious stones	9·40	7·2	6·15	8·2					

N

A Value of United Kingdom exports of item to the Republic of South Africa (£ m.)

B Percentage by value of total exports of item exported to the Republic of South Africa.

C Volume of United Kingdom exports of item to the Republic of South Africa (in units stated)

D Percentage by volume of total exports of item exported to the Republic of South Africa.

X Items for which the Republic of South Africa is the United Kingdom's principal customer by value.

Y Items for which the Republic of South Africa is the United Kingdom's second largest customer by value.

Z Items for which the Republic of South Africa is the United Kingdom's third largest customer by value.

Source: UN Doc. S/6210, 2 March 1965, pp. 109–10.

TABLE 2

United Kingdom Imports from the Republic of South Africa

Description of item		1963 A (£ m.)	1963 B %		First half 1964 A (£ m.)	First half 1964 B %		1963 C	1963 D %	First half 1964 C	First half 1964 D %
Cereals and cereal preparations		15·26	7·1		11·43	9·8	⎫ '000 cwt.	14,034	8·2	9,699	10·7
of which: maize	Y	14·04	18·8	Y	10·25	26·5	⎭	12,960	18·9	8,661	25·5
Fruit and vegetables	X	33·38	11·8	X	20·93	13·5		7,107	10·4	4,197	11·4
of which: oranges, tangerines, etc.	Z	5·55	22·9	Z	1·67	10·9	'000 cwt.	1,707	22·9	591	11·0
apples	Y	3·57	18·4	X	4·42	25·9		835	20·3	992	27·3
tinned or bottled, with sugar	X	12·98	32·1	X	6·53	32·1		2,357	34·9	1,156	34·9
Sugar, honey, etc.		10·16	5·9		2·64	2·7		3,868	6·6	820	2·7
of which: raw sugars		9·84	6·3		2·48	2·7		3,339	7·0	587	2·4
Feedingstuff for animals	Y	0·71	9·8	Z	0·59	10·4	⎫ '000 tons	40	10·5	28	9·6
of which: hay, fodder, bran, etc. fish meal and flour		1·18	8·3		0·56	6·5	⎭	23	8·3	11	6·6
Beverages		1·60	6·2	N	1·06	7·8	'000 galls.	2,477	10·4	1,484	11·8
of which: wine											
Undressed hides and skins		2·34	4·0		1·39	4·3	⎫ '000 cwt.	91	5·8	44	5·1
of which: sheep and lamb skins	Y	1·45	17·3	Z	0·88	14·7	⎭	83	15·8	40	12·3
Oil seeds, oil nuts and oil kernels	Y	1·29	10·0	Y	0·91	14·7	'000 tons	18	9·4	13	14·4
of which: groundnuts											
Pulp and waste paper	X	5·36	28·3	Y	2·51	25·2	'000 tons	102	32·0	47	29·6
of which: chemical wood pulp, dissolving grades											
Textile fibres and their waste		12·77	4·8		9·36	5·5	—				
of which: sheep's or lamb's wool	Z	7·92	5·6	Z	7·27	7·8	million lb.	34	5·4	28	7·8
fine animal hair (other than wool)	Y	3·08	20·7	Y	1·39	23·8	—				
Crude fertilizers and minerals		2·47	6·3		1·34	6·3	'000 tons	25	16·1	16	10·6
of which: asbestos		1·58	14·9	N	0·93	18·5					

Item		A	B		A	B	Units	C	D		D
of which: manganese ore and concentrates	Y	1·05	24·1	X	0·86	27·1	'000 tons	92	29·8	86	28·5
Animal oils and fats	Z	1·28	9·5	Y	1·16	12·6	'000 cwt.	501	10·5	312	12·2
Dyeing, tanning and colouring materials		0·85	7·4		0·58	7·3	—			201	95·7
of which: wattle bark extract		0·82	91·1		0·57	95·0	'000 cwt.	297	95·8	201	95·7
Iron and steel	Y	4·67	6·2	Y	1·64	2·6	'000 tons	105	6·6	40	2·9
of which: ferro-manganese, etc.		2·18	15·0		1·08	11·9		43	20·4	23	17·8
Total, all merchandise		114·72	2·4		69·77	2·5					
Diamonds and precious stones	X	50·10	37·4	X	25·96	34·3	—				

A   Value of United Kingdom imports of item from the Republic of South Africa (£ m.)

B   Percentage by value of total imports of item imported from the Republic of South Africa.

C   Volume of United Kingdom imports of item from the Republic of South Africa (in units stated).

D   Percentage by volume of total imports of item imported from the Republic of South Africa.

X   Items of which the Republic of South Africa is the United Kingdom's principal supplier by value.

Y   Items of which the Republic of South Africa is the United Kingdom's second largest supplier by value.

Z   Items of which the Republic of South Africa is the United Kingdom's third largest supplier by value.

Source: As for Table 1

APPENDIX 4

1962 Production of Minerals in Selected African Countries

	Asbestos (long tons)	Bauxite (long tons)	Chrome ore (long tons)	Cobalt (long tons)	Copper ore (long tons)	Lithium (long tons)	Manganese (long tons)	Columbite (long tons)	Diamonds (£'000)	Gold (Troy oz.)
South Africa	197,591	—	898,369	—	45,638	1,360	1,441,606	4	17,947	25,491,993
S.W. Africa	—	—	—	—	23,000	2,615	—	5	18,635	183
Swaziland	29,311	—	—	—	—	—	—	—	—	2,214
S. Rhodesia	126,961	500	453,294	—	13,524	40,486	7,123	72	—	544,647
Zambia	—	—	—	846	553,442	—	45,983	—	—	3,625
Ghana	—	286,798	—	—	—	—	476,379	—	8,002	888,037
Sierra Leone	—	—	9,350	—	—	—	—	—	13,180	—
Nigeria	—	—	—	—	—	—	—	2,281	—	—
Congo Rep.	—	—	—	9,530	292,296	—	311,203	—	n.a.	203,700
Morocco	—	—	—	1,413	—	—	461,944	—	—	—
Tanganyika	—	—	—	—	15,331	—	—	—	5,508	104,383
Uganda	—	—	—	—	2,289	—	—	13	—	236
UK imports	164,210	563,334	143,894	2,289	—	3,400	415,658	485	n.a.	34,140,428*
World Total	2,700,000	39,000,000	4,200,000	n.a.	4,300,000	n.a.	14,800,000	n.a.	£93,000	36,800,000†

* Ore 59,253; Bullion 34,081,175   † Excluding USSR production

Source: UK, Statistical Summary of the Mineral Industry, 1957–1962 (1964).

SELECT BIBLIOGRAPHY

A comprehensive bibliography of books, articles, and documents on South and South West Africa between 1945 and the end of 1963 will be found in Gerhard Tötemeyer, *South Africa: South West Africa*, published in mimeograph by the Arnold Bergsträsser Institut für Kulturwissenschaftliche Forschung, Freiburg, 1964. The following includes the books cited in the text and additional publications of general interest to the theme.

Ashton, H. *The Basuto*. London, OUP, 1952.
Carnegie Endowment for International Peace. *Apartheid and United Nations Collective Measures : an Analysis*, ed. by Amelia C. Leiss. New York, Mar. 1965, mimeo.
Carter, G. *The Politics of Inequality: South Africa since 1948*. London, Thames & Hudson, 1958.
Commission of Enquiry into South West African Affairs, 1962-3 [Chairman: F. H. Odendaal]. *Report* . . . Pretoria, 1964.
Commonwealth Relations Office. Economic Survey Mission to Basutoland, Bechuanaland Protectorate and Swaziland [Chairman: Chandler Morse]. *Report* . . . London, 1960.
De Kiewiet, C. W. *The Anatomy of South African Misery*. London, OUP, 1956.
De Villiers, H. H. W. *Rivonia: Operation Mayibuye*. Johannesburg, Afrikaanse Pers-boekhandel, 1964.
Doxey, G. V. *The High Commission Territories and the Republic of South Africa*. London, OUP for RIIA, 1963, mimeo.
Hailey, Lord. *The Republic of South Africa and the High Commission Territories*. London, OUP, 1963.
Hancock, W. K. *Survey of British Commonwealth Affairs*, vol. ii, pt 2. London, OUP for RIIA, 1942.
Higgins, R. *The Development of International Law through the Political Organs of the United Nations*. London, OUP for RIIA, 1963.
Hill, C. R. *Bantustans: the Fragmentation of South Africa*. London, OUP, 1963.
Horrell, M. *Survey of Race Relations in South Africa 1963*. Johannesburg, SA Inst. of Race Relations, 1963.
Houghton, D. H. *The South African Economy*. London, OUP, 1964.
Hurley, D. E. *Apartheid: a Crisis of the Christian's Conscience*. Johannesburg, SA Inst. of Race Relations, 1964.
Hutt, W. H. *The Economics of the Colour Bar*. London, Deutsch for Inst. of Economic Affairs, 1964.

International Conference on Sanctions against South Africa, London, Apr. 1964. *Economic Sanctions Against South Africa,* ed. by Ronald Segal. London, Penguin, 1964.

Kuper, H. *Indian People in Natal.* Pietermaritzburg, Natal University Press, 1960.

Kuper, L. *An African Bourgeoisie: Race, Class and Politics in South Africa.* New Haven, Yale University Press, 1965.

Legum, C. and M. *South Africa: Crisis for the West.* London, Pall Mall Press, 1964.

Lewin, J. *Politics and Law in South Africa.* London, Merlin Press, 1963.

Mandela, N. *No Easy Walk to Freedom.* London, Heinemann, 1965.

Mansergh, N. *Documents and Speeches on British Commonwealth Affairs.* London, OUP for RIIA, 1964.

Mansergh, N. *South Africa 1906–1961: the Price of Magnanimity.* London, Allen & Unwin, 1962.

Marais, J. S. *The Fall of Kruger's Republic.* London, OUP, 1961.

Marquard, L. *The Peoples and Policies of South Africa.* Cape Town, OUP, 1960.

Muller, H. *The Role of the Coloured People in the Economic Pattern of the Republic of South Africa.* Cape Town, Combined University Press of Grahamstown & Stellenbosch, 1965.

Munger, E. S. *Bechuanaland.* London, OUP for Inst. of Race Relations, 1965.

Ngubane, J. K. *An African Explains Apartheid.* London, Pall Mall Press, 1963.

Nielsen, W. *African Battleline: American Policy Choices in Southern Africa.* New York, Harper for Council on Foreign Relations, 1965.

Spence, J. E. *Republic under Pressure.* London, OUP for RIIA, 1965.

Vatcher, W. *White Laager.* New York, Praeger, 1965.

World Council of Churches. *The Future of South Africa: a Study by British Christians,* ed. by T. A. Beetham & N. Salter. London, SCM, 1965.

Younger, K. G. *Changing Perspectives in British Foreign Policy.* London, OUP for RIIA, 1964.

UN DOCUMENTS

A/5707, 1964: Report of the Special Committee on Apartheid. (See also previous reports by the Committee.)

S/5658: Report of Group of Experts, 6 May 1964.

S/6210: Report of Expert Committee of the Security Council (established by resolution S/5773), 2 March 1965.

Index

*Printed in Great Britain
by The Broadwater Press Ltd
Welwyn Garden City, Herts.*